THE MEGA TRIVIA BOOK

Compiled by **Joyce Robins**

SIENA

First published in Great Britain in 1994 by
Parragon
13 Whiteladies Road
Clifton
Bristol BS8 1PB
This edition published in 1998

ISBN 0 75252 668 5 (Hardback)
ISBN 0 75252 849 1 (Paperback)

Printed in India

Editorial: Linda Doeser Publishing Services
Design Style: David Rowley Design
Design and DTP: David Rowley and Alan Mckee
Picture Research: Kathy Lockley

Contents

Introd

There are over 100 quizzes in this book to amuse, perplex, absorb and even educate you. Most of us carry far more general knowledge in our heads than we realize. The only problem is tracking down the trivia at the right moment and producing a prompt answer. It can be satisfying and frustrating by turns, but it is always fun.

Some questions are so easy that you will hardly have to think; others will leave you cudgelling your brains. But then, of course, the only way quiz addicts will define an easy question is one where they know the answer. Some readers will romp through the intricacies of American football or Olympic competition, while others find musical

uction

shows or cocktail ingredients more to their taste. In Pot Luck, everyone has an equal chance.

Quizzes are fun for the whole family and if you find the names of dinosaurs impossible to pronounce – let alone remember – just ask your children. The chances are they will be able to answer every question!

Whether you use this book to give your brain a gentle workout or stage a full-scale family-and-friends competition, it will give you many hours of entertainment and you will end up knowing more than when you started.

How to play

There is no 'right' way to play Ultimate Trivia. You can make up your own rules, or simply dip into the book for fun, but we have devised a few games to help you make the most of the 350 questions in each subject category.

Game 1: Single player

Pick your favourite from the seven subject categories (not including Pot Luck) and try to answer each question in order, scoring 1 point for each correct answer. Every time you fail to answer, take a question from Pot Luck 1. If you answer correctly, score 2 points, if not, deduct 1 point from your current score. When you have exhausted the questions in Pot Luck 1, the game is over. Next time you can begin again from where you left off, using Pot Luck 2, and competing against your last score.

Game 2: 2 or more players or teams

Each player or team picks a subject, which can include Pot Luck. You can cut cards or throw dice to decide who chooses first - or you can make the game more difficult by putting all the categories in a hat and making a random choice. Decide in advance how long you want the game to last, then go through the book with each player or team taking turns to answer question 1 in their chosen category, then question 2. Score 2 points for each correct answer. The winner is the person or team with most points when time is up. For the next round, start again where you left off.

Game 3: Several teams with 3 or more members, and a quiz master

Put numbers from 1 to 25 in a hat. Each team draws a number and tries to answer that number in one quiz after another each time their turn comes round. The questions aren't graded for difficulty, so no team is at a disadvantage and team members can confer over their answers. Each correct answer in the subject categories earns 1 point but each time a Pot Luck question is answered correctly, the team score is doubled. The game can be played again with each team drawing a second number and proceeding through the book in the same way.

Qu

iz1

1. King Edward VIII gave up the British throne to marry an American divorcée. What was her name? ▶

2. Whom did filmstar Grace Kelly marry in 1956? ▶

3. Queen Victoria proposed marriage to her cousin Prince Albert at Windsor in 1839. What nationality was he?

4. Who married Robert Browning at a London church, in the utmost secrecy, because her father disapproved of the match?

5. Elizabeth Taylor and Richard Burton fell passionately in love when they were filming a motion picture epic. What was the film?

6. Who was known as the cinema screen's first 'great lover', star of The Sheikh?

7. Lauren Bacall and Humphrey Bogart were known as a devoted couple. Her friends have always called her by her given name, rather than by the glamorous 'Lauren'. What is that name?

8. The close relationship between Spencer Tracy and Katherine Hepburn lasted 25 years. In 1967 they made their last film together, Guess Who's Coming to Dinner. Who was coming to dinner?

9. The man reputed to be the greatest lover of all time lived in the 18th century and his name has passed into the language. Who was he?

10. Who was the love of the Emperor Napoleon's life?

11. Which two royal lovers, parents of the young Princes William and Henry, announced their separation in 1992?

12. When Lord Nelson died, one of his last requests was 'Take care of my dear Lady Hamilton'. What was her first name?

13 Who did assasinated president John F. Kennedy's widow marry in 1968?

14 Which film actress fed her image as a blonde sex symbol with lines like 'Come up and see me some-time,' and 'I never set out to make men a career. It just happened that way!'?

15 Nell Gwyn won the heart of England's 'Merry Monarch'. Who was he?

16 Which of Henry VIII's wives died soon after the birth of her baby while she was still the object of the king's love?

17 Both Julius Caesar and Mark Antony loved Cleopatra. When she ascended the throne she was formally married to a relative. Who was he?

18 What is the name of the village in Scotland where runaway English couples were once married over the blacksmith's anvil?

19 Who is the patron saint of lovers?

20 Name the well-known singer who is Andrew Lloyd Webber's second wife, and who starred in Phantom of the Opera.

21 Of which French king was Madame de Pompadour the influential mistress ?

22 Which group of people were associated with the saying 'Make love, not war'?

23 Which world famous baseball star married Marilyn Monroe in 1954?

24 Winston Churchill married in 1908 and wrote that he and his wife 'lived happily ever after'. What was her Christian name?

25 Mary Queen of Scots supposedly wrote the 'Casket Letters' to her lover with whom she plotted to kill her husband. Name the recipient of the letters.

1 At the climax of North by Northwest, the hero and heroine climb across the faces of American presidents on a famous monument. Name it.

2 Barbara Bel Geddes played James Stewart's down-to-earth girlfriend in Vertigo in 1958. In what television role did she become famous more recently?

3 Who stars opposite Ingrid Bergman as an American agent in Notorious?

4 In Rebecca, Laurence Olivier marries Joan Fontaine and brings her back to his family home in Cornwall. What is the name of his imposing house? ▼

5 Who plays the title role in Rebecca?

6 What nationality was Alfred Hitchcock? ▶

7 Which film has a sequel in which Norman Bates is released from a mental institution?

8 Marnie is the story of a compulsive thief based on a novel by which author?

9 In which country does the action of To Catch a Thief, starring Cary Grant and Grace Kelly, take place?

56

10 In Rear Window , James Stewart plays a news photographer who believes he has witnessed a murder from his window. Why is he confined to his apartment?

11 In an early film, Shadow of a Doubt , Joseph Cotton plays Uncle Charlie, who moves in with his sister and niece, who was named after him. Gradually his niece becomes suspicious of him. What is his guilty secret?

12 Margaret Lockwood is perplexed by the disappearance of an elderly English governess in The Lady Vanishes. Where does the action of the film take place?

13 Jessica Tandy played the hero's mother in The Birds. For which film did the elderly actress win an academy award in 1989?

14 In Spellbound, Gregory Peck suffers from amnesia and fears that he is a murderer. The character played by Ingrid Bergman tries to help him. What is her profession?

15 Jamaica Inn was taken from a novel by a well-known English author. Name her.

16 What was Hitchcock's last film, made in 1976?

17 In Rope, two young men commit murder for the thrill of it and then hold a party, serving food from the chest which contains the body. Who plays the college professor who discovers their secret?

18 Hitchcock freely adapted John Buchan's novel for his film The Thirty-Nine Steps. What are the Thirty-Nine Steps?

19 In Strangers on a Train , Bruno (Robert Walker) believes he has made a bargain with Guy (Farley Granger) whereby Guy is to kill Bruno's father. What does Bruno do for Guy?

20 In Psycho, the first victim is killed in a motel. What is she doing at the time?

21 The crash of a fairground ride provides the climax in Strangers on a Train. Which ride is it?

22 Complete the following Hitchcock quotation. 'The length of the film should be directly related to the endurance of ...'.

23 Hitchcock made two films of the same name and with virtually the same story in 1935 and 1956, the second starring James Stewart and Doris Day. Name the film.

24 From 1955 to 1961 Hitchcock introduced a series of mystery stories on television. What was the series called?

25 Which star do The Birds and Marnie have in common?

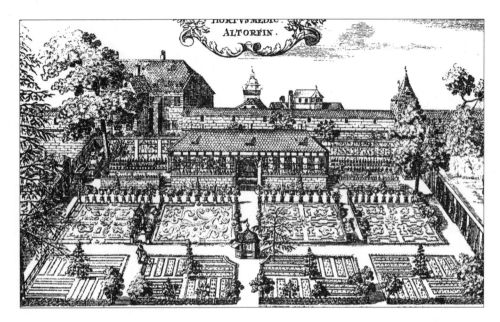

1. In Shakespeare's Hamlet, which herb is said to be 'for remembrance'?

2. Is parsley an annual, biennial or perennial plant?

3. Is French or Russian tarragon normally used in cooking?

4. In which two European countries is caraway often used to flavour breads and pastries?

5. What is the main problem with growing mint in the garden? ▲

6. From which flower does the expensive spice of saffron come?

7. Which of the following plants are hardy annuals: sage, borage, chives, sorrel, dill?

8. In what form is angelica normally used for decorating cakes and desserts?

9. The traditional French blend of 'fines herbes' includes chervil, chives and tarragon. What is the fourth herb?

10. Which herb was regarded as a symbol of immortality by the Greeks and Romans?

11. Fresh coriander leaves are used in Indian cookery and the rest of the plant can also be cooked and eaten. Which vegetable family does it belong to?

12. Which herb is used to flavour the tomato-based sauce on pizza?

13. Sage is now a familiar herb in the kitchen. What was its main purpose in the Middle Ages?

14. Which is milder: American mustard or Dijon mustard?

15. With which of type dish would you use lemon balm as a flavouring?

16 What type of soil does thyme prefer?

17 In the Middle East, cardamom is used in coffee and in Europe it flavours cakes. In France and the United States, its oil is used for a purpose unconnected with cookery. What is it?

18 With what type of food are juniper berries most often used?

19 Which part of the ginger plant does the spice come from? ▼

20 What is a mixture of dried thyme, bay and parsley enclosed in a muslin bag called?

21 Which herb sends cats into ecstasies?

22 What type of flavour does the vegetable fennel have?

23 Camomile is often used in herbal tea. What is it said to promote?

24 The curry plant has a very spicy aroma and silver leaves. What colour are the flowers of the plant?

25 Which of the following is not a herb or spice: savory, soapwort, soy, sassafras?

1 On a darts board, what number is directly opposite No. 1?

2 What colour is the cue ball in pool?

3 What is the craft of making arrows called?

4 In cycle racing, what is a sag wagon?

5 The apparatus used by male gymnasts consists of vaulting horse, pommel horse, horizontal bars, rings and floor. Which of these pieces of apparatus do women use?

6 Essential equipment for a boxer comprises gloves, hand tape, protector below the waist, boots and – what else?

7 Why do American footballers paint black marks across their cheeks? ◄

8 In ice hockey, what are puck-stoppers?

9 In the early days of cricket, a bowler who took three wickets in a row was presented with a top hat. What modern term comes from this practice?

10 What sport has four different colour codes for the balls, ranging from yellow for hot conditions to blue for cold conditions?

11 Apart from body padding, what protection do baseball players wear?

12 In hot air ballooning, how is the manoeuvring or cooling valve used? ▶

13 How many red balls are there in snooker?

14 Which sport uses stones and a house?

15 Starting blocks are used on athletic tracks. Runners push their feet against them to get the fastest start possible. What else can they be used for?

16 In fencing, which is the heavier weapon: the foil or the épée?

17 What is the difference in shape between rugby and soccer balls?

18 Kendo is one of the traditional Japanese martial arts and the participants use a type of sword. From what is the sword made?

19 What type of shots are woods used for in golf?

20 What colour is the centre scoring zone of an archery target?

21 All the hoops in croquet are painted white, except the last one, called the rover, which has a different colour on the crown. Which colour is it?

22 Why are the officials in American football known as zebras?

23 From what fairly light-weight wood is a bat for the sport of cricket traditionally made from?

24 In the ancient sport of archery, what material are the arrows usually made from?

25 Soccer boots have interchangeable studs. The studs for wet and slippery surfaces are made from aluminium. What studs are used for playing on hard ground?

1. Where did the Great Fire of London break out in 1666?

2. Where was the Piper Alpha oil rig belonging to the U.S. Occidental Petroleum Corporation, which exploded in 1988?

3. One of the worst fires in American history gutted the 26-storey MGM Grand Hotel in 1980. In which town was the hotel situated?

4. The ancient Italian town of Pompeii and a great number of its inhabitants were buried when a volcano near Naples erupted in 79AD. Name the great volcano, which is now a tourist attraction.

5. Who was the tyrant leader of the Khymer Rouge whose reign of terror killed some 3 million people in Cambodia in the 1970s?

6. In 1989, the Chinese People's Liberation Army crushed a student pro-democracy protest in Beijing with tanks and machine-gun fire. In which large square did the massacre take place?

7. Which geological fault caused the San Francisco earthquake of 1906?

8. The Welsh mining village of Aberfan suffered a major disaster in 1966 when 81 schoolchildren died. What caused the tragedy?

9. In the 14th century, a plague killed up to one third of Europe's population. What was it called?

10. Both the Hindenburg and the R101 ended in flames. What were they?

11. What is measured on the Richter scale?

12. Which American river caused serious flood damage in 1993?

13. How many voyages had the Titanic made when it hit an iceberg and sank in 1912? ▲ ▶

14. A Pan Am flight, which left London Heathrow bound for New York in December 1988, was blown up by a bomb over a small Scottish town. Name the town.

15 What was Krakatoa?

16 What type of accident happened at Chernobyl in the U.S.S.R. in 1986?

17 Which three sectarian groups are involved in the conflict in Bosnia and Herzogovina?

18 Name the American space shuttle, its crew including a teacher (the first private citizen chosen for a space mission), which exploded killing all on board after lift-off?

19 What is the name given to those who study and predict earthquakes?

20 AIDS has become a worldwide health problem. What do the initials stand for?

21 The American volcano of Mount St. Helens erupted in May 1980. In which state is the volcano?

22 Which Indian city suffered a large death toll after a chemical leak at the Union Carbide (India) factory in December 1984?

23 The worst oil spill ever known in the United States occurred when the Exxon Valdez ran aground. Where did the spill occur?

24 In the 1960s, a tranquillizing drug, thought to have no harmful side effects, was marketed in Britain and other countries as a therapy for morning sickness, resulting in the birth of hundreds of deformed babies. Name the drug.

25 What are the scientists who study volcanoes called?

1. The name 'dinosaur' comes from two Greek words. What do they mean?

2. How long did dinosaurs live on earth?

3. What was remarkable about the fast-running predator the Compsognathos?

4. The dinosaur once known as the Brontosaurus is now known by another name. What is it?

5. The Euoplocephalus had a bony protective layer over its body. What did it have at the end of its tail?

6. Researchers think that the Diplodocus, the longest land animal known, suffered from a painful disease that often affects humans as they grow older. What was it?

7. Why was the Stegasaurus, or 'roofed lizard' so called?

8. What was remarkable about the brain of the Stegosaurus?

9. Was the Brachiosaurus the fastest or slowest of the dinosaurs?

10. Why was the Iguanodon able to use its forefeet as a weapons?

11. What did the Spinosaurus have on its back, which may have played a part in heat regulation?

12. Which was the largest carnivore ever known on earth?

13. What does the name Triceratops mean?

14. Which London park contains models of dinosaurs created by Benjamin Waterhouse Hawkins in the last century?

15. Dinosaurs divide into two main classes: Saurischia and Ornithischia. The Saurischia were lizard-hipped, much like other reptiles. What were the Ornithischia?

16. How did dinosaurs produce their young?

17 In 1960 Irwin Allen directed The Lost World, in which a party of scientists encountered living dinosaurs. Which author wrote the book on which the film was based? ◄

18 The Chinese call fossilized dinosaur teeth 'dragon's teeth'. What are they used for?

19 What ability did the duck-billed dinosaurs share with modern-day hamsters?

20 The name Deinonychus reflects the ability of this fierce flesh-eater to overcome its prey with a large, sickle-like claw on its inner toe. What does the name mean?

21 What are the scientists who study dinosaur fossils called? ▲

22 The first skeleton of the Archaeopteryx or 'ancient wing' was found in Germany in 1861. What is its claim to fame?

23 In the film Jurassic Park, how were the dinosaurs supposed to have been created?

24 Dinosaurs lived in the Mesozoic Era, which is divided into three periods. Two of them are the Jurassic and Cretaceous. What is the third? ▼

25 How long ago did dinosaurs die out?

7 Who was the first woman President of Israel?

8 Who said, 'Je suis la France'?

9 What was British Prime Minister Margaret Thatcher's maiden name? ▼

10 Which Iraqi leader ordered the invasion of Kuwait?

11 Which musical instrument does President Bill Clinton play?

12 By what name was Indian political leader Mohandas Gandhi better known?

13 Who declared war on Britain and France in June 1940?

1 What was the nationality of Adolf Hitler? ▲

2 Which American President ordered the dropping of the first atomic bomb?

3 Who wrote his thoughts in a little red book?

4 Who has been in power in Cuba since declaring the country a socialist nation over 30 years ago?

5 Which British Prime Minister said, 'You've never had it so good' and spoke of the 'wind of change'?

6 Where did the burglary that led to the resignation of an American President take place?

14 What was the slogan of Martin Luther King's famous speech made at the Lincoln Memorial, Washington in 1963 in which he looked forward to understanding between races? ▲

15 Which African leader emerged from prison after 27 years to lead his party again?

16 Which President of the Soviet Union died in 1953, aged 73?

17 What political position did Ronald Reagan hold before becoming President of the United States?

18 Which wartime leader said. 'Never in the field of human conflict was so much owed by so many to so few'?

19 By what military rank is the President of Libya known?

20 Ceylon (now Sri Lanka) had the first female head of government in the modern world when she succeeded her husband after his assassination in 1959. What was her name?

21 In 1941, the Deputy Chancellor of Germany flew to Britain to try to sue for peace. He was later imprisoned in Spandau prison. Who was he?

22 Richard M. Nixon was President of the United States from 1969 to 1974. What does M. stand for?

23 Which Third World leader was assassinated by members of her bodyguard in 1984?

24 Which Russian leader introduced glasnost and perestroika ?

25 Which British Prime Minister said, 'A week is a long time in politics'?

1 Where in the body is the labyrinth?

2 What is the common name for ascorbic acid?

3 Complete this quotation from Voltaire: 'If god did not exist ...'.

4 Americans call it a faucet. What do the British call it?

5 How are the first five books of the Bible known collectively?

6 Who designed the dome of St. Peter's, Rome? ▲

7 What is the unit of currency in Poland?

8 Which two elements make up water?

9 Who was the captain of the Pequod in Moby Dick?

10 What colour is a New York taxi?

11 Which two letters are worth 10 points in the board game Scrabble?

12 Which useful household item is made from naphthalene?

13 What is measured on the Beaufort scale?

14 Which creatures live in a formicary?

15 Which bandleader died in an air crash over the English Channel during World War II?

16 What is the other name for the Jewish Day of Atonement?

17 What was writer Charles Dodgson's pseudonym?

18 If an American footballer talked about his 'zippers' what would he mean?

19 Where would you find the 'ocean of storms'?

20 What is the pirate's flag with the skull and crossbones called?

21 Where is the original Harris tweed spun and woven?

22 What do climbers call a peak higher than 914 m (3,000 ft)?

23 The famous Gurkha soldiers are known for carrying a particular type of large knife. What is this knife called?

24 Which bird is the international symbol of happiness?

25 What is the centuries old art of clipping hedges into various ornamental shapes traditionally called? ▼

TOPIARY WORK AT LEVENS HALL : WESTMORELAND

People and Places   Lovers

1. Wallis Simpson
2. Prince Rainier of Monaco
3. German
4. Elizabeth Barrett
5. Cleopatra
6. Rudolph Valentino
7. Betty
8. Their daughter's black fiancé
9. Casanova
10. Josephine
11. The Prince and Princess of Wales
12. Emma
13. Aristotle Onassis
14. Mae West
15. Charles II
16. Jane Seymour
17. Her brother, Ptolemy
18. Gretna Green
19. Saint Valentine
20. Sarah Brightman
21. Louis XV
22. Hippies
23. Joe DiMaggio
24. Clementine
25. Earl of Bothwell

Entertaining Arts   Hitchcock Films

1. Mount Rushmore
2. Miss Ellie in Dallas
3. Cary Grant
4. Manderley
5. No one. Rebecca is already dead when the story opens.
6. English
7. Psycho
8. Winston Graham
9. France
10. He has a broken leg
11. He murders rich widows
12. On a train
13. Driving Miss Daisy
14. Psychiatrist
15. Daphne du Maurier
16. The Family Plot
17. James Stewart
18. A ring of spies
19. Kills his wife
20. Taking a shower
21. The carousel
22. '... the human bladder'
23. The Man Who Knew Too Much
24. Alfred Hitchcock Presents
25. Tippi Hedren

Food and Drink   Herbs and Spices

1. Rosemary
2. Biennial
3. French
4. Germany and Austria
5. It spreads rapidly
6. Crocus
7. Borage and dill
8. Crystallized
9. Parsley
10. Tansy
11. Carrot family
12. Oregano
13. Medicinal
14. American
15. Fish and poultry
16. Well-drained lime or chalk
17. Bouquet garni
18. Game
19. The underground rhizome
20. Bouquet garni
21. Catnip or catmint
22. Aniseed
23. Relaxation and sleep
24. Yellow
25. Soy is a condiment made from fermented soya beans

Sports and Pastimes   Sports Gear

1. No. 19
2. White
3. Fletching
4. One of the last vehicles following road events and picking up riders who have dropped out
5. Vaulting horse and floor
6. Gumshield
7. It helps protect against the sun's glare
8. Pads protecting knees and shins
9. Hat-trick
10. Squash
11. Helmet and face-mask
12. To release hot air for descent
13. 15
14. Curling
15. To detect false starts
16. The épée
17. A rugby ball is oval; a soccer ball is round
18. Strips of bamboo
19. Long shots
20. Gold
21. Red
22. They wear striped shirts
23. Willow
24. Tubular aluminium alloy
25. Rubber studs

History   Catastrophe!

1. A baker's shop in Pudding Lane
2. North Sea
3. Las Vegas
4. Vesuvius
5. Pol Pot
6. Tiananmen Square
7. San Andreas Fault
8. A slag heap (mine waste) collapsed
9. Black Death
10. Airships
11. Earthquakes
12. Mississippi
13. None; it was her maiden voyage
14. Lockerbie
15. A volcanic island
16. A nuclear reactor caught fire
17. Serbs, Croats and Muslims
18. Challenger
19. Seismologists
20. Acquired immune deficiency syndrome
21. Washington
22. Bhopal
23. Alaska
24. Thalidomide
25. Volcanologists

Natural World   Dinosaurs

1. Terrible lizard
2. 150 million years
3. It was the smallest known
4. Apatosaurus
5. A large lump of bone with which it could club its enemies
6. Arthritis
7. The bony plates on its back looked like roof tiles
8. It was tiny in relation to the creature's size
9. Slowest
10. Its thumbs formed powerful spikes
11. A tall fin
12. Tyrannosaurus rex
13. Three-horned face
14. Crystal Palace
15. Bird-hipped
16. They laid eggs in hollowed-out nests in the ground
17. Sir Arthur Conan Doyle
18. Medicines
19. They could store extra food in their cheeks
20. Terrible claw
21. Palaeontologists
22. It was probably the earliest bird
23. From a DNA sample
24. Triassic
25. 64 million years ago

Twentieth Century   World Leaders

1. Austrian
2. Harry S. Truman
3. Chairman Mao
4. Fidel Castro
5. Harold Macmillan
6. Watergate Building, Washington DC
7. Golda Meir
8. General Charles de Gaulle
9. Roberts
10. Saddam Hussein
11. Saxophone
12. Mahatma
13. General Mussolini of Italy
14. 'I have a dream'
15. Nelson Mandela
16. Joseph Stalin
17. Governor of California
18. Winston Churchill
19. Colonel (Qaddafi)
20. Mrs. Bandaranaike
21. Rudolph Hess
22. Milhous
23. Mrs. Indira Gandhi
24. Mikhail Gorbachev
25. Harold Wilson

Pot Luck

1. The ear
2. Vitamin C
3. '... it would be necessary to invent him'
4. Tap
5. Pentateuch
6. Michelangelo
7. Zloty
8. Hydrogen and oxygen
9. Captain Ahab
10. Yellow
11. Q and Z
12. Mothballs
13. Wind velocity
14. Ants
15. Glenn Miller
16. Yom Kippur
17. Lewis Carroll
18. Scars
19. On the moon
20. Jolly Roger
21. Outer Hebrides
22. A munro
23. The kukri
24. Bluebird
25. Topiary

Quiz

5 Orpheus went down to Hades to rescue his wife. What was her name?

6 What is the usual occupation of the leprechaun of Irish legend?

7 Where did the Greek gods live?

8 Who led the Argonauts in search of the golden fleece?

9 Which Arabian princess saved her life by telling stories for 1001 nights?

10 What nationality was the legendary hero William Tell, who shot an apple from his son's head? ▶

11 Which Roman god gave his name to the month of January?

12 Which hero killed the Gorgon, Medusa?

13 How did the German maiden called Lorelei lure sailors on the River Rhine to their death?

14 The beauty of a woman, the daughter of Zeus, led to a war between Greece and Troy, so her face was said to have 'launched a thousand ships'. What was her name?

15 The Greek forces besieged Troy for 10 years before they devised a plan to smuggle soldiers into the city. How was this accomplished?

16 What was the name of the one-eyed giant of Greek mythology?

17 How was the sword of Damocles suspended?

18 What happens to those who kiss the Blarney Stone in Ireland?

1 Which city was said to have been founded by Romulus and Remus?

2 Name the race of warrior women, famed for their exploits in the Trojan war and ruled by a queen.

3 The Muses were the goddesses of poetry and song. How many Muses were there?

4 Poseidon was the Greek god of the sea. What did the Romans call him? ▲

19 Tales of King Arthur and the Knights of the Round Table have been popular since the Middle Ages. Which musical film, starring Richard Harris, told the story of Arthur and his court?

20 Who was the ancient Egyptian god of the sun?

21 Which character in Greek mythology died when he flew too close to the sun and melted his wings?

22 The Greeks called the goddess of the hunt Artemis. What was the Roman name for this goddess?

23 Which hero did Ariadne, the daughter of the great King Minos, help to escape from the Labyrinth?

24 In ancient Greek mythology, who was the famous winged male messenger who served all gods?

25 In the film *Robin and Marian* (1976) Audrey Hepburn played an elderly Maid Marian. Which male film star played opposite her as Robin Hood?

1. What was Tina Turner's original name? ▲ ▶

2. Who was the drummer who replaced the late Keith Moon in The Who in 1978?

3. Where is Gracelands, the mansion built for Elvis Presley, situated?

4. Which pop star's guitar sold for £198,000 at auction in 1990?

5. In which year did the Live Aid concerts take place?

6. What do the groups En Vogue, Jade and SWV have in common?

7. What is Bruce Springsteen's nickname?

8. Which pop artist recorded the album *True Blue* that topped the charts in 28 countries in 1986?

9. Which rock star became chairman of Watford Football Club in 1980?

10. What is 'acid house'?

11. Johnny Rotten and Sid Vicious belonged to which pop group?

12. Which world famous West Indian rock star, a friend of Jamaican Prime Minister Michael Manley, was shot in the arm by political opponents in 1976?

13. Whose album entitled *Tattoo You* was released in 1981?

14. Which city was the original home of the 1980s pop group U2?

15. Which legendary British singer was awarded the OBE by the Queen in 1980 on his 40th birthday?

16 On which of Michael Jackson's best-selling albums would you find the track *The Girl is Mine*?

17 Which band was the leader of the hard rock movement?

18 Which two artists founded the Eurythmics and recorded the first album in 1981?

19 In what film did pop star David Bowie launch his career as a film actor in 1976?

20 Their album *Synchronicity* became one of the best-selling LPs of all time and, in 1983, they reached No 1 in Britain and the United States with *Every Breath You Take*. Name the group.

21 Which of the Bee Gees are twins?

22 Who left an all-girl vocal group, originally called the Primettes, to begin a solo career in 1969 and has become a top international star?

23 Which American superstar said, 'I don't know anything about music. In my line you don't have to.'?

24 Who had a hit with *I Will Always Love You*?

25 Which American record label was bought by Polygram in August 1993?

1. What is the meaning of the Dutch word *brandewijn* from which we take our word brandy?

2. From which fruit is Calvados made?

3. Which drink has been known as 'Dutch courage' and 'Mother's ruin'?

4. Between 1740 and 1970 British sailors received a daily ration of grog. What is grog? ▼ ▶

5. 5. What is the name of the Japanese spirit made from rice which is served warm?

6. Schnapps is made in Germany from potatoes. What is used for flavouring?

7. Where did the American whiskey 'Bourbon' get its name?

8. What is added to gin to make pink gin?

9. Bottles of spirits should be stored upright. Why? ▶

SIX-WATER GROG.

10 Advocaat is a low-alcohol liqueur made from brandy, sugar and what other important ingredient?

11 Cognac can be made only in a specific area of France. Where can brandy be made?

12 The fermented molasses left over from the sugar-refining process is used in the manufacture of which spirit?

13 A popular Yorkshire liqueur flavoured with herbs is named after the Brontë sisters. On which spirit is it based?

14 In which country is Geneva gin made?

15 What colourless liqueur is made from cherries?

16 Poteen is an illegally distilled spirit made in the west of Ireland. What is it made from?

17 What colour is the Italian liqueur Galliano?

18 Atholl Brose is made from malt whisky, distilled oatmeal, honey and what else?

19 What do the letters VSOP on a bottle of brandy stand for?

20 Southern Comfort is a popular American liqueur with a base of Bourbon whiskey and a fruit flavouring. Which fruit?

21 What is the flavouring of Pernod, the French spirit that turns milky when water is added?

22 Which liqueur is made from the peel of small bitter oranges?

23 What type of spirit is Bacardi?

24 A well-known Balkan spirit is made from plums. What is it called?

25 How old must Scotch whisky be before it can be sold in the U.K.?

1. Where were the 1992 Olympics held?

2. Do Olympic rules allow competitors in athletics events to go without shoes?

3. What distance is the Olympic marathon?

4. How long is the run-up for the Olympic high jump?

5. The modern pentathlon includes fencing, cross-country running, riding, shooting and one other event. What is it?

6. The women's pentathlon has been dominated by East German athletes, but in 1972 there was a British winner. Name her.

7. Which Romanian gymnast won six individual gold medals in 1976-80, sometimes achieving perfect scores?

8. Which country hosted the 1992 Winter Olympics?

9. How many consecutive failures are pole vaulters allowed before they are eliminated?

10. Two styles of wrestling are included in modern Olympics. One is Greco-Roman. What is the other?

11. Ben Johnson of Canada was disqualified in the 1988 Olympic Games in Seoul. Why? ▶

12. Throwing events in the Olympics include javelin, shotput and discus. What is the fourth? ▲

13. In javelin throwing, a red flag indicates a foul. What indicates a fair throw?

14. Which young gymnast from the U.S.S.R. won the hearts of the crowd for her original and individualistic style in the 1972 Munich Olympics?

15. In which decade was judo made an Olympic sport?

16. The three-day event includes three equestrian competitions. Two of them are show-jumping and endurance. What is the third?

17 What is the difference between the vaulting horse used in men's and women's gymnastics?

18 In ice dancing, how long is the free dance programme?

19 How many judges are involved in triple jump events?

20 Mark Spitz won seven gold medals at the 1972 Munich Olympics. In which sport did he compete?

21 What length is the swimming pool in which Olympic competitions are held?

22 What are the two middle distance Olympic track races?

23 How many events are included in the heptathlon?

24 The equestrian events of the Melbourne Olympics in 1956 were held in another country because of Australian quarantine regulations. Where were they held?

25 Who is the most recent British athlete to be simultaneously the World, Olympic, European and Commonwealth champion in his event?

1 What is the holy book of the Islamic religion called?

2 Followers of which religion use prayer wheels?

3 What is the name of the four-cornered headgear worn by Roman Catholic ecclesiastics? ▼

4 Which Christian saint was born at Lourdes in France?

5 What name is given to food prepared in accordance with Jewish ritual?

6 In which country are cows considered sacred?

7 Which religious movement was founded by Mary Baker Eddy in the 19th century?

8 Who was the only Englishman to become pope?

9 What is the tower on top of a Moslem mosque called? ▶

10 In the Islamic world, what is the Hajj?

11 In which country is Zen the leading school of Buddhism?

12 In the Christian religion, what name is given to the first day of Holy Week?

TOMB OF SULTAN KAITBAY

13 In the Jewish faith, what is the religious coming of age of a 13-year-old boy called?

14 In which country did the Dalai Lama rule?

15 Which day of the week is the Moslem Sabbath?

16 Who was the first Christian martyr?

17 Where does the world's largest Mormon Temple stand?

18 How many points does the Star of David have?

19 In which religion is Diwali, the Festival of Light, celebrated?

20 According to the book of Genesis, which common fruit were Adam and Eve forbidden to eat by God?

21 In what type of building would you find a minbar and a mihrab?

22 Who said, the famous words 'Religion is the opium of the people'?

23 How many gospels are there in the New Testament?

24 Vishnu, Shiva and Ganesh play an important part in which religion?

25 What special name was given to the particular-chalice used by Jesus Christ on the evening of the last supper?

1. What is the other name for the Northern Lights?

2. CFCs are said to be damaging the ozone layer. What does CFC stand for?

3. When you cross the international date line from east to west do you gain or lose a day?

4. What are the grasslands of North America called?

5. Which is the world's largest ocean?

6. What is the earth's outer layer called?

7. Why do farmers in parts of China keep ducks in their rice fields?

8. Corals grow in warm, tropical waters. What are corals made from? ▶

9. What is the longest river in Asia?

10. According to scientists, the Himalayas are about 40 million years old. Are the North American Rockies older or younger?

11. What are the chinook, the khamsin and the sirocco?

12. Which limestone formations hang down from the ceilings of caves: stalactites or stalagmites? ▶

13. What is a tsunami?

14. The earth is surrounded by a blanket of air. What is it called?

15. Bamboo forests grow in the south–western mountains of China, but bamboo is not a tree. What is it?

16 Some beaches, for instance in Tahiti, are made from lava. What colour is the sand?

17 In which lake in Peru do people live on islands built from thickly matted totora reeds?

18 What instrument is used for measuring atmospheric pressure?

19 In many countries, farmers cut down and burn a patch of forest, and then use the ash from the fire to fertilize crops. What is this method of cultivation called?

20 What protective function does the ozone layer fulfil?

21 21. What is the only grass that can actually grow in water?

22 22. How long does it take for the earth to revolve once on its axis?

23 23. What is the Hindu Kush?

24 24. What are cone-bearing trees called?

25 25. Half the entire desert area of the world is contained in just a single desert. Name it.

1. During Prohibition, Americans drank illegally in clubs. What were these places called?

2. Who spoke the first words in the first 'all singing, all dancing' film *The Jazz Singer*?

3. What were 'Oxford bags'?

4. By what nickname was French designer Gabrielle Chanel always known? ▲

5. Who followed the yellow brick road in *The Wizard of Oz* along with Dorothy and her dog?

6. What discovery set off the fashions in clothes, fabrics and footwear known as Tutmania?

7. What famous dance of the 1920s shared its name with a city in the southern United States? ▶

8. Which film cartoon character made his debut in *Steamboat Willie* in 1928?

9. Who was the British Prime Minister when King Edward VIII abdicated?

10. What was the other name for the men's fashion of knickerbockers?

11 The struggle for votes for women was finally successful in Britain in 1918. What was the voting age for women at the time?

12 The British called the fashion-conscious young people of the 1920s 'bright young things'. What were they called in America?

13 What film character was portrayed by American Olympic gold medallist swimmer Johnny Weissmuller?

14 In which sport was Frenchwoman Suzanne Lenglen famous, delighting crowds with her fashionable outfits?

15 Who was Ginger Rogers' famous dancing partner in musicals such as *Top Hat*?

16 What were Kickin' the Mule, Truckin' and Peckin' the Apple?

17 What type of skirt was a dirndl?

18 What famous skyscraper with 102 storeys was built in New York in 1931?

19 One of the most famous gangland killings in the United States took place on 14 February, 1929, when members of Al Capone's gang gunned down seven unarmed rivals. What was the killing known as?

20 Which President of the United States brought in the 'New Deal' to revive the American economy in the 1930s?

21 What new fabric replaced rayon for stockings in 1930?

22 German film maker Leni Riefenstahl was commissioned by Hitler to make a documentary of which event, aimed at glorifying Germans as the 'master race'?

23 Which British Prime Minister promised that the treaty signed with Germany in September 1938 meant 'peace in our time'?

24 Who starred as the glamorous nightclub singer in *The Blue Angel*?

25 What record did racing car driver Sir Malcolm Campbell break at Daytona Beach, Florida, in 1932?

1. What is the Decalogue usually called?

2. What is the name of Italy's state airline?

3. Which American golfer has been nicknamed the 'Golden Bear'?

4. Which London tube line is coloured green on the underground map?

5. The handsome peacock belongs to which family of birds? ▲

6. What does a Geiger counter measure?

7 In the fight for racial equality, black people in an American state organized a boycott of buses in 1955 to protest against race laws. Which state?

8 In 1960 Amy, Sally and Mo made a space flight. Who or what were Amy, Sally and Mo?

9 From which ancient game does badminton derive? ▶

10 In which country does the River Rhine rise?

11 In which novel does the parrot called Captain Flint appear?

12 Which young actor died in a car crash in California in 1955?

13 What would you expect to find in a sarcophagus?

14 In the Bible, who was Bathsheba's first husband, at the time when she caught King David's eye?

15 What does the term AWOL mean to a soldier?

16 In World War II, what was the Manhattan Project?

17 In what field was Maria Montessori famous?

18 The film *Ring of Bright Water* told the story of which type of creature?

19 Before British coinage was decimalized, how many old pennies made a florin?

20 In which sport did Mike Gatting become famous?

21 What was Beethoven's first name?

22 Count' was the nickname of which jazz musician?

23 What type of furniture is a davenport?

24 Name the official record of the daily proceedings in the British Parliament.

25 Which country is known as the 'land of the mid-night sun'?

People and Places   Myths

1. Rome
2. Amazons
3. Nine
4. Neptune
5. Eurydice
6. Shoemaker
7. Olympus
8. Jason
9. Sharazad (Shéhérazade)
10. Swiss
11. Janus
12. Perseus
13. She sat on a rock combing her hair and singing
14. Helen
15. They hid inside a wooden horse
16. Cyclops
17. By a single hair
18. They acquire the 'gift of the gab'
19. Camelot
20. Ra
21. Icarus
22. Diana
23. Theseus
24. Hermes
25. Sean Connery

Entertaining Arts   Pop Music

1. Annie Mae Bullock
2. Kenny Jones
3. Memphis, Tennessee
4. Jimi Hendrix
5. 1985
6. All-girl groups
7. The Boss
8. Madonna
9. Elton John
10. A style of fast-beat pop music; also used for a youth cult associated with the music and sometimes with drug-taking
11. The Sex Pistols
12. Bob Marley
13. Rolling Stones
14. Dublin, Ireland
15. Cliff Richard
16. Thriller
17. Led Zeppelin
18. Annie Lennox and Dave Stewart
19. The Man who Fell to Earth
20. The Police
21. Maurice and Robin
22. Diana Ross
23. Elvis Presley
24. Whitney Houston
25. Motown

Food and Drink   The Hard Stuff

1. Burnt wine
2. Apples
3. Gin
4. A mixture of rum and water
5. Sake
6. Caraway seeds
7. It was first made in Bourbon County, Kentucky
8. Angostura bitters
9. To prevent the liquid coming in contact with the metal cap
10. Egg yolks
11. Anywhere in the world
12. Rum
13. Brandy
14. Holland
15. Kirsch
16. Potatoes
17. Yellow
18. Cream
19. Very Special Old Pale
20. Peach
21. Aniseed
22. Curaçao
23. White rum
24. Slivovitz
25. Three years

Sports and Pastimes   The Olympics

1. Barcelona, Spain
2. Yes
3. 42.195 km (26 miles 385 yards)
4. Unlimited
5. Swimming
6. Mary Peters
7. Nadia Comaneci
8. France
9. Three
10. Freestyle
11. Positive drugs test
12. Hammer
13. A white flag
14. Olga Korbut
15. 1960s
16. Dressage
17. The men's is higher; 135 cm compared with 120 cm
18. Four minutes
19. Five
20. Swimming
21. 50 metres
22. 800 metres and 1,500 metres
23. Seven
24. Stockholm, Sweden
25. Lindford Christie

History   World Religions

1. Koran
2. Buddhism
3. Biretta
4. Bernadette
5. Kosher
6. India
7. Christian Science
8. Nicholas Breakspear, Pope Hadrian IV
9. Minaret
10. Pilgrimage to Mecca
11. Japan
12. Palm Sunday
13. Bar Mitzvah
14. Tibet
15. Friday
16. St. Stephen
17. Salt Lake City
18. Six
19. Hindu
20. The fruit of the tree of knowledge of good and evil
21. A mosque
22. Karl Marx
23. Four
24. Hindu
25. The Holy Grail

Natural World   Our Earth

1. Aurora borealis
2. Chlorofluorocarbons
3. Lose a day
4. Prairie
5. Pacific
6. Crust
7. To control insect pests
8. Skeletons of millions of tiny creatures
9. The Yangtze
10. Older
11. Winds
12. Stalactites
13. A sea wave created by an earthquake
14. The atmosphere
15. A type of grass
16. Black
17. Lake Titicaca
18. Barometer
19. Slash and burn
20. It filters out the sun's harmful ultra-violet rays
21. Rice
22. 24 hours
23. A mountain range
24. Conifers
25. Sahara

Twentieth Century   The 1920s and 1930s

1. Speak-easies
2. Al Jolson
3. Wide-legged trousers
4. Coco
5. The cowardly lion, the scarecrow and the tin man
6. The tomb of Tutankhamen, the Egyptian boy king
7. The Charleston
8. Mickey Mouse
9. Stanley Baldwin
10. Plus-fours
11. 30
12. Flappers
13. Tarzan
14. Tennis
15. Fred Astaire
16. Dances
17. A full skirt, loosely gathered onto a waistband
18. Empire State Building
19. The St. Valentine's Day Massacre
20. President Roosevelt
21. Nylon
22. The Berlin Olympic Games in 1936
23. Neville Chamberlain
24. Marlene Dietrich
25. World land speed record

Pot Luck

1. The Ten Commandments
2. Al Italia
3. Jack Nicklaus
4. District
5. Pheasant
6. Radioactivity
7. Alabama
8. Mice
9. Battledore and shuttle cock
10. Switzerland
11. Treasure Island
12. James Dean
13. A corpse
14. Uriah the Hittite
15. Absent without leave
16. Development of the atomic bomb
17. Education
18. Otter
19. 24
20. Cricket
21. Ludwig
22. Basie
23. Writing desk
24. Hansard
25. Norway

Quiz

1. By what name is the Central Criminal Court in London better known?

2. Braemar, near Balmoral, is the site of the most famous of the great clan events, with competitions like caber tossing and hammer throwing. What are these events called?

3. What are Watling Street and Fosse Way?

4. Which Scottish loch is reputedly the home of a prehistoric monster?

5. On which river does the university town of Cambridge stand?

6. Which family trio of writers lived at the Parsonage in Haworth on the wild North Yorkshire moors?

7. Lewis, Harris and Benbecula are part of which group of Scottish islands?

8. Which London street is associated with the medical profession?

9. The Cistercian Abbey of Tintern, founded in 1131, stands beside the River Wye. Which 19th–century poet wrote *Lines written above Tintern Abbey*?

10. Which northern city is the home of the Royal Liver Building, two cathedrals and the Albert Dock?

11. What is the name of the Prime Minister's official country residence?

12. Which is the largest of the lakes in Cumbria's Lake District?

13. Chartwell, in Kent, was the home of which famous statesman for 40 years?

14. In which Midlands town is William Shakespeare buried at St. Mary's Church?

15 What is the nickname of the clock tower on the Houses of Parliament?

16 In which city would you find the Radcliffe Camera, the Sheldonian Theatre and Balliol College?

17 Which is the oldest British royal residence still in use?

18 Which river was the setting for the comic adventures of Jerome K. Jerome's *Three Men in a Boat*?

19 In what part of the British Isles is the Brecon Beacons National Park?

20 What is the most southerly tip of England called?

21 One of Northern Ireland's most famous sights is a collection of basalt columns caused by the cooling and shrinking of lava from an ancient volcano. Legend says they were stepping stones used to reach Scotland. What are they called? ◀ ▲

22 The tors on Dartmoor in south-west Devon are the remains of a three million-year-old mountain system. From what type of rock are the tors formed?

23 In 122AD, a Roman emperor began the building of a wall across the north-west of England to mark the limits of the empire. What was his name?

24 Which Scottish glen is known as the 'Glen of Weeping' because it was the scene of a notorious massacre of the Macdonalds by the Campbells in 1692?

25 The Italianate village of Portmeirion in Wales was designed by Clough Williams-Ellis and provided an atmospheric setting for which 1960s hugely popular television series starring Patrick McGoohan?

1. Which character travelled around the world in 80 days with Passe Partout?

2. What was the girl's school created by Ronald Searle and portrayed in several comedy films?

3. Which author created the aggressive, lethal plants called triffids?

4. Name the Scottish schoolteacher played by Maggie Smith in the film of Muriel Spark's novel?

5. According to Aesop's Fable, which animal did the tortoise beat in a race?

6. Who wrote *The Last of the Mohicans*?

7. Name the young hero of *Treasure Island*.

8. In which book by William Golding are Piggy and Ralph shipwrecked?

9. Victor Hugo wrote *The Hunchback of Notre Dame*. What was his other famous book, the story of an escaped convict, Jean Valjean?

10. Which character in *David Copperfield*, by Charles Dickens, always insisted that he was 'very 'umble'?

11. In what London street did Sherlock Holmes live?

12. Under what name is the author Samuel Langhorne Clemens better known?

13. In which novel does the heroine finally marry Mr. Rochester?

14. Whom did Minnehaha marry in Longfellow's poem?

15. Peter Ustinov has portrayed Agatha Christie's detective Hercule Poirot in films. What nationality was Poirot?

16 In a 17th–century novel, Don Quixote decides to become a knight. What does he begin attacking because he mistakes them for a row of giants?

17 By what romantic name was Sir Percy Blakeney known in Baroness Orczy's novel?

18 Which novelist wrote of a farm run by pigs and of the imaginary world of 1984?

19 Name the character who visits Lilliput and Brobdingnag. ◀ ▼

20 *Carrie* and *The Shining* were both successful films. Who wrote the novels on which they were based?

21 Which character lived at Sunnybrook Farm?

22 Which best-selling novelist was the youngest member of the British House of Commons in 1969?

23 Two novels by Alan Sillitoe were filmed in the 1960s. One was *The Loneliness of the Long Distance Runner*. What was the other?

24 Jeeves was the perfect butler. Who was his employer?

25 In 1991 the sequel to *Gone with the Wind*, written by Alexandra Ripley, was published. What was the title?

1 What type of dried fruit do nomadic tribes call 'bread of the desert'?

2 What colour is the flesh of an ogen melon?

3 The plaintain is a staple food in some areas of East and West Africa. What type of fruit is it exactly?

4 'Plashing' is a term used to describe the collecting of which type of nut?

5 A number of cacti produce edible fruit, but which is the only cactus fruit to be eaten widely? ▲

6 The nursery rhyme says, 'I had a little nut-tree, nothing would it bear, but...'. What did it bear?

7 Which fruit took its name from a shortening of Damascene or 'plum from Damascus'?

8 The people of the Hunza valley in northern Pakistan were said to live to a ripe old age because their diet was based on which dried fruit?

9 What are Blenheim, Lord Derby and Peasgood?

10 Which nut is used to make marzipan?

11 In Edward Lear's poem, on what fruit did the Owl and the Pussycat dine?

12 A nectarine is a smooth-skinned variety of which fruit?

13 What type of fruit is morello?

14 What is the more usual name for a Chinese gooseberry?

15 Mangoes are rich in which vitamin?

16 When the mutiny on the *Bounty* took place, the ship was making for the West Indies with a cargo of fruit trees. Which type of fruit was it?

17 What is the pineapple's top-knot of stiff, spiky leaves called?

18 Bananas grow on stems and the bunches of bananas are called 'hands'. What are individual bananas called?

19 What is the other name for paw-paw?

20 From what type of tree does the delicious pecan nut come?

21 Which fruit got its name because the flowers are said to resemble the crown of thorns worn by Jesus Christ?

22 What fruit sauce is traditionally served with turkey?

23 Which fruit has six sections divided by whitish membranes, each containing many pips embedded in juicy flesh, and causes difficult-to-remove stains?

24 What are 'love apples'?

25 Which type of nut is sometimes called a groundnut or earthnut? ▼

1. Which horse won the Grand National three times?

2. Which famous American horse race is nick-named 'Run for the Roses' because the winner receives a garland of roses in the shape of a horseshoe?

3. What is a baby horse called?

4. When riding, what are 'aids'?

5. In a rodeo, bronco riding is a standard event. What is the only piece of tack worn by the horse?

6. What is a drag–hunt?

7. Which extremely successful racehorse, bred by the Aga Khan, disappeared and was never seen again?

8. Lucinda Green is a well-known British rider in horse trials and holds the record for the most wins at the Badminton Horse trials. What was her double-barrelled maiden name?

9. Three major races make up the legendary American Triple Crown. Two are the Preakness Stakes and the Kentucky Derby. What is the third race?

10 Which major horse race, inaugurated in 1861, is held in Australia on the first Tuesday in November?

11 What is the unit of measurement used for horses?

12 The horse Milton won the King George V Gold Cup in 1990 and the Volvo World Cup in 1990-91, among other competitions. Who was its British rider?

13 What are a horse's parents called?

14 How can a horse's age be determined?

15 On which British race course is Boxing Day's King George VI steeplechase held?

16 In polo, what is a chukka?

17 How many fences are there in the Grand National?

18 In show jumping, how many penalty points are awarded if the rider falls off?

19 How did the Derby get its name? ◀ ▲

20 What, on the race-track, is an 'outsider'?

21 What type of horse is a 'stayer'?

22 How old is a filly?

23 Early races in America were sprints over short distances. Which famous breed was developed for the purpose?

24 In racing, what is a 'maiden'?

25 What happens in the rules of show jumping when two or more riders have tied for first place?

1. In which country were the earliest fragments of paper discovered?

2. Who invented the telephone?

3. In the 1764, an Englishman, James Hargreaves, invented a machine that revolutionized the weaving industry. What was it called?

4. In what decade of the 20th century did electric refrigerators appear, revolutionizing food storage?

5. What were the given names of the Wright brothers, who were the first to achieve power-controlled flight in a full-sized aeroplane? ▲ ▶

6. In 1895 Wilhelm Röntgen made a discovery which was described at the time as 'probably the greatest landmark in the whole history of diagnosis' and is still important in medicine today. What was it?

7. The first hearing aid was invented in 1901. What did people use before that?

8. Many labels still bear the name of the man who invented frozen food. Who was he?

9. In which country were the first bars of chocolate made?

10. What did Louis Braille invent in 1829?

11 Which brothers invented the hot-air balloon, which first carried human passengers in November 1783?

12 The wheel was first used in Mesopotamia over 5,000 years ago. In which modern country is Mesopotamia?

13 What means of transport did Christopher Cockerell invent in the 1950s?

14 What was the very first breakfast cereal, invented by H.D. Perky, who happened to be an American lawyer?

15 When the newly-invented vacuum flask was about to be launched on the market, a competition was held to find a name and 'Thermos' was chosen. What does thermos mean?

16 In which decade of the 20th century was the aerosol invented?

17 Which inventor developed the first radio when experimenting in his parents' attic near Bologna?

18 What did the French brothers Auguste and Louis Lumière demonstrate in the 1890s?

19 The first traffic lights were put up in London in 1868. Where were they situated?

20 In 1909, Leo Baekeland made a plastic from chemicals found in coal tar. What was it called?

21 In which century was movable type first used in Europe?

22 Which doctor discovered penicillin by accident?

23 In the 1920s when Thomas Wall of London manufactured the first wrapped blocks of ice cream and sold them from tricycles in the street. What was the slogan on the front of the tricycles?

24 Who invented the modern ballpoint pen?

25 Who was the German immigrant to the United States who began making trousers out of tough material called 'jean'

1. What is an eagle's nest called?

2. What kind of bird did Noah first release from the ark once the rain had stopped?

3. Which bird sometimes builds its nest on top of a chimney?

4. Baby birds have an 'egg tooth', a small knob on the tip of the beak. What is it used for?

5. Ducks feed in three ways, as grazers, dabblers and divers. To which category do mallards belong?

6. Which bird is the national emblem of the United States? ▼

7. How many toes do most birds have?

8. In ornithology, what is a clutch?

9. Which birds are bred for racing?

10. What is the other name for the long-necked anhinga?

17 In the old song, which bird sang in Berkeley Square?

18 What materials does a swallow use to build its nest?

19 The scientific name of which bird is Pica pica?

20 What is the Californian condor's current claim to fame?

21 Which birds are associated with the Tower of London?

22 Where do wading birds find their food?

23 Which type of swan has a black and yellow face?

24 What is the name for the place where birds sleep?

25 If a bird is diurnal, what are its habits?

11 What is unique about the beak of the wrybill, a New Zealand plover?

12 Which bird lays its eggs in another bird's nest? ▲ ▶

13 What colour is a female blackbird?

14 Which bird lays the largest egg?

15 Name the film in which Burt Lancaster played a bird-loving prisoner.

16 Which African bird is the tallest bird of prey?

1. What was the name of the American Allied Commanding Officer in the Gulf War?

2. What was the name given to the political movement that aimed to create a secure home in Palestine for the Jewish people and which emerged in the early 20th century?

3. What were the Communist guerrillas of the Vietnam war called?

4. The Arabic word 'jihad' literally means 'struggle'. What is the current popular meaning?

5. In 1976, PFLP and Baader-Meinhof terrorists hijacked an Air France plane and landed at a Ugandan airport. The hostages were freed in a successful raid by Israeli forces. Where was the airport?

6. What was the name of the missiles launched by Iraq against Israel in the Gulf War?

7. Members of Britain's SAS stormed the Iranian embassy in London where Arab terrorists were holding hostages in May 1980. What does SAS stand for? ▶

8. An exotic dancer, Margareta-Gertruida Zelle, was arrested and shot for espionage in World War I. By what name is she better known? ▶

9. In 1982 Argentina invaded the Falkland Islands, maintaining that it had a legal claim to sovereignty. What do Argentineans call the islands?

10. On what Jewish religious festival did the Arab-Israeli war of 1973 break out?

11. In the Vietnam war, what was the name of the jellied petrol that sticks to and sets fire to anything it touches?

12. What is the name of the rebel faction waging war in Angola?

13. What group is dedicated to achieving independence of the Basque region of northern Spain?

14. What South African word means 'separate development' or racial segregation?

15. What is semtex?

16 What do the initials IRA stand for?

17 Name the 'red priest' of Haiti, backed in his attempt to regain control of the island by the United States government.

18 Anwar Sadat was assassinated in 1981. In which country?

19 What is the Intifada?

20 Which island was awarded the George Cross for gallantry in World War II?

21 Who was assassinated in June 1914, precipitating the outbreak of World War I?

22 Which side did UN forces support in the Korean War?

23 In what year did Iraq invade Kuwait?

24 Hezbollah is an anti-Israeli and anti-western group of Shi'ite Muslims formed in Lebanon in the 1980s. What does the name mean?

1. What does a herpetologist study?

2. In the United States, how many nickels would you get for a dime?

3. What is a John Dory?

4. Which Scottish school did both the Duke of Edinburgh and his son Prince Charles attend? ▼

5. What does a dermatologist study?

6. Which is the least used letter in the English language?

7. Name the mythological character sentenced to fall in love with his own reflection as a punishment for his pride?

8. In 1908, Kenneth Graham, an English bank clerk, wrote a book which has become a children's classic. What was it called?

9. It is sometimes called a gnu. What is its other name?

10. When milk sours, what acid is formed?

11. Two countries have been the most frequent hosts of the Winter Olympics. One is the United States; what is the other?

16 In medicine. what is known as a 'magic bullet'?

17 What name is given to a baby whale? ▼

18 Which fictional aviator had friends called Ginger and Algy?

19 How do frogs catch flies?

20 Only one American state has a name beginning with 'L'. Name it.

21 For which film and television role is Leonard Nimoy best known?

22 What is measured by the truss?

23 In the book by James Hilton, what was the profession of 'Mr Chips'?

24 The national flag of the Netherlands bears which three colours?

25 On which island did the mutinous crew from the *Bounty* make their home?

12 Which James Bond film starred Honor Blackman? ▲

13 Who was the author of *Our Mutual Friend*?

14 At the time of the French Revolution, what were tumbrels?

15 Which American gangster was known as 'Scarface'?

People and Places   British Isles

1. Old Bailey
2. Highland Gathering or Games
3. Roman roads
4. Loch Ness
5. River Cam
6. The Brontë sisters
7. Outer Hebrides
8. Harley Street
9. William Wordsworth
10. Liverpool
11. Chequers
12. Lake Windermere
13. Winston Churchill
14. Stratford-upon-Avon
15. Big Ben
16. Oxford
17. Windsor Castle
18. Thames
19. Wales
20. Lizard Point, Cornwall
21. Giant's Causeway
22. Granite
23. Hadrian
24. Glencoe
25. The Prisoner

Entertaining Arts   A Good Read

1. Phileas Fogg
2. St. Trinian's
3. John Wyndham
4. Miss Jean Brodie
5. A hare
6. James Fenimore Cooper
7. Jim Hawkins
8. Lord of the Flies
9. Les Misérables
10. Uriah Heap
11. Baker Street
12. Mark Twain
13. Jane Eyre
14. Hiawatha
15. Belgian
16. Windmills
17. The Scarlet Pimpernel
18. George Orwell
19. Gulliver
20. Stephen King
21. Rebecca
22. Jeffrey Archer
23. Saturday Night and Sunday Morning
24. Bertie Wooster
25. Scarlett

Food and Drink   Fruit and Nuts

1. Dates
2. Green
3. Cooking banana
4. Walnut
5. Prickly pear
6. A silver nutmeg and a golden pear
7. Damson
8. Apricots
9. Types of apple
10. Almond
11. Quince
12. Peach
13. Cherry
14. Kiwi fruit
15. Vitamin A
16. Breadfruit
17. Crown
18. Fingers
19. Papaya
20. Hickory tree
21. Passion fruit
22. Cranberry
23. Pomegranate
24. Tomatoes
25. Peanut

Sports and Pastimes   Horses and Riding

1. Red Rum
2. Kentucky Derby
3. A foal
4. Any signals used by the rider to give instructions to the horse
5. A wide leather band round its middle, with a handhold
6. A hunt using an artificial scent
7. Shergar
8. Prior-Palmer
9. Belmont Stakes
10. Melbourne Cup
11. Hand
12. John Whitaker
13. Sire and dam
14. By examining its teeth
15. Kempton Park
16. The 4-6 periods into which the game is divided
17. 30, over two circuits
18. Eight
19. On the toss of a coin between Lord Derby and Sir Charles Bunbury
20. A horse thought to have little chance of winning a race and therefore given long betting odds
21. A horse with great strength and endurance
22. Less than four years
23. The Quarter Horse
24. A horse of either sex which has not yet run a race
25. A jump-off

History   Inventions

1. China
2. Alexander Graham Bell
3. Spinning jenny
4. 1920s
5. Wilbur and Orville
6. X rays
7. Ear trumpets
8. Clarence Birdseye
9. Switzerland
10. A system of raised dots to enable blind people to read printed words
11. Joseph and Etienne Montgolfier
12. Iraq
13. The hovercraft
14. Shredded Wheat
15. It is Greek for hot
16. 1940s
17. Guglielmo Marconi
18. Projected moving images
19. Outside the Houses of Parliament
20. Bakelite
21. 15th century
22. Dr. Alexander Fleming
23. 'Stop me and buy one'
24. Biró
25. Levi Strauss

Natural World   Birds

1. An eyrie
2. Raven
3. Stork
4. To break out of the egg
5. Dabblers
6. Bald eagle
7. Four
8. The number of eggs a bird lays at one time
9. Homing pigeons
10. Snake-bird
11. It is the only bird with a beak that curves sideways
12. Cuckoo
13. Brown
14. Ostrich
15. Bird Man of Alcatraz
16. Secretary bird
17. Nightingale
18. Mud and saliva
19. Magpie
20. It is the rarest vulture in the world
21. Ravens
22. In the mud and sand at the water's edge
23. Bewick swan
24. Roost
25. It is active during the day and sleeps at nights

Twentieth Century   Conflict and Conflagration

1. Norman Schwarzkopf
2. Zionism
3. Viet Cong
4. Holy war
5. Entebbe
6. Scud
7. Special Air Service
8. Mata Hari
9. Las Malvinas
10. Yom Kippur
11. Napalm
12. UNITA
13. ETA
14. Apartheid
15. Plastic explosive often used by terrorists
16. Irish Republican Army
17. Jean-Bertrand Aristide
18. Egypt
19. The Arab uprising in Israeli-occupied territory
20. Malta
21. Archduke Ferdinand of Austria
22. South Korea
23. 1990
24. Party of God

Pot Luck

1. Reptiles and amphibians
2. Two
3. A fish
4. Gordonstoun
5. Skin
6. Q
7. Narcissus
8. Wind in the Willows
9. Wildebeest
10. Lactic acid
11. France
12. Goldfinger
13. Charles Dickens
14. Horse-drawn wagons used to take prisoners to the guillotine
15. Al Capone
16. A drug that will attack only unhealthy cells
17. A calf
18. Biggles
19. They have sticky tongues
20. Louisiana
21. Mr. Spock
22. Hay or straw
23. Schoolteacher
24. Red, white and blue
25. Pitcairn

Quiz

4

1 How did the boy David defeat the giant Goliath?

2 What was the nickname of Ivan IV, Tsar of Russia in the 16th century?

3 Which American soldier, who led the Allied forces to victory in Europe in World War II, later became President of the United States?

4 How did Lawrence of Arabia die? ▼

5 5. Which Roman emperor was said to have fiddled while Rome burned?

6 6. Which people were led by Genghis Khan?

7 7. In 1939 Douglas Bader was flying Spitfire fighter planes for the RAF. Why was this extraordinary?

8 8. Which king of Judea ordered the massacre of male babies under the age of two?

9 How many terms did George Washington serve as the first President of the United States of America?

10 Many legends attach to the English highwayman Dick Turpin, hanged at Tyburn in 1739. According to legend, what was the name of his horse?

11 Who set off on Antarctic expeditions first in *Discovery* and later in *Terra Nova*?

12 Joseph Dzhugashvili, who succeeded Lenin as Soviet leader, took the name of Stalin. What does it mean?

13 The medical missionary Albert Schweizer was awarded the Nobel Peace Prize in 1952. What nationality was he?

14 How did the pirate Captain Kidd meet his end?

15 Which American President announced in 1863 that all slaves in the Confederate states would be freed immediately?

16 Whose secret police force was known as Ton-Ton-Macoutes?

17 Sir Thomas More was tried for high treason when he refused to recognize Henry VIII as Supreme Head of the Church. What high office did More hold?

18 An uprising of slaves against the Romans in 72BC was led by a Thracian gladiator, portrayed by Kirk Douglas in a 1960 film. What was his name? ▶

19 What is the meaning of *Mein Kampf*, the book which set out Hitler's political creed?

20 In which American city did the gangster Al Capone operate?

21 Davy Crockett made his name as a fearless pioneer and a soldier in the Indian wars before he was elected to Congress in 1827. Which state did he represent?

22 Which Hun leader united the Barbarian tribes and attacked the Byzantine Empire in 447?

23 Maximilien de Robespierre was one of the leaders of the French Revolution and ruled the country as a virtual dictator. What name was given to his period of rule?

24 Jean Bedel Bokassa had himself crowned Emperor Bokassa I of his country after it gained independence from the French. Which country was it?

25 Who dissolved the English Parliament and declared himself Lord Protector in 1653?

1. Which artist cut off the lobe of his ear and later shot himself?

2. What nationality were Brueghel and Rubens?

3. Which painter had a 'blue period'?

4. In which type of paintings did Sir Joshua Reynolds specialize?

5. Which legendary artist produced two versions of *The Madonna of the Rocks* between 1483 and 1508?

6. What is the largest oil painting in the world?

7. Where in Britain does Graham Sutherland's tapestry *Christ in His Majesty* hang?

8. Which famous painting by Leonardo da Vinci is also known as *La Gioconda*?

9. What was the great painter Michelangelo's other name?

10. The French Impressionist Edgar Degas is noted for his paintings of horse racing and what other subject?

11. Which actor played Henri Toulouse-Lautrec in the film *Moulin Rouge*?

12. *The Thinker* and *The Kiss* were among the works of which sculptor? ▶

13. Which English landscape artist painted *The Hay Wain* and *Flatford Mill*?

14. What style of painting, in which the subject is reduced to basic geometric shapes, was founded by Picasso and Braque?

15. Domenikos Theotocopoulos was a Greek-born painter who studied under Titian and then lived and worked in Spain. Under what name is he better known?

16. To which school of painting did Dante Gabriel Rossetti belong?

17. Sir Jacob Epstein established himself as a sculptor in Britain after studying in Paris. Where was he born?

18. To which school of painting did Claude Monet belong?

19. Canaletto was famous for his paintings of which city?

20. Who designed St. Paul's Cathedral in London?

21. Which artist was commissioned by the Italian city of Florence, to sculpt the figure of David?

22. What nationality was the painter Goya?

23. The French painter Paul Gauguin went to live and paint on a Pacific island. Which island was it?

24. For what subject was the painter Stubbs best known?

25. In which branch of the arts did Barbara Hepworth achieve fame?

1. What substance is added to some jams and marmalades to make them set so they are firm in consistency?

2. Fruit should never be cooked in a copper pan. Why not?

3. What is it called when fat and juices from the roasting tin are spooned over meat while it is cooking?

4. If you cook food at 220° Celsius, what Fahrenheit temperature would you use?

5. In Chinese cooking, what is the name of the curved–bottomed iron pan, in which food cooks very quickly? ▲

6. When cooking with eggs, what can be tested by putting the egg in water containing 10 per cent salt, to see if it sinks or floats?

7 Why would you decant red wine?

8 On which shelf of the refrigerator should raw meat be stored?

9 Blackcurrants are a good source of which vitamin?

10 In cooking, what is dredging?

11 What is the small ovenproof dish used to serve individual savoury portions of food called?

12 How many fluid ounces are there in an American pint?

13 How many fluid ounces are there in an Imperial pint?

14 What is parboiling?

15 In what food is collagen found?

16 In degrees Fahrenheit, the boiling point of water is 212°. What is it in degrees Celsius?

17 What is the food made when fresh milk is artificially curdled by bacteria?

18 When you pit a cherry, what do you do?

19 What does rechauffé mean?

20 Name the red colouring matter obtained from a small Mexican beetle used to give shades of red and pink to food?

21 What is the name of the bowl used to help grind food and spices, used with a pestle? ▼

22 How would you reduce a liquid?

23 What are small cubes of fried or toasted bread sprinkled on soup called?

24 In Indian cooking, what is the name given to butter after it has been heated and then left to set?

25 Which word describes the action of tying or skewering a turkey into a good shape before cooking?

1. How many playing cards are there in a standard pack?

2. How do players advance around the board in a game of Snakes and Ladders?

3. 3. In bridge, what are the major suits?

4. 4. What are the tiles used to play dominoes often called?

5. 5. The game of chess is probably 14 centuries old. In which country did it originate? ▶

6. 6. A backgammon board is marked out in saw-tooth 'points' in two colours. How many points?

7. What game was officially ruled by Hoyle's Laws from its publication in 1760 to 1864?

8. In draughts, how many draughtsmen does each player have?

9. In which card game would you 'meld'?

10. What is the letter Q worth in Scrabble?

11. How many games are there in a rubber of contract bridge?

12. For what are tarot cards used?

13 In which board game would you buy and sell property?

14 How is the score usually kept in cribbage?

15 In gin rummy, how many cards are dealt to each player at the beginning of the game?

16 In mah jong, what combination of tiles is called a kong?

17 In chess, what is a gambit?

18 In pontoon, what is the point value of the picture cards?

19 In which game do you have to deduce who committed a murder?

20 How many picture cards are there in a standard pack of playing cards?

21 In the famous French game of boules, what is a baguette actually used for when one is playing?

22 How many blank tiles are there in the game of Scrabble?

23 What is the other name given to a castle in chess?

24 If you win a rubber in bridge, what have you done?

25 In darts, what does a dart in the outer bull score? ◄

1. Name two of the brothers of lawman and gun-fighter Wyatt Earp.

2. The notorious Judge Roy Bean dispensed his form of justice from a Texas saloon that he named 'The Jersey Lily', after an actress he admired. Who was she?

3. Which two army officers led the expedition which was to open up the American West in 1804 and establish the Oregon Trail?

4. In 1953 Doris Day played the title role in a film about a tough woman of the early West who reckoned she could out-shoot and out-drink any man. What was her name? ▼

5. What would a cowboy do with 'chaps' – a word taken from the Mexican *chaparejos*?

6. What was the surname of the notorious outlaw brothers Frank and Jesse?

7. Gold was first found in California on land belonging to pioneer John Sutter in 1848. What were the thousands of prospectors who joined the Gold Rush called?

8. Kit Carson was one of the best known of the 'mountain men', who worked as fur trappers. As the settlers moved west, he made himself invaluable in another capacity. What work did he choose?

9. Where did General Custer make his ill-fated 'last stand'?

10. Name one of the two great heroes of the American west who died in the battle of the Alamo at San Antonio, Texas.

11. What was the profession of gunfighter and gambler 'Doc' Holliday?

12. The following advertisement appeared in the newspapers of 1860. 'Wanted: Young, skinny, wiry fellows not over 18. Must be expert riders willing to risk death daily. Orphans preferred.' What was on offer to the applicants? ▲

13 Joseph Smith founded the Church of Jesus Christ of Latter Day Saints (the Mormons), but who led the Mormon pioneers on the trek west to the Salt Lake basin?

14 When the Plains people folded their tepees and prepared to follow the buffalo herds to better hunting grounds, they loaded their belongings onto sledges mounted on runners. We still use the Indian word for such sledges today. What is it?

15 Sitting Bull (1834-90) was one of the most famous native Americans of his time. What was his tribe?

16 What was the name of the gang headed by Butch Cassidy and the Sundance Kid? ▼

17 By what name was Colonel William Cody better known?

18 What were the Shawnee, Chisholm and Goodnight-Loving?

19 In 1939, John Wayne starred in John Ford's classic western *Stagecoach*. What role did he play?

20 In 1881 Sheriff Pat Garratt killed a young outlaw in Fort Sumner, New Mexico, after hunting him for a year. Who was he?

21 According to tradition, Davy Crockett habitually wore a particular item of dress. What was it?

22 In 1873 a new invention by Joseph Glidden made fencing land for cattle ranching much easier. What was it?

23 Name the celebrated gunfight that took place in Tombstone, in Arizona in October 1881.

24 The building of the great Pacific railway was called 'the grandest enterprise under God'. What did the Native Americans call the train?

25 What was the usual nickname of the graveyard outside town where the victims of gunfights were buried?

1. How many known planets are there in our solar system?

2. What was the name of the first man in space?

3. In what state in America is Cape Canaveral, one of the world's most important launching sites for space travel? ▶

4. A 'supernova' occurs every few hundred years. What is it?

5. Who, in 1962, was the first American launched into orbit?

6. Why is it impossible to get an overall picture of Venus using telescopes?

7. What is the name of the spaceship in the *Star Trek* films?

8. Neil Armstrong was the first man to step onto the moon in 1969. Who was the second? ▶

9. How many men have walked on the moon?

10. Once a rocket has left the launch site at Cape Canaveral, Johnson Space Centre takes over. Where is it?

11. Who was the Polish born founder of modern astronomy?

12. How long does it take for the Moon to pass through a complete cycle from new Moon to new Moon?

13. Who was Britain's first cosmonaut?

14. What 'first' did Soviet cosmonaut Alexei Leonov achieve in 1965?

15 Which planet was named after the Roman messenger of the gods?

16 When does a meteoroid actually become a meteorite?

17 The Strategic Defence Initiative (SDI) was launched in 1983 by United States President Ronald Reagan. What was the project nicknamed?

18 Which is in fact the solar system's largest planet?

19 Which is the solar system's smallest planet?

20 Who was the first American woman in space?

21 In 1971, Mariner 9 sent back to earth the first close-up pictures of which planet?

22 What do we call the event when the moon passes across the face of the sun.

23 Name the world's first satellite, launched in 1957 by the U.S.S.R.

24 Who directed the film *Star Wars* in 1977?

25 For what is Edmund Halley the second British Astronomer Royal best known?

1. How often are Presidential elections held in the United States?

2. In which state was the first successful atomic bomb test held in July 1945?

3. What was the name given to the post-war rivalry between the Communist and non-Communist superpowers?

4. Which senator led the anti-Communist witchhunt of the early 1950s?

5. In the late 1960s demonstrators used to shout 'LBJ, LBJ, how many kids have you killed today?' About what were they protesting?

6. What were the first two names of Secretary of State Dulles, who served in Eisenhower's administration?

7. Who became President when Nixon was forced to resign in 1974?

8. What was the policy of transporting children from their own neighbourhood to school in other areas called?

9. Which singer made a comment on American society in *Times They Are A–Changin'* in 1965?

10. Under Jimmy Carter's presidency, the country suffered from 'stagflation'. What is 'stagflation'? ▲

11 What maximum speed limit was imposed on all roads after the oil shortages of the late 1970s?

12 The United States withdrew its athletes from the Moscow Olympics of 1980 as a protest against which action by U.S.S.R.?

13 Which President was nicknamed the 'great communicator'?

14 In which decade did Hawaii and Alaska become states of the Union?

15 By what name was the religious cult led by the Reverend Sun-Myung Moon popularly known?

16 Where in Washington does the United States Congress meet?

17 What do the initials CIA stand for?

18 Which city suffered an earthquake measuring 8.8 on the Richter scale in 1989? ▼

19 What did the press call the secret deal to sell arms to Iran in return for Iranian aid in freeing American hostages in the Lebanon?

20 Which United States Secretary of State engaged in 'shuttle diplomacy' in the conflict between Britain and Argentina over the Falkland Islands?

21 What street in New York is associated with financial dealings?

22 In the 1980s and 1990s drug abuse became a major issue. From what drug is the highly addictive 'crack' derived?

23 What is the name of New York's principal airport?

24 In the summer of 1980, a wave of race riots hit which American city?

25 The wreck of which famous ocean liner was found by an American and French team of divers in 1985?

1. In heraldry, what is the colour black called?

2. What famous Washington building would you find at 1600 Pennsylvania Avenue?

3. Which animal appears on the flag of Sri Lanka?

4. How many lines does a sonnet have?

5. Fronds are the leaves of what type of plant?

6. In which French city was Joan of Arc burned at the stake? ▼

7. To which country do the Atlantic islands, the Azores, belong?

8. The fantastically wealthy owner of a diamond mine gave his name to a southern African country that has since been renamed. Who was this man?

9. The Beatles founded their own record label. What was it called?

10. Name the virus that was deliberately introduced into Europe to control the rabbit population.

11. Where in the human body would one locate the cochlea?

12 What is the title of Beethoven's only opera?

13 What was the name of the lioness raised by Joy Adamson? ▲

14 One of Queen Elizabeth's four children was born at Clarence House. Which one?

15 The English call them nappies. What do the Americans call them?

16 What is non-rhyming poetry called?

17 In which country was Treblinka concentration camp?

18 Which district in Spain gave its name to sherry?

19 What is the common name for sodium hydroxide?

20 In architecture, what name is given to the horizontal beam over a door or window?

21 Name the type of cheese usually sprinkled on minestrone soup and spaghetti Bolognese?

22 What was Popeye the Sailor's favourite food?

23 At the wedding of Prince Charles, who acted as his best man?

24 What is pyrophobia?

25 Which organization has the motto 'Fidelity, Bravery, Integrity'?

People and Places   Heroes and Villains

1. He stunned him with a stone from a sling, then slew him with a sword
2. Ivan the Terrible
3. Dwight D. Eisenhower
4. In a motorcycle accident
5. Nero
6. Mongols
7. He had lost both legs
8. Herod
9. Two
10. Black Bess
11. Captain Scott
12. Man of Steel
13. French
14. He was hanged
15. Abraham Lincoln
16. 'Papa Doc' Duvalier
17. Lord Chancellor
18. Spartacus
19. My Struggle
20. Chicago
21. Tennessee
22. Attila
23. The Reign of Terror
24. Central African Republic
25. Oliver Cromwell

Entertaining Arts   Art and Artists

1. Vincent van Gogh
2. Flemish
3. Picasso
4. Portraits
5. Leonardo da Vinci
6. Paradise by Tintoretto
7. Coventry Cathedral
8. Mona Lisa
9. Buonarroti
10. Ballet dancers
11. Jose Ferrer
12. Rodin
13. John Constable
14. Cubism
15. El Greco
16. Pre-Raphaelite
17. United States
18. Impressionists
19. Venice
20. Sir Christopher Wren
21. Michelangelo
22. Spanish
23. Tahiti
24. Racehorses
25. Sculpture

Food and Drink   Kitchen Know-how

1. Pectin
2. Acid can dissolve the copper and cause poisoning
3. Basting
4. 425°
5. A wok
6. Freshness
7. To clear the sediment
8. Bottom shelf
9. Vitamin C
10. Sprinkling with sugar, flour, seasoning, etc.
11. Ramekin
12. 16
13. 20
14. Part cooking food which will then be cooked by another method
15. Meat and fish
16. 100°
17. Yogurt
18. Remove the stone
19. Reheating cooked food
20. Cochineal
21. Mortar
22. Boil it rapidly
23. Croûtons
24. Ghee
25. Trussing

Sports and Pastimes   A Quiet Game

1. 52
2. On rolls of a die
3. Spades and hearts
4. Bones
5. India
6. 24
7. Whist
8. 12
9. Canasta
10. 10 points
11. Three
12. Fortune-telling
13. Monopoly
14. On a pegboard
15. 10
16. A set of four identical tiles
17. Sacrifice of a piece or pawn at the opening
18. 10
19. Cluedo
20. 12
21. Measuring distance and tracing lines and marks
22. Two
23. Rook
24. Won two out of three games
25. 25

History   The Wild West

1. Morgan, Virgil, Jim, Baxter
2. Lillie Langtry
3. Lewis and Clark
4. Calamity Jane
5. Wear them
6. James
7. The Fortyniners
8. Scout
9. Little Bighorn
10. James Bowie and Davy Crockett
11. Dentist
12. A job as rider for the Pony Express
13. Brigham Young
14. Toboggan
15. Sioux
16. The Hole in the Wall gang
17. Buffalo Bill
18. Cattle trails
19. The Ringo Kid
20. Billy the Kid
21. Coonskin cap
22. Barbed wire
23. Gunfight at the OK Corral
24. The iron horse
25. Boot Hill

Natural World   Out in Space

1. Nine
2. Yuri Gagarin
3. Florida
4. The explosion of a star
5. John Glenn
6. The planet's surface is covered by thick cloud
7. Enterprise
8. Buzz Aldrin
9. 12
10. Houston, Texas
11. Copernicus
12. 29 days, 13 hours
13. Helen Sharman
14. First ever space walk
15. Mercury
16. When it strikes a planet
17. Star Wars
18. Jupiter
19. Pluto
20. Dr. Sally Ride
21. Mars
22. Solar eclipse
23. Sputnik I
24. George Lucas
25. His work on comets

Twentieth Century   The United States since 1946

1. Every four years
2. New Mexico
3. Cold War
4. Joseph McCarthy
5. Vietnam War
6. John Foster
7. Gerald Ford
8. Busing
9. Bob Dylan
10. A combination of stag2 nation and inflation
11. 55 mph
12. Invasion of Afghanistan
13. Ronald Reagan
14. 1950s
15. Moonies
16. Capitol Building
17. Central Intelligence Agency
18. San Francisco
19. Irangate
20. Alexander Haig
21. Wall Street
22. Cocaine
23. Kennedy airport
24. Miami
25. Titanic

Pot Luck

1. Sable
2. The White House
3. Lion
4. 14
5. Ferns
6. Rouen
7. Portugal
8. Cecil Rhodes
9. Apple
10. Myxomatosis
11. Inner ear
12. Fidelio
13. Elsa
14. Princess Anne
15. Diapers
16. Blank verse
17. Poland
18. Jerez
19. Caustic soda
20. Lintel
21. Parmesan
22. Spinach
23. No one. His two brothers were his 'supporters'
24. Fear of fire
25. FBI

Quiz

1. Cosa Nostra is another name for which secret society?

2. To which religion does a person with the surname Singh belong?

3. What has been the most frequent name for popes?

4. The first and last wives of Henry VIII had the same given name. Who were they?

5. In which sport did partners McNamara and McNamee compete?

6. What was the nickname of the landscape gardener Lancelot Brown?

7. In which film did Warren Beatty and Faye Dunaway play a pair of notorious outlaws?

8. Which United States President had the middle name Baines?

9   What was Judy Garland's real name? ◄

10   What was Iran called before 1935?

11   Name the three musketeers in the novel by Alexandre Dumas.

12   What was the artist Picasso's first name?

13   From which American President do teddy bears get their name?

14   What name did Peggy Hookham take for her career as a dancer?

15   What name is given to a community farm in Israel?

16   Which British politician was called 'the Welsh Wizard'?

17   The name of which Biblical character is given to someone thought to bring bad luck?

18   Which writer's given names were Pelham Grenville?

19   Who gave his name to the internationally known system of communication where letters appear as dots and dashes?

20   Which country has the name 'Hellas' on its postage stamps?

21   What was musician Louis Armstrong's nickname? ▼

22   Give the first name of German Field Marshall Goering.

23   What nickname is often given to people with the surname White?

24   In the Bond film Goldfinger what was the name of Goldfinger's bodyguard, who had a lethal hat?

25   What was the actual pen name of the world famous American writer William Sidney Porter?

1. What was the surname of Wendy and her brothers in Peter Pan?

2. In The Jungle Book, what type of animal is Baloo?

3. Who bullied Tom Brown at Rugby school?

4. The television series Little House on the Prairie was based on a series of books by Laura Ingalls Wilder. Who plays Laura in the series?

5. Who wrote about Christopher Robin and his friends, including Tigger and Piglet? ▲ ▶

6. In which pantomime does Widow Twankey appear?

7. Which is the first book to tell the story of Meg, Jo, Beth and Amy March?

8. What school did Billy Bunter, the 'fat owl of the Remove' attend?

9. In Enid Blyton's Famous Five stories, how many of the five are boys and how many are girls?

10. Which American author wrote Are you there, God?, It's me, Margaret and It's not the end of the World?

11. How many Dalmatians are there in the book and animated film titles?

12. Which book was written because C.L. Dodgson enjoyed telling stories to 10-year-old Alice Liddell and her sisters on an Oxford boat trip?

13. Who found a house made of bread and cake with window panes of sugar in a forest, and began eating bits of it?

14. What was the signature tune of the American cartoon character, Felix the cat?

15. In the Disney film Snow White and the Seven Dwarfs, the dwarfs were given names, including Happy, Sleepy, Doc, Bashful and Sneezy. Who were the other two?

16. Who lived at Green Gables?

17. How did Doctor Dolittle learn how to talk to animals?

18. Where was Superman born?

19. Which book, published in 1876, told the story of a boy who lives with his Aunt Polly in St. Petersburg, a village on the Mississippi?

20. In the film Bambi, what type of animal was Thumper?

21. Who created Skimbleshanks the cat?

22. In which film does Julie Andrews play a nursemaid with magic powers?

23. In the poem The Pied Piper of Hamelin by Robert Browning, the piper was engaged to rid the town of rats. When he was cheated of his payment, what did he do?

24. Which famous storyteller did Danny Kaye play in a film in 1952?

25. In the classic Uncle Tom's Cabin, who said 'Never had no father, nor mother, nor nothin'. I 'spect I growed'?

1 Which country is the world's largest producer of cheese? ▲

2 How many bottles of Champagne are there in a magnum?

3 From which country does 'Blood's Blood' come?

4 What type of milk goes into Roquefort cheese?

5 Commandaria St. John is the oldest known named wine and has been made since the 12th century. In which country is it made?

6 What do wine buffs call the scent given off by wine?

7 The bland cheese called Baby Bel was invented in 1931 in which country?

8 In which country are the wine-producing areas of Little Karoo, Ladysmith, Worcester and Montagu?

9 Which type of wine usually accompanies fish?

10 What word is used to describe a wine with a high alcohol content?

11 What do the Portuguese call the 'Englishman's wine'?

12 Which cheese, eaten all over the world, is transported in cylindrical wood-chip boxes?

13 What colour grapes are used to make white wine? ▼

14 The Rhenish wine, hock, takes its name from which German town?

15 What type of cheese is Dolcelatte?

16 How should bottles of wine be stored?

17 Which hard cheese is made from unpasteurized milk in certain provinces of the Po valley in Italy and matured from one to four years?

18 What does Appellation Origine Contrôllée on a bottle of French wine signify?

19 What is a non-vintage wine?

20 What is stored in a bodega?

21 Which European country is the world's largest wine producer?

22 What type of cheeses are native American products such as Colby, Monterey Jack and Tillamook?

23 The quality of Champagne, which is made only in a small area of France, is due to the great depth of what type of soil?

24 When sold in the United States, the Italian cheese Bel Paese has a map of the western hemisphere on the packet. What does the British packaging show?

25 Which English cheese, factory-made as early as 1870, is better known in its sage-flavoured, green-coloured version than in its original form?

1. How many times did Björn Borg win the men's singles finals at Wimbledon?

2. In which year did Monica Seles win her first U.S. Open?

3. Which championships make up the 'Grand Slam'?

4. What was Australian player Evonne Cawley's maiden name?

5. At what score does a tie-break come into operation?

6. What is the first score in a tennis match?

7. Jennifer Capriatti was Olympic singles champion in 1992. Which country does she represent?

8. What is the name given to a short, quick stroke when the ball is hit before it bounces?

9 Who was the only Afro-American man to win major tennis championships?

10 If part of the ball touches the baseline, is it in or out?

11 Name the film actress who married John McEnroe.

12 Which woman has won most Wimbledon singles titles?

13 In doubles matches the Australian formation is when both members of the serving team stand on the same side of their half of the court. What is the other name used for this formation?

14 Who was known as 'Little Mo'?

15 Name the woman tennis player who was undefeated on clay courts for 125 matches from August 1973 to May 1979?

16 In which country did the game of tennis originate in the Middle Ages?

17 Who was the youngest and the first unseeded player to win the men's singles at Wimbledon?

18 What is the name given to the centre of the racket strings, the best place to hit the ball?

19 Who was nicknamed 'Horrible Hana' by the British press?

20 American teams have recorded most wins in the Davis Cup tennis competion. Which country comes second?

21 Rod Laver is considered one of the best ever players. What was his home country?

22 How many Wimbledon singles titles did John McEnroe win? ◀ ▶

23 In the 1984 final of the French Open, John McEnroe took the first two sets and it looked as though the United States might win the title for the first time in 29 years. However, his opponent beat him to win his first major title. Who was he?

24 What is an 'ace'?

25 In practice, 'shadow stroking' is often used as a way of improving technique. What is it?

1. Where in the world was the Thirty Years War fought?

2. In which country did the Boxer Rebellion take place?

3. In the Second Punic War, a Carthaginian general led a whole army, including elephants, across the Alps and defeated the Romans at Cannae. What was his name?

4. The houses of York and Lancaster fought the War of the Roses. Which side had the white rose as its symbol?

5. In which war did Florence Nightingale lead a team of nurses? ▲

6. Kaiser Wilhelm I was ruler of Germany when World War I broke out. What did the British nickname him?

7. The Boston Tea Party contributed to the start of a war. Which war?

8. Which English king was killed at the Battle of Hastings in 1066?

9. Who fought the 100 Years War?

10 What contribution did Copenhagen make to the Battle of Waterloo?

11 The battle of Spion Kop was fought in Natal in 1900 in which war?

12 At the battle of Passchendaele in 1917, the British forces suffered 265,000 dead and wounded and gained only a few kilometres of mud. Where is Passchendaele? ▼

13 What type of weapon was the tomahawk, used by native North Americans?

14 In what year did the Russian Revolution take place?

15 Which war was named after an incident when an English sea captain lost an ear in a skirmish with the Spanish?

16 What were the two sides in the English Civil War called?

17 Which war was the longest in history?

18 What battle between the French and the English took place on St. Crispin's Day in 1415?

19 The film A Bridge too Far is about which battle?

20 After it had lost the War of American Independence, which part of North America did Britain retain?

21 Which famous English admiral died at the Battle of Trafalgar, living just long enough to hear that the battle was a great victory?

22 Who sent the Armada to conquer England?

23 Which famous battle in the American Civil War was the beginning of the end for General Robert E. Lee and the Confederate forces?

24 What colour was the Confederate uniform in the American Civil War?

25 Who invaded England in 55BC?

1. What organs enable fish to breathe under water?

2. What happens to a starfish if it loses an arm?

3. Which is the fastest sea mammal?

4. What are the tiny plants and animals that float in the top layer of the sea called?

5. Which birds breed on the soda lakes of East Africa?

6. What is an otter's home called?

7. How many tentacles has an octopus?

8. Dolphins often travel in family groups. What are they called? ▼

9. Why do spoonbills and flamingos swing their heads from side to side in water or mud?

10. Many fish have a swim bladder, like a bag of air, inside their bodies. What is its purpose?

11. Which river-living mammal has a duck-like beak and lays eggs?

12. The giant Victoria water lily of South America is the largest water plant. Which is the smallest?

13. What is the other name for a manatee?

14. What group of fish do lampreys and hagfish belong to?

15 What are limpets?

16 What does the huge (up to 12 metres long) whale shark eat?

17 What is a male swan called?

18 How do whales breathe?

19 What is unusual about the way the sea horse hatches its young? ▲

20 Where do demersal fish live?

21 What actually is the world's smallest living species of fish?

22 Which type of shark is the most dangerous to people?

23 Very rarely an occasional oyster miraculously produces a pearl. What causes this to happen?

24 Small fish almost always swim in groups for protection from predators. What are these groups called?

25 What is the correct terminology for an infant eel?

1. Which pop singer faced allegations of child sex abuse in California in 1993?

2. The Ayatollah Khomeini issued a death threat against novelist Salman Rushdie after the publication of which novel?

3. Why did Britain's Trade Secretary Cecil Parkinson resign during the Tory party conference in 1983?

4. In 1981 lorry driver Peter Sutcliffe pleaded guilty to 13 killings in the north of England. By what name is Sutcliffe popularly known?

5. Two reporters, Carl Bernstein and Bob Woodward, uncovered the Watergate scandal. Which newspaper employed them? ▲

6. Where was the Archbishop of Canterbury's special envoy Terry Waite kidnapped in 1987?

7. British MP John Stonehouse was arrested in Australia in 1974 on charges of theft and forgery. How had he attempted to cover his disappearance?

8. What controversial book did former intelligence officer Peter Wright publish in 1987?

9. Which foreign office Soviet spy defected to Moscow in 1951?

10. On which day of the week was John Lennon shot in New York?

11. Who was Joyce McKinney accused of kidnapping and forcing to make love to her in 1977?

12. What was the nickname given to Jack Kevorkian, the retired American pathologist who helped several people to commit suicide in the 1990s?

13 In October 1990 Marion Barry, Mayor of Washington DC, was given a six–month prison sentence and a $5,000 fine. What was his offence?

14 Intimate taped conversations allegedly between the Prince of Wales and an old friend caused a furore when they were published in the British press. What is the friend's name?

15 Which British politician won a libel action against a magazine that linked his name with that of caterer Clare Latimer in 1993?

16 16. In 1969 Senator Edward Kennedy's car plunged over a bridge at Chappaquiddick and a girl was killed. What was her name?

17 Which eminent judge conducted the British 'arms for Iraq' enquiry in 1993?

18 From what position was John Profumo forced to resign in 1963 after revelations about his affair with Christine Keeler?

19 Which American TV evangelist was sentenced to 45 years in prison in 1989 on 24 counts of fraud and conspiracy?

20 Which bank, in 1988, was charged with laundering money for cocaine traffickers?

21 Of what was Judge Clarence Thomas accused when he stood for appointment to the United States Supreme Court in 1991? ▼

22 Who was the 'Queen of Mean', wife of an American property tycoon, quoted as saying, 'only little people pay taxes', and eventually sent to prison for tax evasion?

23 Woody Allen's divorce made headline news when he was accused of child abuse. Who was his wife?

24 Which American rock singer died of a drugs' overdose at the age of 27 in October 1970?

25 In Britain, the Director of Public Prosecutions, Sir Allan Green, resigned his post after a caution from the police. What was his alleged offence?

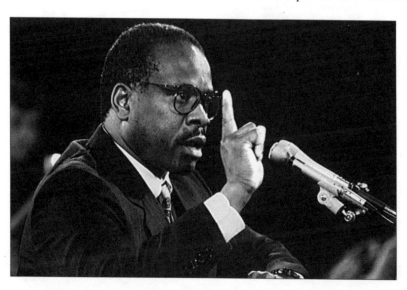

1. In Alice's Adventures in Wonderland, whom did Alice join at a tea party, along with the Mad Hatter?

2. Which of the Seven Wonders of the Ancient World stood at Olympus?

3. The film Silkwood was based on a true case about nuclear industry safety hazards. Who played Karen Silkwood?

4. Which is the largest joint in the body?

5. According to the nursery rhyme, who is made from 'sugar and spice and all things nice'?

6. The backbone is a flexible chain of how many bones?

7. What is the fundamental oath usually associated with doctors?

8. Which designer created the fashion called the 'New Look'? ▼

9. Which extremist terrorist group coldly killed 11 world-class Israeli athletes at the Munich Olympics of 1972?

10. Which carnivorous animal lives wild in the Australian outback?

11 Who was 'The Equalizer' in the popular television series?

12 Into which ocean does the Zambesi river flow?

13 Where would you normally find a gavel?

14 Who wrote The Unfinished Symphony?

15 The centaur is a mythological creature, part man and part what?

16 Which school did Princess Anne attend?

17 What was Ringo Starr's original name? ▲

18 Who said 'If you can count your money, you're not really a rich man'?

19 To which group of mammals do apes and monkeys belong?

20 Which was the very first birth the Bible ever records?

21 What are the punched holes at the side of postage stamps called?

22 If you saw 'AP' on a print, what exactly would it mean?

23 What was Louise Brown's unique claim to fame- this century?

24 They may be complex, vulgar or mixed. What are they?

25 In the Book of Genesis, how many days did the Creation take?

People and Places   Names and Such

1. Mafia
2. Sikh
3. John
4. Catherine of Aragon and Catherine Parr
5. Tennis
6. Capability
7. Bonnie and Clyde
8. Lyndon Johnson
9. Frances Ethel Gumm
10. Persia
11. Athos, Porthos and

Aramis
12. Pablo
13. Theodore Roosevelt
14. Margot Fonteyn
15. Kibbutz
16. David Lloyd George
17. Jonah
18. P.G. Wodehouse
19. Samuel Morse
20. Greece
21. Satchmo
22. Hermann

23. Chalky
24. Oddjob
25. O. Henry

Entertaining Arts   Children's Corner

1. Darling
2. Brown bear
3. Flashman
4. Melissa Gilbert
5. A.A. Milne
6. Aladdin
7. Little Women
8. Greyfriars
9. Two of each
10. Judy Blume
11. 101
12. Alice's Adventures in

Wonderland
13. Hansel and Gretel
14. Felix Kept on Walking
15. Grumpy and Dopey
16. Anne
17. His parrot, Polynesia, taught him
18. The planet Krypton
19. The Adventures of Tom Sawyer
20. Rabbit
21. T.S. Eliot

22. Mary Poppins
23. He took the children of the town
24. Hans Christian Andersen
25. Topsy

Food and Drink   Cheese and Wine

1. United States
2. Two
3. Hungary
4. Ewe's milk
5. Cyprus
6. Bouquet
7. France
8. South Africa
9. Dry white wine
10. Robust
11. Port
12. Camembert

13. Any colour
14. Hochheim, on the River Main
15. Soft blue cow's milk cheese
16. On their sides, preferably in the dark
17. Parmesan
18. It is a guarantee that quality wine comes from a defined area
19. A blend of wine from

different years
20. Sherry
21. Italy
22. Cheddar
23. Chalk
24. Map of Italy
25. Derby

Sports and Pastimes   Tennis

1. Five
2. 1991
3. Wimbledon, U.S. Open, French Championship and Australian Championship
4. Goolagong
5. When the score reaches six games all
6. 15-love or love-15
7. United States
8. Volley

9. Arthur Ashe
10. In
11. Tatum O'Neal
12. Martina Navratilova
13. Tandem
14. Champion player Maureen Connolly
15. Chris Evert
16. France
17. Boris Becker
18. Sweet spot
19. Hana Mandlikova

20. Australia
21. Australia
22. Three
23. Ivan Lendl
24. A service too fast and accurate for the opponent to hit
25. Practising the motions of groundstrokes without hitting the ball

History   Wars and Battles

1. Germany
2. China
3. Hannibal
4. York
5. Crimean War
6. Kaiser Bill
7. War of American Independence
8. Harold
9. France and England
10. Copenhagen was a horse; he carried the

Duke of Wellington
11. Boer War
12. Flanders
13. Short-handled axe or hatchet
14. 1917
15. The war of Jenkins' Ear
16. Cavaliers or Royalists and Roundheads or Parliamentarians
17. The Hundred Years War 1338-1453

18. Battle of Agincourt
19. Arnhem
20. Canada
21. Nelson
22. Philip II of Spain
23. Gettysburg
24. Grey
25. The Romans under Julius Caesar

Natural World   At Home in the Water

1. Gills
2. It grows a new one
3. Killer whale
4. Plankton
5. Flamingos
6. Holt
7. Eight
8. Pods
9. They are filtering out food
10. It makes them lighter and helps them to float

in the water
11. The platypus
12. Algae
13. Sea cow
14. Agnatha or jawless
15. Sea snails
16. Plankton
17. A cob
18. Through blowholes on the top of the head
19. The male keeps the eggs in his pouch until

they hatch
20. At the bottom of the sea
21. A type of goby
22. The great white shark
23. A sand grain inside the shell
24. Shoals
25. Elver

Twentieth Century   Alarm and Scandal

1. Michael Jackson
2. Satanic Verses
3. His affair with Sara Keays had become public
4. The Yorkshire Ripper
5. Washington Post
6. Beirut
7. He faked suicide
8. Spycatcher
9. Guy Burgess
10. Monday

11. Mormon missionary Kirk Anderson
12. Dr. Death
13. Possession of cocaine
14. Camilla Parker-Bowles
15. John Major
16. Mary Jo Kopechne
17. Lord Justice Scott
18. British Secretary of State for War
19. Jim Bakker
20. Bank of Credit and

Commerce International
21. Sexual harassment
22. Leona Helmsley
23. Mia Farrow
24. Janis Joplin
25. Kerb-crawling

Pot Luck

1. The March Hare and the Dormouse
2. Statue of Jupiter
3. Meryl Streep
4. Knee joint
5. Little girls
6. 26
7. Hippocratic oath
8. Christian Dior
9. Black September
10. Dingo
11. Edward Woodward

12. Indian ocean
13. An auction room
14. Schubert
15. Horse
16. Benenden
17. Richard Starkey
18. Paul Getty
19. Primates
20. Cain
21. Perforations
22. Artist's proof
23. The world's first test-

tube baby
24. Fractions
25. Six

Quiz

5 Which singer was known as the Swedish Nightingale?

6 What did Harriet Beecher Stowe do to help the lot of black slaves in America?

7 With what slogan are Emmeline Pankhurst and her daughters associated?

8 In which country was Israeli leader Golda Meir born?

9 Who was nicknamed 'the iron lady'?

10 The Nobel Peace prize was awarded to two Irish women in 1976. Maired Corrigan was one; who was the other?

11 What was Nancy Reagan's occupation before she devoted herself to helping her husband's political career? ◄

12 Which dancer, a soloist with Diaghilev's Ballet Russe, formed a London company which became, in 1957, the Royal Ballet?

13 Which 19th-century Englishwoman campaigned for prison reform?

14 Which of the Brontë sisters wrote The Tenant of Wildfell Hall?

15 Which famous opera singer left her husband for Greek shipping magnate Aristotle Onassis, who in turn left her to marry Jacqueline Kennedy?

16 In which film did Elizabeth Taylor achieve child stardom in 1944?

17 Joan Armatrading has achieved worldwide success as a vocalist and guitarist. Where was she born?

1 What nationality was Catherine the Great?

2 Which novelist wrote Emma and Mansfield Park?

3 Andrée de Jongh, known as Dédée, was 24 years old when she set up the Comet Line and was later awarded the George Medal by King George VI. What was the Comet Line?

4 In what field did Sarah Siddons achieve fame in the 18th century?

18 In the last nine years of her life, Sarah Bernhardt suffered from a physical disability, although she continued to act. What was the disability?

19 Who was the legendary 19th-century pioneer of women's rights in the British medical profession in which she qualified and was eventually finally allowed to practise as a doctor and after whom a very famous women's hospital in London was named?

20 Which young woman stabbed Jean Paul Marat, one of the leaders of the French Revolution, in his bath?

21 Gladys Aylward became famous for her missionary work in China. Who portrayed her in the film Inn of the Sixth Happiness?

22 Which American state is named for Queen Elizabeth I?

23 Who was the only person to win Nobel Prizes for Physics and Chemistry?

24 What is Mother Teresa's given name? ▼

25 Name the woman who was elected President of the Philippines after Ferdinand Marcos fled?

1 Which musical was derived from George Bernard Shaw's play Pygmalion?

2 Which New York composer wrote the score for A Chorus Line?

3 In the film Oklahoma, who played the villain Jud Fry?

4 An 'American Tribal Love-Rock Musical' first shocked and delighted audiences in the 1960s. What was it called? ▲

5 Which musical includes the songs Marrying for Love and Hostess with the Mostes' on the Ball?

6 On Broadway, Glynis Johns sang Send in the Clowns in A Little Night Music. On the London stage it was sung by Jean Simmons. Who sang it on screen?

7 In South Pacific, heroine Nellie Forbush falls in love with a plantation owner. What was Nellie's profession?

8 The Sound of Music, starring Julie Andrews on screen, told the story of which real-life family? ▶

9 In the film Oliver, Mark Lester played the title role. Who played the Artful Dodger?

10 Which musical, inspired by a comic strip, tells the story of an orphan who is eventually adopted by a millionaire?

11 Richard Rodgers and Oscar Hammerstein II formed the most successful of musical partnerships. Which was the lyricist?

12 Which author wrote the book on which the musical Les Misérables was based?

13 Who starred with Dorothy Dandridge in the 1959 film Porgy and Bess?

14 Which film musical, starring Liza Minelli, is set in Berlin during the rise of the Nazis?

15 The characters Gus, Skimbleshanks and Growltiger appear in which musical?

16 The film High Society, starring Grace Kelly, was a musical remake of which film?

17 The King and I told the story of a real-life English governess who went to teach the children of the King of Siam in Victorian times. What was her name?

18 Which musical told the story of a Scottish town that appears only once every 100 years?

19 Name the composer and lyricist who produced Gigi, Coco and Paint Your Wagon.

20 The songs June is Bustin' Out All Over and You'll Never Walk Alone come from which musical?

21 Who went 'Singin' in the rain' in the film of the same name?

22 Evita was based on the life of the wife of a South American dictator. Who was she?

23 Who starred as the young Gypsy Rose Lee in the film Gypsy?

24 Richard Harris starred in the film Camelot. Who sang his songs?

25 The actress Tammie Grimes played the title role in The Unsinkable Mollie Brown on Broadway. Who actually played Mollie Brown in the film?

1. What type of soup is a julienne?

2. The Italians and Americans call them zucchini. What do the French and British call them?

3. At what stage of the meal would you eat a charlotte?

4. Which region of France is the original home of Calvados?

5. What type of delicious food are the French langues de chat?

6. What name is given to a pan of hot water which stands on top of the cooker and in which other pans stand, so that their contents will cook gently?

7. What is Coquille St. Jacques a fancy name for?

8. What is the head waiter in a French restaurant called?

9. How is a drink served when it is described as frappé?

10. What name is given to a ham and cheese sandwich dipped in beaten egg and deep-fried?

11. When food is cooked en croûte, what does it mean?

12. What is the difference between pommes and pommes de terre?

13. What have you ordered if a thin pancake is cooked in butter, sugar, orange juice and Curaçao, and then flambéed at your table? ▲

14 Petit fours means literally 'little ovens', but what are they?

15 What is the main ingredient of a soufflé?

16 In a French restaurant, what describes a dish that is specially recommended that day?

17 Bénédictine has been made by the Bénédictine order since the 16th century. On what is it based? ▼

18 At what stage of the meal would you eat cassoulet?

19 What is a sorbet?

20 How is boeuf bourguignon cooked?

21 What type of stew is a navarin?

22 What is the most famous guide to the best restaurants in France called?

23 What is a clafouti?

24 If you ordered carré d'agneau, what would be served?

25 François-René de Chateaubriand was a novelist, poet and politician. What type of food was named after him?

1. What sport has a 'beach start' and a 'dock start'?

2. In boxing, which is lighter: bantamweight or featherweight?

3. In which sport are competitors forbidden to play left-handed?

4. Two methods are used in weight-lifting. One is the clean and jerk. What is the other?

5. When a referee in karate calls shobu sanbon hajime, what happens?

6. In curling, what is a broom used for?

7. How many rounds are there in a professional boxing title contest?

8. In which sport does one player take black and blue balls and another red and yellow?

9. In Rugby, which players form the scrum? ▼

10. How many games make up a match in squash?

11. Which piece of sporting equipment shares its name with a character from A Midsummer Night's Dream?

12. In table tennis, what is the name given to a rally where no points are scored? ▶

13. What is the value of the black ball in snooker?

14. On which hand does a right-handed hammer competitor wear a glove?

15 Which three events are included in the Olympic triathlon?

16 In the sport of sled-dog racing, what exactly is a musher?

17 In athletics, how many obstacles would you find in the 3,000 metres steeplechase?

18 Rifle shooting is divided into three basic categories. Two of them are smallbore and bigbore. What is the third?

19 What is the minimum height by which the bar of the Olympic pole vault is raised for each round?

20 How many players make up each team in volley-ball?

21 Which is the first stroke in a medley relay in swimming?

22 A player called a 'goal attack' is found in which game?

23 How old must a horse be before it can take part in steeplechasing?

24 What do orienteering competitors often carry for use in an emergency?

25 Which sport includes coxless pairs and quadruple sculls?

1. Who invaded England during the reign of Alfred the Great, King of Wessex?

2. At the centre of a medieval castle, surrounded by walls and moats, was a tall tower. What was it called? ▲

3. Charlemagne was crowned Emperor in Rome in 800. What did his name mean?

4. Oxford and Cambridge universities were both founded in the Middle Ages. Which came first?

5. The Vikings were pirates who raided European lands in the 8th and 9th centuries. Where did they come from?

6. Thursday takes its name from one of the gods worshipped by the Vikings. What was the name of the god?

7. Which famous tapestry tells the story of the Battle of Hastings?

8. What was the name given to the mock fights between two mounted knights at tournaments? ▶

9. What building became a place of pilgrimage after Thomas a Becket was murdered there in the 12th century?

10. In 1096 Pope Urban II called for a crusade or 'war of the cross'. Where were the crusades fought?

11. Which country was ruled by the Shoguns from 1192?

12. Which young woman was known as the Maid of Orleans?

13. The Renaissance began in Italy around 1300. What does Renaissance mean?

14. In the Middle Ages, every monastery had its Physick garden. What grew there?

15 What was kept in a reliquary?

16 Every medieval castle would have its own bakery, granary and buttery. What was the buttery?

17 Who was the red-headed king who succeeded William I?

18 In the Middle Ages, what was a 'hospice' or hospital?

19 Which city did the Medicis rule?

20 In Norman England, knights leased small pieces of land to men who had to give free labour and obedience in return. What were these men called?

21 William the Conqueror ordered a detailed register of the lands of England. What was the resulting survey called?

22 What 14th century event does the nursery rhyme 'Ring a ring of roses' commemorate?

23 Which Englishman led the Peasants' Revolt in 1381?

24 The English writer Geoffrey Chaucer wrote The Canterbury Tales in 1388. Who told the tales in this work?

25 Apprenticeship spread throughout England in the 13th century. How long did an apprenticeship last before a worker became a journeyman?

1 The Sahara is the largest of the world's deserts. What is the second largest? ▼

2 Snakes do not have external ears. How do they 'hear'?

3 What is the name given to a dry stream bed that fills with water briefly after a desert storm?

4 How does a cactus plant actually survive in a desert?

5 What is a large group of locusts called?

6 A desert is an area with only a certain amount of rain per year. How much rainfall?

7 How do the large ears of animals like American jackrabbits or African fennec foxes help to keep them cool?

8 The Takla Makan desert, the 'place from which there is no return', is in which country?

9 Only around 20 per cent of the world's deserts consist of sand. What is the commoner surface?

10 What can be transverse, seif or star?

11 Which desert is the driest on earth?

12 What proportion of the land on Earth is desert?

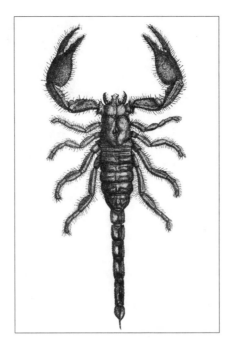

13 Which precious stones are found in the Namib desert in Africa?

14 What is the name given to flat-topped islands of rock when the face of a rock plateau is worn away?

15 Desert scorpions are dangerous creatures; how do they kill their prey? ▲

16 What type of creature is a skink?

17 In which country would you find the Simpson and Gibson deserts?

18 Out of which desert do the Hoggar (or Ahaggar) mountains rise?

19 The welwitschia plant grows where no rain has fallen for years. How does it obtain moisture?

20 What actually is the process called desertification?

21 When rock is near the surface of a desert, any water in the sand can collect and form a small area where vegetation can grow. What is such an area called?

22 Some powerful rivers run through desert areas. Which river runs through the Grand Canyon in the United States?

23 Which type of camel has two humps, the Arabian or the Bactrian?

24 How do sand dunes move?

25 In which country in the world can the Negev desert be located?

1. Who was given the nickname 'Tricky Dickie'?

2. How long is the term for which the French President is elected?

3. In 1986 the Swedish Prime Minister was shot dead as he and his wife walked home from the cinema. What was his name?

4. Which woman became Prime Minister of Pakistan in 1988 and again in 1993?

5. Who was Hitler's minister of propaganda during World War II?

6. Which British statesman spoke in 1946 of an Iron Curtain that had descended across Europe?

7. Who was leader of the Labour Party in 1983?

8. In 1979, U.S. President Jimmy Carter signed the SALT II Treaty in Vienna along with which leader?

9. Which President of Austria and former United Nations Secretary-General was accused of involvement in Nazi war atrocities?

10. Dictator Idi Amin was forced to flee his country in 1979 when Tanzanian forces invaded. What was his country?

11. Harold Wilson and Harold Macmillan were two of Britain's Prime Ministers in the 1960s. Who was the third?

12. Which country's Parliament is called Storthing?

13. Who was Mrs. Indira Gandhi's father?

14. Pierre Trudeau was Prime Minister in which country?

15. In 1981 the 'Gang of Four' left the British Labour Party to form the new Social Democratic Party. Two of them were Roy Jenkins and William Rogers. Who were the other two?

16. Which American statesman wrote his memoirs in two volumes entitled The White House Years and Years of Upheaval? ◀

17. After whose death was Prince Juan Carlos I sworn in as King of Spain? ▼

18. Which country did President Kaunda lead?

19. Name the Rhodesian Prime Minister who made the Unilateral Declaration of Independence from Britain in 1965?

20. Who prepared the blueprint for reform of America's health care system under President Clinton's administration?

21. In which European country did workers only finally obtain the right to join free trades unions in 1979?

22. Who was American Vice-President in the years 1989-93?

23. Who was Israeli Prime Minister before Yitzhak Rabin, sharing the same first name?

24. In which country was Eamonn de Valera a prominent statesman?

25. Which British journalist disappeared from Beirut and was granted asylum in the U.S.S.R. in 1963?

1 What is the name given to the killing of a brother?

2 In which film do Paul Newman and Robert Redford jump into a river holding hands?

3 3. What is the name given to a female deer?

4 Why was a young American girl, Karen Anne Quinlan, in the headlines in 1976?

5 Who gave his name to the seventh month of the year?

6 What are the names of Princess Anne's two children? ▲

7 Where would you find the Guggenheim museum?

8 What would you do with a Lee Enfield?

9 The film Gone with the Wind was based on a novel by which author? ▶

10 In Moscow, where does the Church of St. Basil stand?

11 According to the proverb, what do too many cooks do?

12 Which saint is the patron of fishermen?

13 By what name is the author H.H. Munro better known?

14 Which was the first war to be photographed?

15 In the well-known saying, 'He who can, does; he who cannot...' does what?

16 This port is known as the 'gateway to India'. What is it?

17 Which are the two smallest continents?

18 Who is considered to be the first of the classical economists?

19 What does the name Antarctica mean?

20 Which youth organization held its first jamboree in 1920?

21 Name the 23-year-old filmstar who died of suspected drug abuse in 1993.

22 Which person wrote 'a little learning is a dangerous thing'?

23 What is the actual Italian name for the great city of Venice?

24 Which zodiac sign has the symbol of the bull?

25 A religious sect, which was founded in Ireland, moved to Devon, England in 1831 and took its name from its new home. Name it.

People and Places   Notable Women

1. German
2. Jane Austen
3. An escape route through Nazi occupied Europe, which ran from Brussels to the Pyrenees, that helped Allied forces escape to freedom
4. Acting
5. Jenny Lind
6. She wrote Uncle Tom's Cabin
7. 'Votes for women'
8. Russia
9. Margaret Thatcher
10. Betty Williams
11. Film actress
12. Ninette de Valois
13. Elizabeth Fry
14. Anne
15. Maria Callas
16. National Velvet
17. West Indies
18. She had a leg amputated
19. Elizabeth Garrett Anderson
20. Charlotte Corday
21. Ingrid Bergman
22. Virginia
23. Madame Curie
24. Agnes
25. Corazon Aquino

History   Middle Ages

1. The Danes
2. The keep
3. Charles the Great
4. Oxford
5. Scandinavia
6. Thor
7. Bayeaux tapestry
8. Jousts
9. Canterbury Cathedral
10. Palestine
11. Japan
12. Joan of Arc
13. Rebirth
14. Herbs for medicinal purposes
15. A relic of Christ or the saints
16. Wine and ale store
17. William Rufus
18. A place where guests were received
19. Florence
20. Serfs
21. Domesday Book
22. The Black Death
23. Wat Tyler
24. A group of pilgrims
25. Seven years

Entertaining Arts   Musicals

1. My Fair Lady
2. Marvin Hamlisch
3. Rod Steiger
4. Hair
5. Call Me Madam
6. Elizabeth Taylor
7. Army nurse
8. Von Trapp
9. Jack Wild
10. Annie
11. Hammerstein
12. Victor Hugo
13. Sidney Poitier
14. Cabaret
15. Cats
16. The Philadelphia Story
17. Anna Leonowens
18. Brigadoon
19. Lerner and Loewe
20. Carousel
21. Gene Kelly
22. Eva Perón
23. Natalie Wood
24. Richard Harris
25. Debbie Reynolds

Natural World   Deserts

1. Australian desert
2. They pick up vibrations through the ground
3. Arroyo
4. Its waxy stems expand and store water
5. A swarm
6. Less than 25 cm (10 in)
7. They lose heat from the many blood vessels close to the surface
8. China
9. Broken stone and rock
10. Sand dunes
11. Atacama desert
12. One seventh
13. Diamonds
14. Mesas
15. With the sting in their tails
16. Lizard
17. Australia
18. Southern Sahara
19. Overnight fogs leave dew on the plants
20. The expansion of deserts into areas which previously supported vegetation
21. Oasis
22. Colorado
23. Bactrian
24. Sand is blown to the top of the ridge, then trickles down the other side
25. Israel

Food and Drink   French cuisine

1. Clear soup with thin strips of vegetables
2. Courgettes
3. Dessert
4. Normandy
5. Biscuits
6. Bain-marie
7. Scallops
8. Maître d'hôtel
9. With finely crushed ice
10. Croque Monsieur
11. In a crust; food inside
12. The first are apples, the second potatoes
13. Crêpes Suzette
14. Small cakes or biscuits
15. Egg whites
16. Plat du jour
17. Cognac
18. Main course; it is a meat and bean stew
19. Water-ice
20. Braised in red pastry
21. Lamb or mutton, with vegetables
22. Guide Michelin
23. Thick, batter pancake
24. Rack of lamb
25. Thick fillet of beef Burgundy

Twentieth Century   Modern Politics

1. Richard Nixon
2. Seven years
3. Olaf Palme
4. Benazir Bhutto
5. Joseph Goebbels
6. Winston Churchill
7. Neil Kinnock
8. Leonid Brezhnev
9. Kurt Waldheim
10. Uganda
11. Sir Alec Douglas-Home
12. Norway
13. Jawaharlal Nehru
14. Canada
15. Shirley Williams and David Owen
16. Henry Kissinger
17. Generalissimo Franco
18. Zambia
19. Ian Smith
20. Hillary Clinton
21. Poland
22. Dan Quayle
23. Yitzhak Shamir
24. Eire
25. H.A.R. (Kim) Philby

Sports and Pastimes   Rules of the game

1. Water-skiing
2. Bantamweight
3. Polo
4. Snatch
5. The match begins
6. Sweeping frost and moisture to clear the path for the stone
7. 12
8. Croquet
9. The forwards of each side
10. Five
11. Puck: a rubber disc used in ice hockey
12. A let
13. Seven
14. Left hand
15. Swimming, cycling and running
16. Driver
17. 35
18. Air rifle
19. 5 cm
20. Six
21. Backstroke
22. Netball
23. Four
24. Whistle
25. Rowing

Pot Luck

1. Fratricide
2. Butch Cassidy and the Sundance Kid
3. Doe
4. She was in a coma and her parents fought a successful legal battle to have her removed from the respirator
5. Julius Caesar
6. Peter and Zara
7. New York
8. Shoot with it
9. Margaret Mitchell
10. Red Square
11. Spoil the broth
12. St. Peter
13. Saki
14. American Civil War
15. Teaches
16. Bombay
17. Australia and Europe
18. Adam Smith
19. Opposite the Arctic
20. Boy Scouts
21. River Phoenix
22. Alexander Pope
23. Venezia
24. Taurus
25. Plymouth Brethren

Quiz

1 To which European country does the island of Madeira belong?

2 Mount Etna, the tallest volcano in Europe, stands on which island?

3 In which ocean is the area known as Polynesia?

4 The island of Taiwan is off the coast of which country?

5 Which island in the Pacific was discovered by Captain Cook in December 1777?

6 Name the island in Paris on which Notre Dame stands. ▼

7 To which group of islands does Corfu belong?

8 Which island did Turkish troops invade in 1974?

9 What is the name of the small volcanic island in the East Pacific which has some 600 strange stone statues? ▶

10 On which island are Bob Marley and Noël Coward buried?

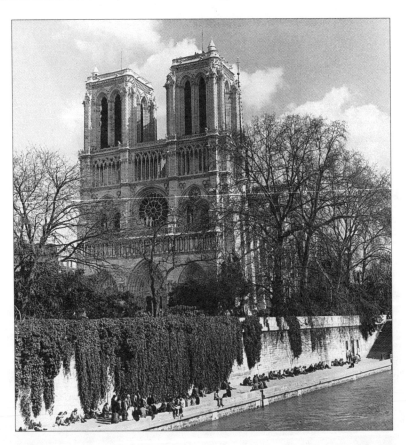

11 The Faroes are an isolated group of islands in the North Atlantic. How many islands are there in the group?

12 Las Palmas and Santa Cruz de Tenerife are the two main groups of which islands?

13 The Zaïre (or Congo) river flows into which ocean?

14 On which island would you find the tourist resorts of Nusa Dua, Sanur and Kuta?

15 In which ocean are the islands of Mauritius and Madagascar?

16 What language is chiefly spoken by the inhabitants of what is the largest island in the Mediterranean?

17 Where was Napoleon imprisoned after his defeat at Waterloo?

18 The island of Zealand is part of which country?

19 What are the inhabitants of Sardinia called?

20 What is the world's largest island?

21 How did the Dead Sea get its name?

22 Which island country has two official languages: Sinhalese and Tamil?

23 Name the largest island belonging to Greece.

24 Where are the volcanoes Mount Erebus and Mount Terror?

25 Into which ocean does the Amazon flow?

1 An attempted assassination is the subject of *Day of the Jackal*. Who is the target?

2 The actor William Henry Pratt played the definitive monster in *Frankenstein* in 1931 and has a whole string of horror roles to his credit. Under what name is he better known?

3 In *The Omen*, an American diplomat brings up a child who is not his own. Who does the child turn out to be?

4 Name the director of *The Godfather*.

5 In which film does Popeye Doyle, played by Gene Hackman, make his debut?

6 Lycanthropy exists in the folklore of many lands and has given rise to many films. What is the popular name for a lycanthrope?

7 What character is played by Orson Welles in *The Third Man*?

8 The 1957 film *Witness for the Prosecution* was based on the play by which author?

9 Mr Hyde is the alter-ego of a respectable professional man. Who is his other half?

10 Which two actresses starred in *Whatever Happened to Baby Jane*? ▲

11 In which film did Steve McQueen star as a fire chief battling with a blaze in a skyscraper? ▶

12 Which author created the legendary vampire Count Dracula in his world famous novel published in 1897?

13 Which 1933 film told the story of a giant ape brought to New York, where it escapes and terrorizes the city before being shot down by an aircraft from the summit of the Empire State Building?

14 What was the extremely odd thing about the Stepford Wives?

15 Which male Hollywood star appeared as the Terminator?

16 Who produced, wrote the screenplay and directed *A Clockwork Orange*?

17 A 1979 film told the story of a family living in a Long Island house for a month, while they are terrorized by supernatural forces and put to flight. Where was the house?

18 Which actress starred as Rosemary in *Rosemary's Baby*?

19 *Jaws* was based on a best-selling novel by which author?

20 What type of criminals are Mel Gibson and Danny Glover chasing in *Lethal Weapon*?

21 Which film role has been played by Sean Connery, George Lazenby, Roger Moore and Timothy Dalton?

22 What event was re-told in the movie *A Night to Remember*?

23 Who starred as the villain in the remake of *Cape Fear* in 1991?

24 In which city was the atmospheric thriller *Don't Look Now* set?

25 A British star won a Best Actor Oscar in 1991 for his performance in *Silence of the Lambs*. Name him.

1. Bean sprouts are usually the sprouts of which bean?

2. Calabrese is a variety of which vegetable?

3. Americans say 'walk slowly to pick it, run back to the kitchen to cook it'. What is it?

4. Which vegetable is traditionally served with the cheese board?

5. If you were using nettles as a vegetable, how would you destroy the sting?

6. Which vegetable was regarded by the ancients as a symbol of eternity because of its many layers?

7. Laver is fried and eaten with bacon and eggs in Wales. What is it?

8. By what name is chicory better known in the United States?

9. What is often described as the 'aristocrat' of the cabbage family? ▲

10. Which type of pea can be eaten whole, including the pod?

11. Which vegetable has trench and self-blanching varieties?

12. Some vegetables contain enzymes which cause oxidation on contact with the air. What does this cause?

13. In the film starring Jessica Tandy, what was served at the Whistle Stop Café? ▶

14. What is another name for the delicious vegetable okra or bindi?

15. Which vegetable, resembling broccoli, grows wild along the seashores of northern and western Europe and is eaten like asparagus?

16 What vegetable has varieties called aquadulce, relon and red epicure?

17 The leek is the national emblem of which country?

18 What is called 'batala' in South America, 'kumara' in New Zealand and is sometimes loosely referred to as 'yams' in the United States, though yams are a different vegetable?

19 When a recipe calls for 'green beans', what would you be likely to use?

20 What is another name for the eggplant?

21 Which vegetable fruit is traditionally served in pies on the American festival of Thanksgiving?

22 Who wept in the desert as they remembered the food such as cucumbers, melons, leeks, onions and garlic?

23 Courgettes are the young version of which vegetable?

24 What is sometimes called the oyster plant or vegetable oyster?

25 Which particular type of vegetable has the name kohlrabi?

1. What is the highest number on a roulette wheel? ▼

2. What is pontoon called when it is played in a casino?

3. In the game of craps, what is the first shoot or throw of the dice called?

4. At a race meeting, what is the call over?

5. What game has suits called bamboos, characters and circles?

6. In which card game are the expressions 'for his nob' and 'for his heels' used?

7. Which American state is famous for its gambling casinos?

8. Which game is the modern version of Pope Joan, sometimes called Michigan or Saratoga in the United States and Boodle or Stops in Britain?

9. In poker, which hand is more valuable: flush or full house?

10. What is 'form' in horse-racing?

11. Which of Ian Fleming's Bond books describes the glittering world of gambling?

12. In baccarat, what is a 'natural'?

13. Keno is an American casino form of which game?

14. The 1965 film *The Cincinnati Kid* starred Edward G. Robinson and Steve McQueen. Around which card game did the film revolve? ▶

15. What is a 'straight up' bet in roulette?

16. What, in a casino, is a croupier?

17 What, in a casino, is a kibitzer?

18 In bingo, what number would a caller be giving if he said 'Key of the door'?

19 If you saw the letters 'EP' against the name of a runner on a greyhound racecard, what would it mean?

20 When playing craps, who is the 'shooter'?

21 What does it mean when a player in blackjack decides to 'stand'?

22 In the game of roulette, what is a bet on numbers 1-18 called?

23 What is the main object of the popular card game of pontoon?

24 At a race meeting, what is an 'also ran'?

25 According to the old song, all the girls used to wink an eye at 'The man who broke the bank...' where?

1. Which of the Great Train Robbers escaped from a British prison and now lives in Brazil?

2. How did Anne Bonney become notorious in the 18th century?

3. By what name is the unknown murderer who killed five women in the East End of London in 1888 remembered? ▲

4. What was the nickname of the infamous bank robber Charles Floyd, killed in a shoot-out with the FBI in 1934?

5. Which British spy, who confessed his treachery in 1964, kept his job on the Queen's payroll until he was publicly unmasked in 1978?

6. Ned Kelly, son of a convict transported to Australia from Ireland, became known in which field of crime?

7. Who is a 'fence'?

8. By what names are partners-in-crime Robert Parker and Harry Longabaugh better known?

9. Which murderer was the first to be caught by the use of ship-to-shore telegraph?

10. What was the surname of brothers Ron and Reg who ruled London's underworld for a decade and were sentenced to life imprisonment? ▶

11. When a defendant 'coughs', what does he do?

12. Forensic pathology is the investigation of what?

13. Phoolan Devi, known as the 'Beautiful Robber', was a feared bandit leader in which country?

14 Which man founded the world's famous detective agency in the United States of America in 1850?

15 Nathan Leopold and Richard Loeb killed a 14-year-old boy, Robert Franks, in Chicago in 1924. What was their motive?

16 Gangster Al Capone, boss of the Chicago underworld, was finally gaoled for 11 years for what crime?

17 Vlad V of Transylvania, the original 'Dracula', was a sadistic killer who drank the blood of his victims. His method of killing earned him what grim nickname?

18 In 1932, the Lindbergh baby was kidnapped and killed. For what was his father Colonel Charles Lindbergh famous?

19 What is toxicology?

20 Name the notorious pair of bodysnatchers who robbed graves in Scotland in the 1820s to sell bodies for dissection, and later murdered at least 15 people?

21 The science of ballistics is concerned with what?

22 What is the method of identification that uses the genetic material from our cells to produce a virtually unique pattern or 'fingerprint' called?

23 Madeleine Smith was tried for the murder by poison of her lover in Edinburgh in 1857. What was the verdict?

24 The 15th century Cesare Borgia was an expert in which type of killing?

25 Which woman thief and bank robber later reformed and became a society columnist in New York and was eventually murdered in her own home by burglars in 1924?

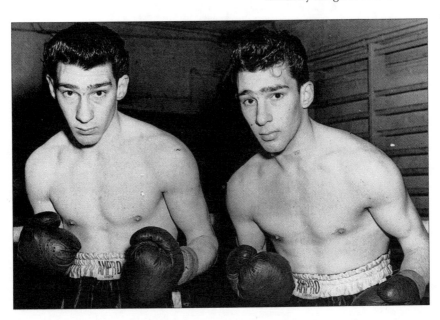

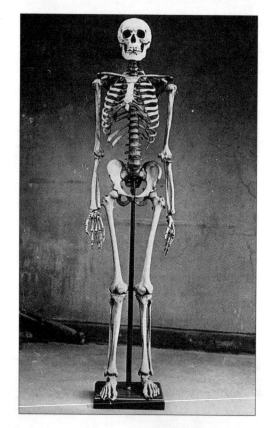

1. Which organ of the body is affected if someone is suffering from Bright's disease?

2. Where did the 'funny-bone' get its nickname?

3. Blood is classified in four main groups. A, B, and AB are three of them; what is the fourth?

4. Shallow sleep, which is the time when we dream, is also known as REM sleep. What does REM stand for?

5. What are the phalanges?

6. Muscles account for what percentage of total body weight?

7. How many litres of blood are contained in an adult's body?

8. The top bone of the backbone is called the atlas bone, after the Greek god Atlas. In legend, what did Atlas do?

9. What is the normal body temperature?

10. How many separate bones are there in the body of an adult? ▲

11 Which side of the brain governs creative skills?

12 What colour eyes is a baby likely to have if one parent has blue eyes and the other brown?

13 The retina of the eye has light-sensitive nerve cells called rods and cones. Which of these enable us to see colour?

14 Which gland in the body secretes the hormone responsible for growth?

15 What does the abbreviation IVF stand for?

16 Where would you find the coccyx?

17 Most people are right– or left-handed but what word describes those who can use either hand with equal ease?

18 What is the common name for the scapula?

19 Identical twins come from a single fertilized egg which splits in two; non-identical twins come from two fertilized eggs. What are non-identical twins called? ▼

20 Where would you find the femur in the human body?

21 What is the world's commonest contagious disease?

22 Give the scientific name for the jawbone.

23 What particular name is given to the study of character by feeling the lumps and bumps of the head?

24 What is a specialist in skin disorders called?

25 Hairs grow out of pits in the skin. What are these pits called?

1. What made Christiaan Barnard of Cape Town famous in 1967?

2. Rhodesia, in 1964, declared UDI. What does UDI stand for?

3. The first Bond movie was released in 1962. What was the title?

4. What device, aimed at cutting drink–driving accidents, was introduced in Britain in October 1967?

5. What were the proprietary names of the widely prescribed tranquillizing drug diazepam, first used in the 1960s?

6. 'The eagle has landed' reported Edward (Buzz) Aldrin in July 1969. What was he talking about?

7. Who killed American Civil Rights leader Martin Luther King in 1968?

8. Which of London's streets became famous with fashion-conscious youngsters throughout the world?

9. Ho Chi Minh, who led the independence struggle against the French, was the first president of which country?

10. In the 1960s the Beatles were among the followers of Maharishi Mahesh Yogi. What technique did he teach?

11. Muhammed Ali was professional world heavyweight champion 1964-67. What was his catch-phrase?

12. The Cockney model Twiggy was one of the top models of the 1960s. What was her real name? ◄

13. Who was the star with the wholesome and feminine image who proved a big box office draw in films like *The Thrill of it All* and *Move over Darling*?

14. What was the name of the group put together especially for a TV series as an American answer to the Beatles and which achieved a surprising level of success?

15. Who was the captain of the spaceship that went where 'no man has gone before'?

16. In 1960 South African police fired on an anti-apartheid demonstration killing 56 and injuring 162. Where did this massacre take place?

17. What was held at Woodstock, New York, in 1969?

18. What style of hat did Jackie Kennedy wear for her husband's inauguration ceremony that set a new fashion trend?

19 With which fashion style was British designer Mary Quant associated?

20 American Professor Timothy Leary, author of *The Politics of Ecstasy* claimed that a psychedelic drug could enhance the spiritual quality of life. Which drug?

21 What was the title of the first Beatles' single? ▲

22 *Barbarella*, a space fantasy based on a comic strip, helped to inspire fashions like cat-suits and high boots for some years to come. Who starred as Barbarella?

23 At the 1968 Olympics in Mexico, several American medal-winning black athletes rebelled during the playing of their national anthem. What did they do?

24 Who fought the Six Day War in 1967?

25 Name the American exponent of 'pop art' who used ordinary objects, such as soup cans and soap packets, in his creations.

5 If a government claims that it has a mandate from the electorate, what does it mean?

6 With which sport is William 'the Refrigerator' Perry associated?

7 U Thant was the Secretary General of the UN from 1962 to 1971. What was his home country?

8 Which planet is known as the 'red planet'?

9 In 1957, the first black player won the ladies' singles title at Wimbledon. Name her. ◀ ▶

10 Blanket and honeycomb are the two main types of what?

11 In the rhyme about birthdays, a child born on which day is said to be 'full of grace'?

12 Which English city exports cutlery all over the world?

13 The bite of which insect can spread sleeping sickness?

14 What would you do with a *dhoti*?

15 'Mayday' is the word used as a distress signal. Where does the word come from?

16 Which writer wrote *Jude the Obscure* and *Return of the Native*?

17 On which day of the year are hot cross buns traditionally eaten?

18 Which series of 15th–century wars ended with the battle of Bosworth Field?

19 What happened to British Prime Minister Spencer Perceval in May, 1812?

1 The picture of which American President appears on the one dollar bill?

2 Which musician was known as 'the king of swing'?

3 Name the silent screen comedian who was writer, director and star of *The Navigator*?

4 The Hare Krishna sect is an orthodox exponent of which religion?

20 What instrument does Ravi Shankar play?

21 To which royal house did Marie Antoinette belong?

22 On which book was the musical *Cabaret* based?

23 Roald Dahl wrote the book called *BFG*. What do the initials stand for?

24 According to the song, what did Molly Malone sell on the streets of Dublin?

25 Whose seaplane was called *The Spruce Goose*?

People and Places   Seas and Islands

1. Portugal
2. Sicily
3. Pacific
4. China
5. Christmas Island
6. Ile de la Cité
7. Ionian Islands
8. Cyprus
9. Easter Island
10. Jamaica
11. 18
12. Canary Islands
13. Atlantic
14. Bali
15. Indian
16. Italian; the island is Sicily
17. St. Helena
18. Denmark
19. Sards
20. Greenland
21. The salt content is so high that no vegetation can live there
22. Sri Lanka
23. Crete
24. On Ross Island in Antarctica
25. Atlantic

Entertaining Arts   Screen Thrills

1. General de Gaulle
2. Boris Karloff
3. The Anti-Christ
4. Francis Ford Coppola
5. The French Connection
6. Werewolf
7. Harry Lime
8. Agatha Christie
9. Dr. Jekyll
10. Bette Davis and Joan Crawford
11. The Towering Inferno
12. Bram Stoker
13. King Kong
14. They were robots
15. Arnold Schwarzenegger
16. Stanley Kubrick
17. Amityville
18. Mia Farrow
19. Peter Benchley
20. Drug dealers
21. James Bond
22. Sinking of the Titanic
23. Robert de Niro
24. Venice
25. Anthony Hopkins

Food and Drink   Vegtables

1. Mung beans
2. Broccoli
3. Sweetcorn
4. Celery
5. Cook them
6. Onions
7. Seaweed
8. Endive
9. Cauliflower
10. Mangetout or sugar peas
11. Celery
12. Discoloration
13. Fried green tomatoes
14. Ladies' fingers
15. Seakale
16. Broad beans
17. Wales
18. Sweet potato
19. French or runner beans
20. Aubergine
21. Pumpkin
22. Children of Israel after leaving Egypt
23. Marrow
24. Salsify
25. Cabbage

Sports and Pastimes   Betting and Gaming

1. 36
2. Blackjack
3. The comeout
4. Naming of horses with the latest betting odds
5. Mah jong
6. Cribbage
7. Nevada
8. Newmarket
9. Full house
10. The record of performance of what a horse
has and has not achieved
11. Casino Royale
12. A score of 8 or 9 with two cards
13. Bingo
14. Stud poker
15. A bet on a single number
16. An employee who runs the game
17. An onlooker
18. 21
19. Early pace
20. The first person to throw the dice
21. The player takes no more cards
22. Manque
23. To score 21 or as near as possible
24. A horse that has finished out of the money
25. Monte Carlo

History   Crime and Criminals

1. Ronnie Biggs
2. She was a pirate
3. Jack the Ripper
4. Pretty Boy
5. Anthony Blunt
6. Bank robbery
7. Someone who sells stolen goods on behalf of thieves
8. Butch Cassidy and the Sundance Kid
9. Dr. Crippin
10. Kray
11. Confesses
12. Suspicious or criminal causes of death or injury
13. India
14. Alan Pinkerton
15. Thrills
16. Tax evasion
17. Vlad the Impaler
18. The first non-stop transatlantic flight
19. Study of poisons
20. Burke and Hare
21. Firearms
22. DNA profiling
23. Not proven
24. Poisoning
25. Sophie Lyons

Natural World   The Human Body

1. Kidney
2. From the scientific name, the 'humerus'
3. O
4. Rapid Eye Movement
5. Finger and toe bones
6. 40 per cent
7. Over 4.5 litres
8. Supported the world on his shoulders
9. 37° C (98.6° F)
10. 206
11. Left
12. Brown
13. Cones
14. Pituitary
15. In vitro fertilization
16. The lower end of the spinal column
17. Ambidextrous
18. Shoulder blade
19. Fraternal
20. The thigh
21. Common cold
22. Mandible
23. Phrenology
24. Dermatologist
25. Follicles

Twentieth Century   The 1960s

1. He performed the first heart transplant
2. Unilateral Declaration of Independence
3. Dr. No
4. Breathalyzer
5. Valium and Librium
6. The first moon landing
7. James Earl Ray
8. Carnaby Street
9. North Vietnam
10. Transcendental
Meditation
11. 'I am the greatest'
12. Lesley Hornby
13. Doris Day
14. The Monkees
15. James Kirk
16. Sharpeville
17. Rock festival
18. Pill-box
19. Mini-skirt
20. LSD
21. Love Me Do
22. Jane Fonda
23. They gave a clenched fist 'black power' salute
24. Arabs and Israelis
25. Andy Warhol

Pot Luck

1. George Washington
2. Benny Goodman
3. Buster Keaton
4. Hinduism
5. It has the authority to carry out certain policies
6. American football
7. Burma
8. Mars
9. Althea Gibson
10. Tripe
11. Tuesday
12. Sheffield
13. Tsetse fly
14. Wear it
15. From the French m'aidez, meaning 'help me'
16. Thomas Hardy
17. Good Friday
18. Wars of the Roses
19. He was assassinated
20. Sitar
21. Hapsburg
22. I am a Camera by Christopher Isherwood
23. Big Friendly Giant
24. Cockles and mussels
25. Howard Hughes

Quiz

1 What, in New York City, is known as the lungs of the city?

2 Which country is the leading world producer of tobacco?

3 Before it was bought by the United States in 1867, which country owned Alaska?

4 In which cemetery, just outside Washington DC, have soldiers been buried since American the Civil War?

5 The Spanish explorer Ponce de Leon discovered Florida in 1513. What was he seeking at the time?

6 Texas, Idaho and Oklahoma all have panhandles. What are they?

7 What is the language of Uruguay?

8 President Alfonsin was ruler in which South American country?

9 In the United States, Thanksgiving Day is celebrated each November. Why did the early settlers begin the festival?

10 The New Orleans festival of Mardi Gras, with its parades, floats and general revelry, is world famous. When does it take place? ▶

11 Which city in Tennessee is known as the home of country music?

12 Who are the Dallas Cowboys?

13 What unit of currency is used in the country of Bolivia?

14 Which city in Michigan, United States, is known as Motor City because of the large number of cars built there?

15 For what crop is the Napa Valley in California best known?

16 Which South American country has the world's highest cable car?

17 The Astrodome in Houston, United States, was the first air-conditioned indoor stadium in the world. What is played there?

18 Which legendary film director made several westerns, including *Stagecoach*, in Monument Valley, Utah?

19 What is the official language of Surinam?

20 Which famous university is located in Cambridge, Massachusetts?

21 Yellowstone National Park, in the northern United States, is famous for springs that spout boiling water and steam. What are they called? ◀

22 Olympia is the capital of which American state?

23 The world's second longest river flows through South America. Name it.

24 One of the largest sculptures in the world, showing the heads of four presidents, is at Mount Rushmore in South Dakota. Three of them are George Washington, Thomas Jefferson and Abraham Lincoln. Who is the fourth?

25 The harbour of which South American city is dominated by the Sugar Loaf and Corcovado mountains?

1. Which silent movie actress, known as 'America's Sweetheart', later became Vice-President of United Artists?

2. Who played Eliza in *My Fair Lady* on Broadway only to lose the role to Audrey Hepburn in the film?

3. How was Elizabeth Taylor's husband, film producer Mike Todd, killed in 1958?

4. For which flamboyant actress did Noël Coward write *Private Lives*? ▲

5. Name the two actress daughters of John Mills.

6. Ingrid Bergman won Best Actress Oscars for *Gaslight* and *Anastasia*. In 1974 she won a Best Supporting Actress award for a role in which film? ▶

7. Which child actress played opposite her father in *Paper Moon*?

8. Who took a year off after filming *Hook*, then married Lyle Lovett and signed a multi-million dollar contract to film a Gothic horror tale *Mary Reilly*?

9. Which actress won a coveted role in a blockbuster picture when she arrived on the set to watch a city burn?

10. Who was nominated as Best Actress for her first film *The Color Purple* in 1985?

11. Judy Garland's daughter became a famous singer and actress. Name her.

12. In which 1989 film did Pauline Collins play a middle-aged woman who goes to Greece to find adventure?

13. When Winston Churchill saw *Mrs Miniver* he said that it would prove more valuable for the war effort than the combined efforts of six divisions. Who played Mrs Miniver?

14. Which singer did Sissy Spacek play in *Coal Miner's Daughter*?

15. How was Norma Jean Baker better known in public life?

16. Which 93-year-old actress played opposite Bette Davis in *The Whales of August*?

17. Name the established Broadway star who made her home at London's Savoy Hotel for some years and was a great success in the TV series *Two's Company* with Donald Sinden, before returning to the United States in 1982?

18. How is Mrs. Charles Black better known?

19. Who plays the mute wife in an arranged marriage in *The Piano*?

20 Which leading lady has written several books on reincarnation?

21 In *The Avengers*, Honor Blackman and Diana Rigg both played John Steed's side-kick. Which actress appeared in *New Avengers*?

22 Who won her fourth Tony award in 1979 for her performance in Sondheim's *Sweeney Todd* and is now better known as a TV sleuth?

23 Which young actress played a juvenile prostitute at the age of 14 and later played the victim of a gang rape?

24 Jean Marsh was one of the originators of the TV series *Upstairs Downstairs*. What role did she play in the series?

25 Who lodged in an L-shaped room and danced with puppets in *Lili*?

1. Name the delicacy made from the liver of specially fattened geese.

2. What is the usual name for the alligator pear?

3. At what particular stage of a meal is a *bombe* usually served?

4. Which type of fish is known as an Arbroath smokey?

5. What is the meaning of *rijstaffel*, a banquet with up to 25 dishes?

6. What type of fruit is a kumquat?

7. Stilton, known in Britain as the 'king of cheeses' is traditionally served with which drink?

8. What are the fungi used in gourmet cooking and found growing wild among tree roots mainly in France and Italy?

9. If you were eating fish 'a la Normande', how would the fish be cooked?

10. In Japanese cooking, why must the chef be very careful when preparing the globe fish, *fugu*? ▲

11. What is the main ingredient of the dish called 'angels on horseback'?

12. From which fish does caviar come?

13. What is the world's most expensive spice?

14. The Italian name is scampi and this is often used on international restaurant menus, but what is the English name?

15 What type of food is 'bouillabaisse'?

16 What is the name given to poached and glazed chestnuts?

17 Which fruit is often served with Parma ham as a first course?

18 What is the 'glorious twelfth'?

19 What is the main ingredient of Tía María liqueur?

20 From which country do the cheeses Marscarpone, Ricotta and Provolone come?

21 What type of oven, used to cook marinated meat, is a tandoor?

22 Beef stroganoff was first made in the 1700s for Count Alexander Stroganoff. After the meat is cooked, what is added?

23 What do we call young herring and sprats, when coated in flour and deep-fried until crisp and golden-brown?

24 What are the main ingredients of hollandaise sauce?

25 Pheasants are now found all over the northern hemisphere, but what is their native country? ▼

1. The first woman to run a mile in under five minutes was Diane Leather. What nationality was she?

2. How many spikes do the shoes of discus and hammer throwers have?

3. How many spikes do the shoes of contestants in the javelin event have?

4. For how many years did Jesse Owens' long jump record, set in 1935, stand? ▶ ▶

5. Which British athlete won every decathlon he entered between 1979 and 1984 and was known for his rivalry with Germany's Jurgen Hingsen?

6. If the baton is dropped as it is changing hands in a relay race, who must pick it up?

7. Serge Bubka has broken 29 outdoor and indoor records in pole vaulting. Which country does he represent?

8. The Marathon commemorates the run of a courier who took the news of the victory over the Persians from Marathon to which city?

9. Kenyan athlete Ibrahim Hussain won which marathon in 1991 and 1992?

10. What is a heat?

11. In which event might a competitor use the 'Fosbury Flop'?

12. How many obstacles would you find in the 110 metres hurdles event?

13. In which athletic event do the contestants aim to move only backwards?

14. What is the venue for the 1994 Commonwealth Games?

15. Who was the first British athlete to set a world record in a field event when she set a new javelin world record in 1986?

16. In which field event did Brazil's Adhemar Ferreira da Silva win every title from 1951 to 1959?

17. Who won the 1960 Olympic Marathon, running without shoes?

18. In running events, what is a break?

19 19. What is the scratch line?

20 Ed Moses of the United States is one of the legendary champions of track and field. In which event was he twice Olympic Champion?

21 What is the largest number of Olympic gold medals in athletics to be won by a woman?

22 The only walker to win three Olympic gold medals was Ugo Frigerio. Which country did he represent?

23 What close relation is gold medal winner Jackie Joyner-Kersee to the great athlete Florence Griffith-Joyner?

24 In what class of athletic events have Steve Ovett, Sebastian Coe and Steve Cram achieved fame?

25 The American Mary Decker-Slaney claimed that she had been tripped by another athlete when running in the 1984 Olympics. Who was that athlete?

1. Which famous bridge stands at the entrance to San Francisco Bay?

2. Name the building that stood as the centrepiece of the Paris Exhibition of 1899 and for 40 years was the world's tallest man-made edifice?

3. Which is the only one of the seven wonders of the ancient world to survive?

4. What is the world's largest amusement park?

5. What is the name of the arena in Rome which was the site of gladiatorial contests and Christian martyrdom?

6. Which Australian city is famous for the Opera House and the Harbour Bridge? ▲

7. What great engineering feat was completed in 1914, providing a short route for shipping between the Atlantic and Pacific oceans?

8. The tallest building in the world is the Sears tower. In which American city does it stand?

9. What would you find in Gorëme, in the Turkish region of Cappadocia?

10. Which French king built the palace of Versailles outside Paris, its splendour becoming famous throughout Europe?

11. What is the name of the 'lost' city of the Incas, in Peru, which was rediscovered by Hiram Bingham in 1911?

12. What is the only man-made structure on Earth which is visible from the moon?

13. The Tower of London began with a fortress built by William the Conqueror. What is the oldest structure within the Tower? ▶

14. For what purpose was the Taj Mahal built by Mogul Emperor Shah Jahan?

15 In 1974 farm labourers in China were drilling a well when they discovered a large collection of life-size figures. What are they called?

16 For what is the Sistine Chapel chiefly famous?

17 Name the massive prehistoric stone circle which stands in the middle of England's Salisbury Plain.

18 The famous Egyptian rock temples built in honour of Rameses II were dismantled and reassembled at a new site when the Aswan dam was built. By what name are the temples known?

19 What famous classical site, once a stronghold of the Athenian kings, stands on a rocky outcrop above Athens?

20 The world's largest concrete dam stands on the Columbia River in Washington state, United States. What is it called?

21 What is the height, in feet, of St. Paul's Cathedral in London?

22 Where in St. Petersburg is the Hermitage art collection housed?

23 The world's largest telescope is on the volcano Mauna Kea. Where is the volcano?

24 Which of the seven wonders of the ancient world stood in Ephesus?

25 What splendid building stands in Jerusalem, on the spot from which Mohammed was said to have ascended to heaven?

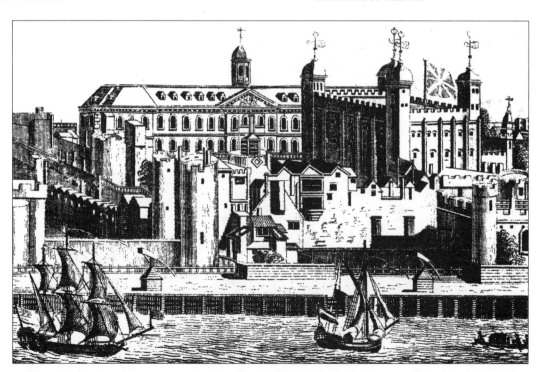

1 Where is the largest of the world's rainforests?

2 Elephants and buffaloes are herbivores. What does this mean they feed on? ▼

3 To which family of animals does the ocelot belong?

4 Twenty per cent of all drugs contain extracts of rainforest plants. From what does the malaria drug quinine derive?

5 What do scientists call plants or animals that are studied to check the health of a particular environment?

6 What particular type of animal is the very agile tree-climbing tamandua from South America?

7 What is the other name for the animal known as the flying fox (so called because of its fox-like face) which feeds on fruits such as figs, bananas, mangoes, etc.?

8 Why does the Australian animal the koala not need to drink?

9 How does the male cricket attract a mate?

10 What type of plants are epiphytes?

11 Which is the largest of the tree-dwelling apes, whose name means 'forest man'?

12 What are the proper names for male and female badgers?

13 Which is the world's biggest deer?

14 If you were escaping from an angry black bear, could you do this by climbing a tree?

15 From what part of the oil palm tree is the oil used to make soap, margarine and candles taken?

16 Why is the Midwife Toad so–called?

17 What is the annual rainfall of the 'rainforest'?

18 What purpose do the vivid orange and black stripes of the tiger centipede fulfil?

19 What is the principal food of the giant panda? ▲

20 Which Australian bird is often called the 'alarm bird' or 'breakfast bird' because its call is particularly loud in the morning?

21 What is the dominant feature of the pot-bellied, tree-living proboscis monkey?

22 What is the largest parrot in the rainforest?

23 What substance, taken from forest trees, goes into the making of rubber?

24 Where is the largest tropical forest in Africa?

25 The skin on the throat of a frog can expand like a balloon for what purpose?

1. With which charity is Princess Anne particularly associated?

2. How old was Princess Elizabeth when she became Queen? ▲

3. The Duke and Duchess of York married in Westminster Abbey. Where did the Prince and Princess of Wales marry?

4. Whom did Princess Margaret marry in 1960?

5. Which are the two private residences of Queen Elizabeth II?

6. At which university did Prince Charles read archaeology and anthropology?

7. Which member of the British royal family did Baroness Marie Christine von Reibnitz become on her marriage?

8. How did Michael Fagan come into contact with the royal family in 1982?

9. Which male member of the royal family served with the Royal Navy in the Falklands war against Argentina?

10. Who wrote the children's story *The Old Man of Lochnagar*?

11. Who was the governess to Princess Elizabeth and Princess Margaret who angered the royal family by publishing a book of reminiscences when she left royal service?

12. What is the name of the 18th–century mansion bought by the Queen as a home for the newly married Princess Anne and Captain Mark Philips in 1976?

13. Which major anniversary did the Queen celebrate in 1977?

14 Which of the Queen's children was the first royal baby to be born at Buckingham Palace for 62 years?

15 Which royal wife's jewellery was auctioned at Sotheby's in 1987?

16 What was the Duchess of Kent's maiden name?

17 Which designers created Lady Diana Spencer's wedding dress? ▼

18 Where did the investiture of Prince Charles as Prince of Wales take place in 1969?

19 Which sport did the Duke of Edinburgh take up when he retired from polo?

20 What was Elizabeth the Queen Mother's maiden name?

21 What connection has London-born Jeannette Charles with the royal family?

22 In which year did Princess Anne compete in Great Britain's equestrian team in the Olympics Games?

23 Whose daughter is Lady Helen Windsor?

24 Name the Duke of York's two children.

25 Who is third in line of succession to the throne?

1 Whose biography is called *Waxmaker Extraordinary*?

2 Walter Mondale was appointed to which office by President Clinton in 1993? ▼

3 What is the capital of Turkey?

4 In which country are the ruins of the city of Carthage situated?

5 Who said that 'in the future everyone will be famous for 15 minutes'?

6 Which part of the eye determines its colour?

7 Who followed Charles de Gaulle as President of France in 1969? ▶

8 Trichology is the study of what?

9 In *Hamlet*, Polonius is stabbed behind an arras. What is an arras?

10 In the Morse code, which letter is indicated by one dash?

11 To what was the Trojan prophetess Cassandra doomed?

12 Which bird lays the smallest egg?

13 Who retired after four years as Chairman of United States Joint Chiefs of Staff in September 1993?

14 Who wrote *The Tale of Peter Rabbit*?

15 What is a crack in a glacier called?

16 In the British Parliament, who sits on the Woolsack in the House of Lords?

17 Paul McCartney has always used his middle name. What is his first name?

18 Which stunning film actress, daughter of a famous father had children by Roger Vadim and Marcello Mastroianni without being married to either of them at the time?

19 In Britain, how many old pennies made up a 'tanner'?

20 The instruments which make up the brass section of the orchestra are trombone, trumpet, tuba and which other instrument?

21 Who is the patron saint of children?

22 Where would you find the medieval illuminated manuscript the *Book of Kells*?

23 Which American city is nicknamed the 'Windy City'?

24 Name the 1988 film that told the story of the trial of Stephen Ward and the Profumo affair?

25 How long must a dog arriving in Britain from abroad spend in quarantine?

People and Places   The Americas

1. Central Park
2. Brazil
3. Russia
4. Arlington Cemetery
5. The fountain of youth
6. Strips of land stretching into another state
7. Spanish
8. Argentina
9. To celebrate their first harvest
10. Shrove Tuesday
11. Nashville
12. American football team
13. Peso
14. Detroit
15. Grapes
16. Venezuela
17. Baseball and American football
18. John Ford
19. Dutch
20. Harvard
21. Geysers
22. Washington
23. Amazon
24. Theodore Roosevelt
25. Rio de Janeiro

Entertaining Arts   Leading Ladies

1. Mary Pickford
2. Julie Andrews
3. Plane crash
4. Gertrude Lawrence
5. Hayley and Juliet
6. Murder on the Orient Express
7. Tatum O'Neal
8. Julia Roberts
9. Vivien Leigh in Gone with the Wind
10. Whoopi Goldberg
11. Liza Minnelli
12. Shirley Valentine
13. Greer Garson
14. Loretta Lynn
15. Marilyn Monroe
16. Lillian Gish
17. Elaine Stritch
18. Shirley Temple
19. Holly Hunter
20. Shirley MacLean
21. Joanna Lumley
22. Angela Lansbury
23. Jodie Foster
24. The maid, Rose
25. Leslie Caron

Food and Drink   Gourmet Fare

1. Pâté de foie gras
2. Avocado pear
3. Dessert
4. Haddock
5. Rice table
6. Orange
7. Port
8. Truffles
9. Braised in white wine
10. The flesh is poisonous – some parts more than others
11. Oysters
12. Sturgeon
13. Saffron
14. Dublin Bay Prawns
15. Fish stew
16. Marrons glacés
17. Melon
18. The beginning of the grouse-shooting season – August 12
19. Coffee beans
20. Italy
21. A charcoal-fired clay oven
22. Sour cream
23. Whitebait
24. Butter and egg yolks
25. China

Sports and Pastimes   Athletics

1. British
2. None
3. A maximum of 11
4. 25 years
5. Daley Thompson
6. The runner who dropped it
7. U.S.S.R., now C.I.S
8. Athens
9. Boston
10. A preliminary round
11. High jump
12. 10
13. Tug of war
14. Victoria, Canada
15. Fatima Whitbread
16. Triple jump
17. Abebe Bikila
18. When a runner establishes a gap between himself and the other competitors
19. The line an athlete must not cross at the
end of the runway for the javelin, long jump and triple jump events
20. Hurdles
21. Four
22. Italy
23. Sister-in-law
24. Middle distance running
25. Zola Budd

History   Man-made Wonders

1. Golden Gate Bridge
2. Eiffel Tower
3. The pyramids of Giza
4. Disney World, Florida
5. Colosseum
6. Sydney
7. Panama Canal
8. Chicago
9. Rock temples with frescoes
10. Louis XIV
11. Machu Picchu
12. Great Wall of China
13. White Tower
14. A mausoleum for his wife
15. Terracotta warriors of Xi'an
16. Frescoes by Michelangelo
17. Stonehenge
18. Abu Simbel
19. Acropolis
20. Grand Coulee
21. 365
22. The Winter Palace
23. Hawaii
24. Temple of Artemis
25. Dome of the Rock

Natural World   Woods and Forests

1. Amazon basin
2. Plants
3. Cats
4. Tree bark
5. Indicator species
6. Anteater
7. Fruit bat
8. It obtains sufficient moisture from eucalyptus leaves
9. It stridulates (rubs parts of its body together to
make a shrill sound)
10. They live on other plants but do not damage them
11. Orangutan
12. Boar and sow
13. Moose
14. No; they can climb
15. The fruit
16. The male carries the eggs on its hind legs
17. 300-600 cm (120-240 in)
18. They warn enemies that it is poisonous
19. Bamboo shoots
20. Kookaburra
21. A huge, bulbous nose
22. Macaw
23. A milky white juice called latex
24. Congo Basin
25. To make its mating call louder

Twentieth Century   British Royals

1. Save the Children Fund
2. 25
3. St. Paul's Cathedral
4. Antony Armstrong-Jones
5. Balmoral and Sandringham
6. Cambridge
7. Princess Michael of Kent
8. He managed to get into the Queen's bed-
room in Buckingham Palace
9. Prince Andrew
10. Prince Charles
11. Marion Crawford (Crawfie)
12. Gatcombe Park
13. Silver Jubilee
14. Prince Charles
15. Duchess of Windsor
16. Katharine Worsley
17. Elizabeth and David
Emanuel
18. Caernarfon Castle
19. Carriage driving
20. Bowes-Lyon
21. She has made a career out of being the Queen's look-alike
22. 1976
23. Duke and Duchess of Kent
24. Beatrice and Eugenie
25. Prince Henry

Pot Luck

1. Madame Tussaud's
2. Ambassador to Japan
3. Ankara
4. Tunisia
5. Andy Warhol
6. The iris
7. Georges Pompidou
8. Hair and scalp
9. A wall hanging
10. T
11. To tell the truth and never be believed
12. Bee hummingbird (0.35 cm/1/4 inch long)
13. General Colin Powell
14. Beatrix Potter
15. Crevasse
16. Lord Chancellor
17. James
18. Catherine Deneuve
19. Six
20. Horn
21. St. Nicholas
22. Trinity College, Dublin
23. Chicago
24. Scandal
25. Six months

Quiz

1. What is the world's most southerly capital?

2. In Jerusalem, what important Jewish memorial is the last remaining part of the Jewish temple built by Herod?

3. What is housed in the Prado, Madrid?

4. Columbo is the capital of which Commonwealth country?

5. Which building in Moscow has a name meaning 'citadel'?

6. Honolulu is the capital of the state of Hawaii. What is the name of its famous beach?

7. In Paris, what name is given to the artists' and writers' quarter?

8. How long was the original lease of Hong Kong from China, that ends in 1997?

9. Name the Lebanese capital which reduced to anarchy in the 1980s as factions fought for supremacy?

10. In London it is called the tube or the underground. What is it called in Paris?

11. Which country has Vaduz as its capital?

12. In which capital city is the Humboldt University, the Brandenburg Gate and the Kaiser Wilhelm Memorial Church? ▲

13. On the island of Malta, Valetta is the capital but what is the largest and most modern city?

14. Where would you find the Tivoli Pleasure Gardens?

15. What is the world's highest capital city?

16. Oscar Wilde died and was buried in which city?

17 Washington DC, named after George Washington, is the capital of the United States. What does DC stand for?

18 In which city would you walk through the Gate of Heavenly Peace and find yourself in front of the monument to the People's Heroes?

19 Name the capital city of Zambia.

20 In which city could you travel on the Chao Phraya river to see Wat Po and the Wat Arun?

21 What is the world's northernmost capital?

22 On which river do the cities of Vienna, Budapest and Belgrade stand?

23 The Trevi fountain is one of Rome's tourist attractions. What is promised to any visitor who throws a coin into the fountain? ▼

24 In which city are the headquarters of the Arab League?

25 Which European city is the headquarters of Sabena World Airlines?

1 Who played Count Dracula most times on film?

2 Which 'hero of Arabia' had appalling notices for his Macbeth on the London stage and resigned from the board of the Old Vic when the directors disowned the production?

3 For which film, the last before his death, did Henry Fonda achieve an Oscar?

4 Zero Mostel played the lead role in Fiddler on the Roof on Broadway. Who took over the film role?

5 Who is Bernard Schwartz?

6 Which screen star had his feet insured for $150,000?

7 John Wayne, receiving an Oscar after 42 years in the business, said 'If I'd known, I'd have put the eyepatch on 35 years earlier'. What film was he talking about? ◄

8 Which actor is married to Joanne Woodward?

9 Who played the bogus instrument salesman in The Music Man on Broadway and on the screen?

10 Which filmstar became Mayor of Carmel?

11 In which musical did Laurence Olivier take a singing role?

12 Which actor dressed as a woman in one movie and played an autistic savant in another?

13 In 1946, Humphrey Bogart played Philip Marlowe in The Big Sleep. Who took the role in the 1978 version?

14 Which star of Brighton Rock and Morning Departure went on to direct Oh What a Lovely War and Young Winston?

15 Name Steve McQueen's last film?

16 Who refused his Academy Award for his role in Patton?

17 Which actor, who founded the Mercury Theater and directed Citizen Kane, later took to voice-overs on TV commercials?

18 In Reversal of Fortune the actor Jeremy Irons played a multi-millionaire tried for the attempted murder of his wife.
Who was he actually playing? ▶

19 Which famous Hollywood actor, once, remarkably, a circus acrobat, played a king on Broadway for 1,246 performances and then revived the role in 1972?

20 Which famous British wit, in the famous song, advised Mrs. Worthington not to put her daughter on the stage?

21 In which two films did Marlon Brando win an Oscar?

22 Whose Indian name was Dances with Wolves in the 1990 film?

23 Which Welsh miner's son starred as the Archbishop of Canterbury in Becket?

24 Who was catapulted to stardom in Alfie?

25 By what name is John Carter better known?

1 The French call it sabayon. What do the Italians call it?

2 If you ordered Cherries Jubilee, how would you expect them to be cooked?

3 What name is given to a custard whisked with gelatine, with whipped cream added?

4 A Linzer torte, named after an Austrian town, has a ground nut pastry base spread with jam. What type of topping does it have?

5 On the dessert menu, what is a compôte?

6 What type of pastry is used for profiteroles?

7 What type of pastry is used for jam roly-poly?

8 For what was liquorice used in ancient Egypt?

9 Halva is made from sugar, water, butter, nuts and what else?

10 The Australian biscuits called Anzac biscuits, containing rolled oats and golden syrup, got their name in World War I. Where did the name come from?

11 What colour is the pistachio nut, often used in ice cream and confectionery?

12 Marshmallows are now made from sugar, egg white and gelatine. From what were they made originally?

13 Crème brûlée is a rich custard topped with sugar. How is the topping prepared?

14 The root of sarsaparilla, a plant native to South America, is used to flavour confectionery, desserts and drinks. What flavour is it?

15 Baked Alaska has meringue on the outside. What does the meringue cover?

16 What sweet can be made from the sap of the South American sapodilla tree?

17 Banbury cakes come from a town in the Midlands of England. The sweet pastry has what kind of filling?

18 What food has a name that means 'baked twice'?

19 Baklava, a Middle Eastern pastry, has layers of buttered filo pastry with chopped nuts, sugar and cinnamon. What process does it undergo after cooking?

20 What type of sweets did American President Reagan have on his desk?

21 How does the French cake dessert millefeuille get its name?

22 What name is given to sweetened cream beaten to the consistency of a mousse, sometimes flavoured with vanilla?

23 Which German chocolate cake with a filling of cherries, cream and kirsch, has become internationally popular?

24 What type of dessert is cassata?

25 A popular Australian dessert, consisting of meringue topped with cream and fruit, is named after a famous ballet dancer. What is it called?

1. In cricket, which batsman holds the record for the most first-class runs in a career?

2. Which United States baseball team holds the record for the most wins in a World Series?

3. What is the playing time in basketball?

4. Who is the world's most capped goalkeeper in soccer?

5. What sport would you be watching if a 'chain crew' appeared on the field?

6. What sport would you be watching if a fireman comes on as a relief?

7. In which sport would you compete for the Cowdray Cup?

8. Australians Ray Lindwall and Keith Miller were famous in which team sport?

9. In what sport could you use an Iron Mike in training?

10. Which ice-hockey player was bought by Los Angeles Kings from Edmonton Oilers for $15 million?

11 Where does the umpire-in-chief stand in baseball?

12 Why did the selection of Basil d'Oliveira for the English cricket tour of 1968 cause an international furore?

13 Which famous American team has featured in two films and a cartoon series since being formed in 1927 by Abraham Saperstein? ◀

14 How many innings for each side will there be in a game of baseball?

15 In which team sport was Holland's Johan Cruyff famous?

16 Which great baseball star set 76 batting and pitching records in his 22-year career? ▼

17 Fast pitch and slow pitch are types of the indoor version of baseball. What is it?

18 Who is the only test cricketer to be created a life peer?

19 In which particular sport are penalties awarded to the opposing team for hooking, holding and clipping?

20 How many players does men's lacrosse have on each side?

21 Britain's world famous Lords cricket ground was founded in 1787. The present ground was first opened in 1814, in which area of London can it be found?

22 Pato is a version of which game?

23 What are the most runs scored off one over in first class cricket?

24 The sport of water polo is played by two teams of up to 13 people a side. How many of each team may actually be in the water at one given time?

25 In which sport are Dev, Lillee and Crowe famous?

1 The ancient Egyptians wrote on papyrus. What was it made from?

2 Who was the Queen of the Iceni who fought the Romans and who, according to legend, had knives on the wheels of her chariot?

3 Where was the Hittite empire?

4 Who was the first Emperor of Rome, who came to power in 27BC?

5 Which of the Seven Wonders of the World did Nebuchadnezzar, King of Babylon from 605 to 562 BC, build?

6 The English king Harold was killed in the battle against William the Conqueror. How, according to popular tradition, was he killed?

7 The tomb of 18th dynasty Pharaoh Tutankhamun, containing rich treasure, was discovered in 1922. How old was Tutankhamun when he died? ▼ ▶

8 What was the first Roman name for London?

9 Who was the first Christian missionary?

10 Name the god of the underworld worshipped by the ancient Egyptians?

14 The Roman emperor Caligula created a new consul, Incitatus, in the year 41 AD. Why did this cause consternation?

15 St. Patrick, the patron saint of Ireland, was the Romano-British son of an army officer. How did he first arrive in Ireland?

16 Which Roman general became Cleopatra's lover and ruled Egypt with her?

17 What happened to Julius Caesar on the Ides of March?

18 What was the name given to money demanded by the Vikings from kings in the countries they invaded, as a bribe to leave them and their lands in peace?

19 How many cohorts would actually make up a Roman legion?

20 A spectacular British archaeological find was made in 1939 in Sutton Hoo, Suffolk. What was uncovered?

21 Offa's Dyke was built to divide England from Wales, possibly to mark an agreed border, possibly as part of a defensive system. Where did King Offa rule?

11 In which country was Brian Boru king?

12 Moses led the Hebrew people out of Egypt but died before he could lead them into Canaan. Who was his successor?

13 The Greek philosopher Socrates made many enemies by questioning accepted beliefs and he was eventually tried for corruption of the young and sentenced to death. What was the exact sentence?

22 Plato was a celebrated philosopher. What was his home city?

23 As what did Homer become famous?

24 The Anglo-Saxons wrote with letters they believed to have magical properties. What were they called?

25 Which ancient people did the Romans call barbarians?

1. What is another name for the rowan tree?

2. Which flower is named after the botanist Dr Leonhard Fuchs?

3. From which plant does the pain-killing drug morphine come?

4. What name is given to the Japanese art of growing miniature trees? ▲

5. Which plant is the national emblem of Ireland?

6. Who is said to have worked out the theory of gravity as a result of sitting under an apple tree?

7. What do yew, laburnum seeds and mistletoe berries have in common?

8. Give the popular name for the antirrhinum.

9. What are plants that flower every year called?

10. Which plant takes its name from the Italian phrase for 'beautiful woman'?

11. What name is given to a flowerhead made up of many tiny flowers?

12. Which Swedish naturalist introduced the present-day system of plant classification?

13 By what name is the plant 'digitalis' popularly known?

14 Trees that do not shed their leaves in winter belong to which group?

15 Which salad vegetable has varieties called iceberg and cos?

16 What is the loss of water from the leaves of plants called?

17 How is it possible to tell the age of a tree?

18 Which flower takes its name from the Turkish word for 'turban'?

19 What is the common name for Prunus domestica?

20 Which particular part of the flower is called the anther?

21 What is the difference between dicotyledon and monocotyledon plants?

22 Name the liquid made by a flower to attract insects? ▼

23 In the world classification system for plants, what are aquatic plants containing chlorophyll always called?

24 What is the popular name for the most deadly fungus, the exremely poisonous Amanita phalloides?

25 What is the sacred flower of the Buddhist tradition?

ERISTALIS TENAX AND ITS RAT-TAILED LARVA.

1. Businessman Asil Nadir left Britain after accusations of fraud over the running of his Polly Peck empire. To which country did he flee?

2. Which president of the Philippines was forced to flee the country after the United States withdrew support for him?

3. Live Aid was one of the largest ever fund-raising concerts in 1985. What was it in aid of? ▲ ▶

4. In 1985, Palestinian terrorists hi-jacked an Italian cruise liner in the Mediterranean and murdered a disabled American tourist. Name the ship.

5. Shortly after his inauguration, Ronald Reagan was shot by John Hinckley. Why did Hinckley claim that he attempted assassination?

6. Who led the fundamentalist Islamic regime in Iran at the time of the United States hostage crisis?

7. What was the scene of America's worst nuclear accident, in 1979?

8. Which party did Jimmy Carter represent?

9. Who was known as Stormin' Norman?

10. The Symbionese Liberation Army kidnapped an American heiress, daughter of a millionaire newspaper tycoon in 1974. What was her name?

11. Who was murdered by the IRA at Mullaghmore in Ireland on 27 August, 1979?

12. What post was held by H.R. Haldeman at the time of Watergate?

13. Which militant black American leader was assassinated in 1965?

14 Why did Patricia Cahill and Karen Smith feature in the British headlines in July 1993?

15 Who succeeded Mikhail Gorbachev as Russian leader in 1991?

16 The British government broke off diplomatic relations with which country after the shooting of WPC Fletcher in 1984?

17 How did Provisional IRA member Bobby Sands die in May 1981?

18 Which British newspaper tycoon, his empire deep in debt, was lost overboard from his yacht in November 1991?

19 Which Soviet dissident, husband of Yelena Bonner, was released from internal exile in December 1986?

20 Name the Argentinean cruiser sunk by the British during the Falklands conflict.

21 In December 1989, United States troops invaded Panama and the country's dictator was ousted from power. Name him.

22 The agreement signed between the Israelis and Palestinians in September 1993 gave the Palestinians autonomy in which areas?

23 Of what was John Demjanjuk cleared in 1993?

24 Name the Australian prime minister who discussed severing constitutional ties with Britain with the Queen during a visit to Britain in 1993?

25 Over what incident did the Princess of Wales take legal action in November 1993?

1 In which film did Elvis Presley play the role of a boxer? ▼

2 Which outlaw was killed by Bob Ford?

3 Who was Tsar Nicholas II's youngest daughter?

4 Who won the Pulitzer Prize for his Profiles of Courage?

5 In the Bible, whose parents were Zacharias and Elizabeth?

6 Tariffs and quotas are some of the weapons used in which kind of war?

7 Of which country was Sir Keith Holyoake Prime Minister?

8 From which inn did Chaucer's pilgrims set out in Canterbury Tales?

9 If you had tinnitus, from what would you be suffering?

10 Who was the creator of fictional detective Mike Hammer?

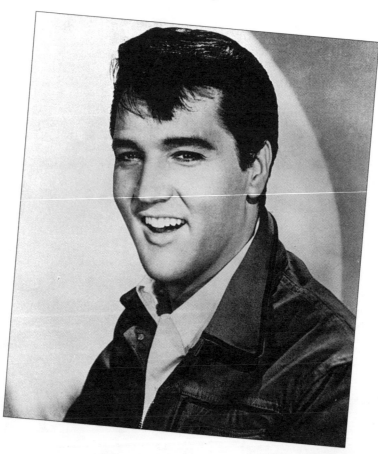

11 In which sport has Stephen Roche achieved success?

12 Which country is the home of feta cheese?

13 Name the 1969 'road' movie starring Dennis Hopper and Peter Fonda as two nonconformist motorcyclists.

14 Larry Hagman is the son of which famous actress? ▲

15 Whose autobiography was entitled Is that it?

16 In which American state is the university of Princeton?

17 What was once called brimstone?

18 In which war were the battles of Bunker Hill and Brandywine Creek fought?

19 Which well-loved cartoon animal made his debut in 1937?

20 What does a protractor measure?

21 What name is given to the person authorized to vote on behalf of someone else?

22 Who said the famous phrase 'An army marches on its stomach'?

23 Iceland and England broke off diplomatic relations in 1976. What particular problem caused the split?

24 Fats Waller was famous as a player of which instrument?

25 Who defined democracy as 'government of the people, by the people, for the people'?

People and Places   Capitals

1. Wellington, New Zealand
2. Western (Wailing) Wall
3. A famous art collection
4. Sri Lanka
5. Kremlin
6. Waikiki
7. Rive Gauche (Left Bank)
8. 99 years
9. Beirut
10. Métro
11. Liechtenstein
12. Berlin
13. Sliema
14. Copenhagen
15. La Paz, Bolivia
16. Paris
17. District of Columbia
18. Beijing (Peking)
19. Lusaka
20. Bangkok
21. Reykjavik, Iceland
22. River Danube
23. A return visit
24. Cairo
25. Brussels

Entertaining Arts   Leading Men

1. Christopher Lee
2. Peter O'Toole
3. On Golden Pond
4. Topol
5. Tony Curtis
6. Charlie Chaplin
7. True Grit
8. Paul Newman
9. Robert Preston
10. Clint Eastwood
11. The Beggar's Opera
12. Dustin Hoffman
13. Robert Mitchum
14. Richard Attenborough
15. The Hunter
16. George C. Scott
17. Orson Welles
18. Claus von Bulow
19. Yul Brynner
20. Noël Coward
21. On the Waterfront and The Godfather
22. Kevin Costner
23. Richard Burton
24. Michael Caine
25. Charlton Heston

Food and Drink   Desserts and Sweets

1. Zabaglione
2. Flambéed in kirsch
3. Bavarois
4. Criss-crossed pastry strips
5. A mixture of fresh or dried fruit in syrup
6. Choux
7. Suet crust
8. As medicine
9. Semolina
10. They were sent to the Anzacs troops, the Australia, New Zealand Army Corps
11. Pale green
12. The root of the marshmallow plant
13. The sugar is caramelized under a high grill
14. Liquorice
15. Ice-cream
16. Chewing gum
17. Currants, peel and sugar
18. Biscuit
19. It is steeped in honey or sugar syrup
20. Jelly-beans
21. It has several layers of crisp puff pastry, hence 'a thousand leaves'
22. Chantilly cream
23. Black forest cherry cake (Schwarzwälder Kirschtorte)
24. Ice cream
25. Pavlova (named after Anna Pavlova)

Sports and Pastimes   Team Games

1. Jack Hobbs
2. New York Yankees
3. 60 minutes with three intervals
4. Pat Jennings
5. American football
6. Baseball
7. Polo
8. Cricket
9. Baseball
10. Wayne Gretzky
11. Behind the catcher
12. South Africa objected because he was 'coloured'
13. Harlem Globetrotters
14. Nine
15. Soccer
16. Babe Ruth
17. Softball
18. Leery Constantine
19. Ice hockey
20. Ten
21. St. John's Wood
22. Polo
23. 36
24. Seven
25. Cricket

History   Ancient Days

1. Reeds
2. Boudicca (Boadicea)
3. Anatolia, Turkey
4. Augustus
5. Hanging Gardens of Babylon
6. With an arrow through the eye
7. 18
8. Londinium
9. The apostle Paul
10. Osiris
11. Ireland
12. Joshua
13. Death by drinking hemlock
14. Incitatus was a horse
15. He was captured by Irish pirates and sold as a slave
16. Mark Antony
17. He was assassinated
18. Danegeld
19. 10
20. Anglo-Saxon burial ship
21. Mercia
22. Athens
23. Poet and storyteller
24. Runes
25. All those who lived outside the Empire

Natural World   Plants

1. Mountain ash
2. Fuchsia
3. Opium poppy
4. Bonsai
5. Shamrock
6. Isaac Newton
7. They are all poisonous
8. Snapdragon
9. Perennial
10. Belladonna
11. A composite flower
12. Karl Linnaeus
13. Foxglove
14. Evergreens
15. Lettuce
16. Transpiration
17. From the rings within the trunk
18. Tulip
19. Plum
20. The top of the stamen, where the pollen is found in pollen sacs
21. The dicotyledon has two seed leaves; monocotyledon has only one
22. Nectar
23. Algae
24. Death cap
25. Lotus

Twentieth Century   Headline News

1. North Cyprus
2. Ferdinand Marcos
3. Victims of the Ethiopian famine
4. Achille Lauro
5. To impress actress Jodie Foster with whom he was obsessed
6. Ayatollah Khomeini
7. Three Mile Island
8. Democratic
9. General H. Norman Schwarzkopf
10. Patty Hearst
11. Earl Mountbatten
12. Presidential Chief of Staff
13. Malcolm X
14. They were released from a prison sentence for drug offences in Thailand
15. Boris Yeltsin
16. Libya
17. He was on hunger strike in prison
18. Robert Maxwell
19. Andrei Sakharov
20. General Belgrano
21. Manuel Noriega
22. Jericho and Gaza Strip
23. Of being the Nazi war criminal, Ivan the Terrible
24. Paul Keating
25. Unauthorized photos of her exercising in a gym

Pot Luck

1. Kid Galahad
2. Jesse James
3. Anastasia
4. John F. Kennedy
5. John the Baptist
6. Trade
7. New Zealand
8. The Tabard at Southwark
9. Ringing or buzzing in the ears
10. Mickey Spillane
11. Cycling
12. Greece
13. Easy Rider
14. Mary Martin
15. Bob Geldof
16. New Jersey
17. Sulphur
18. War of American Independence
19. Bugs Bunny
20. Angles
21. Proxy
22. Napoleon
23. Cod-fishing rights
24. Piano
25. Abraham Lincoln

Quiz

10

1. Woody Allen said, 'It was the most fun I ever had without laughing!' To what was he referring?

2. What was the famous sign on United States President Harry S. Truman's desk?

3. According to film producer Sam Goldwyn, 'a verbal contract is not worth...'. What? ▲

4. Which TV cop would say 'Who loves ya, baby?'

5. 'You can fool all of the people some of the time and some of the people all of the time but...'. Complete this quotation from Abraham Lincoln.

6. Which British monarch said 'We are not amused'?

7. Whom did H.G. Wells say was king in 'the country of the blind'?

8. Oscar Wilde said that fox-hunting was the 'unspeakable in pursuit' of what?

9. 'Frankly my dear, I don't give a damn'. In which film were these words spoken?

10. Whom did Churchill describe as a 'sheep in sheep's clothing'?

11. Who resigned from the Hollywood Club, saying that he would not want to belong to any club that would accept him as a member?

12. Which music-hall star sang, 'A little of what you fancy does you good'?

13. Which blonde bombshell said 'Keep a diary and one day it will keep you'?

14. British fashion designer Mary Quant said 'A woman is as young as ...'. What?

15. Jean Jacques Rousseau said 'Man was born free and everywhere he is ...'. Complete the quotation.

16. Who sang that 'Mad dogs and Englishmen go out in the midday sun'?

17. Marilyn Monroe, after posing for a revealing photograph, was asked 'Didn't you have anything on?' What was her reply? ▶

18. Which Nazi said in a 1936 broadcast 'Guns will make us powerful – butter will only make us fat'?

19. The saying 'May the force be with you' comes from which film?

20. Maurice Chevalier said 'I prefer old age ...' to what?

21. Which famous Hollywood actress said she had never hated a man enough to give him back his diamonds?

22 Which world leader said in September 1993, 'Enough of blood and tears, enough'?

23 In which film did the main character, played by Bette Davis, say 'Fasten your seatbelts. It's going to be a bumpy night'?

24 Karl Marx said that the workers had nothing to lose but what?

25 Sophie Tucker said the famous lines 'I have been poor and I have been rich.' Complete the quotation.

1. What is the subject of a mystery play?

2. Who sold his soul to the devil in a play by Goethe?

3. Who wrote Separate Tables, The Winslow Boy and The Browning Version?

4. In what type of stage production would you find a dame?

5. Who became the first director of Britain's National Theatre?

6. The first big popular success of the Off-Broadway musical came with a revival of the Threepenny Opera in 1954. Who wrote it?

7. Who goes mad and commits suicide in Hamlet?

8. What is the name of the space above the proscenium in the theatre, from which the scenery is controlled?

9. What type of plays did the French dramatist Molière write? ▼

10. Who was Joseph Grimaldi?

11. Which Shakespearean play concerns the fortunes of the Montagues and the Capulets?

12. Name the Australian performer who has become famous as Dame Edna Everage?

13 What play holds the record for the longest continuous run in Britain?

14 Name the Irish dramatist who wrote Juno and the Paycock and The Plough and the Stars?

15 Which was Shakespeare's shortest play?

16 In which country is a type of play called kabuki performed?

17 Who were the hero and heroine of the Italian Commedia dell'arte?

18 Oscar Wilde said 'The play was a great success but the audience ...'. Complete the quotation. ▲

19 What is the name of the Mr. Punch's wife in the puppet play?

20 Which early theatre performed its dramas in verse, with the action punctuated by a chorus and with the actors wearing masks?

21 What is the part of the stage that projects into the auditorium called?

22 In which pantomime does the main character 'turn again' with his faithful cat?

23 What happened to London's original Globe Theatre in 1613?

24 Who wrote the music for The Phantom of the Opera?

25 Which of the great writer Shakespeare's plays is the subject of great superstition among actors, so that many will not use its name for fear of disaster?

1 What is the name given to a small field used for rice cultivation?

2 Sugar cane is the largest member of which family?

3 3. From what is chocolate and cocoa made?

4 What is the other name for vegetables known as legumes?

5 From which substance do bees manufacture honey?

6 The people of which country consume most beef?

7 In which century was margarine invented?

8 Mutton comes from sheep of what age?

9 Geese are bred for their meat and for what else?

10 What type of foodstuff is sorghum, used as a staple diet in Africa and parts of Asia, though rarely in the west?

11 What are Brown Swiss, Finn and Normandy?

12 Which meat was once the staple diet of sailors and early settlers because it could be salted and kept without refrigeration?

13 What is the name for the system of keeping chickens in tiers of cages, with the eggs they lay running down into containers outside the cages?

14 What is a male duck called?

15 In which century was tea drinking introduced into Europe?

16 What are Andalusian, Berkshire and Duroc?

17 When raising beef cattle, what is the name of the system where animals are provided with fodder rather than being allowed to graze?

18 In which country were pigs first used for food?

19 What was normally used as a sweetener before sugar was available?

20 Which country provides about half the coffee consumed in the world?

21 What crop is attacked by the Colorado beetle?

22 Which cereal forms the staple diet of three-quarters of the world's population?

23 Where does maple syrup come from?

24 What are Plymouth Rocks, Barnevelder and Leghorns?

25 The meat veal comes from very young dairy cattle. At what particular age are they usually slaughtered?

1. Which boxer had the most world title fights in his career?

2. Which black American won four gold medals in track and field events in front of Adolf Hitler at the 1936 Berlin Olympics?

3. In golf, who was the first European to win the U.S. Masters?

4. In which ball sport is the U.S. sportsman Magic Johnson famous?

5. Which English woman cricketer has played in the most test matches?

6. Who was the first man to run a mile in under four minutes?

7. Which Portuguese woman has won the Boston Marathon twice and the London Marathon once?

8. Since 1977 the World Snooker Championships have been played at a theatre in northern England. Name it.

9. Which Wimbledon tennis champion was nick-named 'Superbrat'? ▲

10. Paavo Nurmi won nine Olympic medals for distance running in the 1920s and set 29 world records in his career. Which was his home country?

11. The story of which British runners is told in the film Chariots of Fire? ▶

12. By what first name is Frances Morgan Thompson better known?

13 Name the American who won Olympic gold medals in the long jump in 1984, 1988 and 1992?

14 Who did Pete Sampras beat in the 1993 Wimbledon Finals?

15 Which motor racing driver has won most Grand Prix races in his career?

16 Which American athlete is known as 'Flo-Jo'?

17 Who skated to victory to the strains of Ravel's Bolero?

18 What was tennis star Billie Jean King's maiden name?

19 Which East German girl broke the world record for the 400 metres seven times between 1978 and 1985?

20 Mark Todd rode his horse Charisma to victory in the three day event in the Olympics of 1984 and again in 1988. Which country did he represent?

21 Which two West Indian cricketers have been knighted?

22 In which sport are the Cincinnati Reds, Toronto Blue Jays and Los Angeles Dodgers winning teams?

23 Which golfer has most wins in the world's major golf tournaments?

24 Whom did Britain Steve Davis defeat in his very first World Championship snooker final in 1981?

25 In which sport did the Brazilian Pelé achieve fame?

1. Who, in 1895, first fitted pneumatic tyres to a car? ▲

2. In which country did the bullet train – at the time, the fastest train in the world – start running in 1964?

3. What is the distance between the two rails of a railway track called?

4. What, in car production, is CAD?

5. What is a Ro-Ro vessel?

6. In air travel, what do the initials ATC stand for?

7. In which year did the jumbo jet make its maiden flight?

8. What form of transport, mainly made of wood, was invented by Gottlieb Daimler in 1885?

9. It took seven years to build the first railroad from east to west across America and teams of workers started from each end. In which state did they meet? ▶

10. In the 1920s and 1930s, the Orient Express was one of the most glamorous trains in the world. Some carriages have been restored and run to various exotic locations. What is the train now called?

11. In San Francisco tubes run under the Bay on a system called BART. What do the initials stand for?

12. Lagos, in Nigeria, has introduced its own method of traffic control. What happens on Mondays, Wednesdays and Fridays?

13 Who invented the first internal combustion engine to run on petroleum in 1885?

14 What were the Rainhill trials, held in England in 1829?

15 In 1891, the Tsar of Russia ordered the building of a railway between Moscow and Vladivostock and the first train ran in 1901. What was the railway called?

16 What is given the name 'piggy-back transport'?

17 Which new type of passenger ferry appeared in 1959?

18 What make of car featured in Back to the Future?

19 In which year did Concorde, the world's only successful supersonic airliner, first fly?

20 In 1986 Dick Rutan and Jeana Yeager piloted Voyager around the world. What 'first' did they achieve?

21 What is the national civil aircraft mark of the United Kingdom?

22 Where does the new motorway called the Autoput run?

23 Which building is known as the world's largest railway station?

24 The train of the future is the Maglev, which has no wheels but floats above a magnetic track. What does 'Maglev' stand for?

25 Where is the highest railway line in the world to be found?

1. The world's highest waterfall is in Venezuela. What is it called?

2. Which island is famous for its giant tortoises?

3. In Antarctica, an active volcano is covered with snow but still spouts steam. Name it.

4. Where is the world's longest fjord: Iceland, Greenland or Norway?

5. The Grand Canyon, in the United States, is a geologist's paradise. Is the youngest of its rock formations 100 million, 175 million or 225 million years old? ▼

6. Caverns formed in what type of rock have stalactites and stalagmites?

7. What was named after Sir Henry Ayers, Premier of South Australia in 1873?

8. Which is the world's longest river?

9. Rotorua, nicknamed 'sulphur city', has large areas of spectacular geothermal activity – geysers, steam vents and hot springs. In which country is it?

10. What is the most distinctive feature of the Auvergne in France's Massif Central?

11 Which author was inspired by the remote Hunza valley in northern Pakistan to create the idyllic Shangri-La in Lost Horizon?

12 Which animal has become a symbol for the endangered species of the world and is used in the logo of the Worldwide Fund for Nature (formerly World Wildlife Fund)?

13 What is the Perseid shower?

14 Which part of the world is advertised in tourist brochures as 'the land of the midnight sun'?

15 Where is the world's largest coral reef to be found?

16 Which country has the highest navigable lake in the world?

17 Which of the world's trees has the longest lifespan?

18 The largest lizards in the world, growing to nearly 4 metres (12 feet) and able to feed on pigs and deer, are found in Indonesia. What are they called? ▲

19 Which musician was inspired by the cave on the Hebridean island of Staffa to write the overture Fingal's Cave?

20 The deepest of the world's lakes is in south-eastern Siberia. What is it called?

21 The Petrified Forest National Park, where ancient forests have turned into minerals, is in which 'desert' in Arizona in the United States?

22 Bungle Bungle, a wild expanse of striped black and orange beehive-shaped rocks, was proclaimed as a rediscovered 'lost world' in 1982. In which country is it?

23 Conservationists believe that the destruction of the rainforests, resulting in increased carbon dioxide in the atmosphere, is contributing to what harmful effect?

24 Which sacred river has a special place in the Hindu religion because it is believed to be a goddess, commanded to flow down from heaven to give immortal life to those whose ashes are covered by her waters?

25 The beautiful Phang Nga Bay in southern Thailand was the setting for the Bond film The Man with the Golden Gun. Who played the villain Scaramanga, who had a private island here?

1 Henri Landru killed a series of women in France in the early years of the century after advertising in 'lonely hearts' columns. What was his nickname?

2 What was the name of Dr. Crippen's secretary and lover?

3 At which fast food restaurant did James Huberty gun down men, women and children in San Ysidro, United States in 1984?

4 Name the mother convicted and later pardoned in the Australian 'dingo baby' case.

5 Who was the last woman hanged for murder in Britain?

6 Name the pregnant actress, wife of Roman Polanski, who was murdered, along with four others by members of the Charles Manson 'family'?

7 In which city was John F. Kennedy assassinated?

8 Christopher Craig shot a British policeman in 1952 but was too young to face the death penalty. Name his 19-year-old companion, who was hanged.

9 Which English lord disappeared after the killing of his children's nanny and has never been heard of again?

10 I want to Live! was the title of a 1958 film telling the story of the murderess Barbara Graham. Who played Graham?

11 American headmistress Jean Harris shot her lover Dr. Herman Tarnower in 1980. For what diet was the doctor world famous?

12 Marguerite Fahmy shot her Egyptian husband Prince Ali Kemal Fahmy Bey in which luxury hotel in London?

13 How old was ex-Beatle John Lennon when he was shot dead in New York? ▼ ▶

14 Who was Ian Brady's female accomplice in the horrific 'Moors Murders'?

15 Which murderer did Richard Attenborough play in the film 10 Rillington Place?

16 For what was Adolf Eichmann tried and convicted in 1961?

17 Who was the toddler killed in Britain by two 11-year-old boys in 1993?

18 In Cold Blood was an account of the murder of the Clutter family in Kansas, United States. Who was the writer?

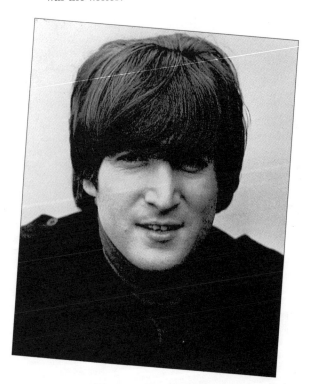

19. Albert De Salvo spread panic through an American city as he raped and strangled 13 women over 18 months. By what name is he better known?

20. Who shot Robert Kennedy in 1968?

21. Marcel Petiot was found guilty of murdering 25 people in Paris in 1946; he had pretended to help those who wanted to escape the Nazis, but killed them for their cash. How was he executed?

22. Who was the young black man convicted in 1982 of two murders and suspected of the string of killings of black children in Atlanta, United States?

23. Donald Neilson, who killed three sub-postmasters and heiress Lesley Whittle in northern England in the 1970s, earned what nickname because of the hood he wore to commit his crimes?

24. Who was the British MP, shadow Northern Ireland Secretary, killed by a terrorist bomb as he drove from the House of Commons car park in 1979?

25. David Berkowitz, the infamous killer who shot a number of young couples for no apparent reason, taunted the police with strange letters signed by what name?

1 Where is the Dewey classification system used?

2 In what field did Sir Alexander Korda make his name? ▲

3 A tithe was a tax paid to support the clergy. What proportion of income was a tithe?

4 What nationality is the novelist Patrick White?

5 What is the common name for rubella?

6 In which year was the state of Israel created?

7 How old was Rose Kennedy, mother of J.F.K., in July 1993?

8 In which country was Archbishop Makarios President?

9 In the 1992 summer Olympics, three new medal events were added. Two of these were Badminton and Baseball. What was the third?

10 What was Bob Hope's signature tune?

11 Which English Prime Minister once edited The Church Times?

12 Who is the chief god of Scandinavian mythology?

13 For what purpose was the Leaning Tower of Pisa originally built? ▶

14 What was the name of the Mafia patriarch played by Marlon Brando in The Godfather?

15 For what was the Haight-Ashbury area of San Francisco famous in the 1960s?

16 Which Scandinavian country achieved its independence from Sweden in 1905?

17 If you were ailurophobic, what would you fear?

18 After how many years of marriage is a ruby wedding celebrated?

19 Where in London would you find the Whispering Gallery?

20 Which Nobel prize-winning writer shot himself in 1961?

21 In Italy, what is the capital city of Tuscany?

22 Veni, vidi, vici wrote Julius Caesar. What is the translation?

23 Which comedy team included John Cleese, Michael Palin, Graham Chapman and Terry Jones?

24 What would you do with an ocarina?

25 Name the lawyer in Dickens' Tale of Two Cities who finally goes to the guillotine in place of another.

People and Places   Who Said What

1. Sex
2. 'The buck stops here'
3. '... the paper it's written on'
4. Kojak, played by Telly Savalas
5. '... you can't fool all of the people all of the time'
6. Queen Victoria
7. The one-eyed man
8. The uneatable
9. Gone with the Wind
10. Clement Attlee
11. Groucho Marx
12. Marie Lloyd
13. Mae West
14. Her knee
15. '... in chains'
16. Noel Coward
17. 'I had the radio on'
18. Goering
19. Star Wars
20. '... the alternative'
21. Zsa Zsa Gabor
22. Yitzhak Rabin, Premier of Israel
23. All About Eve
24. Their chains
25. 'Rich is better'

Entertaining Arts   Treading the Boards

1. Bible stories or the lives of saints
2. Faust
3. Terence Rattigan
4. Pantomime
5. Peter Hall
6. Bertolt Brecht
7. Ophelia
8. Flies
9. Comedies
10. A clown
11. Romeo and Juliet
12. Barry Humphries
13. The Mousetrap
14. Sean O'Casey
15. The Comedy of Errors
16. Japan
17. Harlequin and Columbine
18. '... was a disaster'
19. Judy
20. Greek theatre
21. Apron
22. Dick Whittington
23. It burned down
24. Andrew Lloyd Webber
25. Macbeth

Food and Drink   Feeding the World

1. Paddy
2. Grass
3. The pods of cacao trees
4. Pulses
5. Nectar
6. United States
7. 19th century
8. Over two years
9. Feathers and down
10. Grain
11. Types of dairy cow
12. Pork
13. Battery
14. Drake
15. 18th
16. Pigs
17. Lot-feeding·
18. China
19. Honey
20. Brazil
21. Potato
22. Rice
23. The sap of maple trees
24. Hens
25. Before three months

Sports and Pastimes   The Winners

1. Joe Louis
2. Jesse Owens
3. Seve Ballesteros
4. Basketball
5. Rachael Heyhoe-Flint
6. Roger Bannister
7. Rosa Mota
8. The Crucible Theatre, Sheffield
9. John McEnroe
10. Finland
11. Harold Abrahams and
Eric Liddell
12. Daley
13. Carl Lewis
14. Jim Courier
15. Alain Prost
16. Florence Griffith-Joyner
17. Jayne Torvill and Christopher Dean
18. Moffitt
19. Marita Koch
20. New Zealand
21. Garfield Sobers and
Frank Worrell
22. Baseball
23. Jack Nicklaus
24. Doug Mountjoy
25. Soccer

History   Transport

1. Edouard Michelin
2. Japan
3. Gauge
4. Computer-aided design
5. Roll on, roll off
6. Air traffic control
7. 1969
8. Motorbike
9. Utah
10. Venice Simplon Orient Express
11. Bay Area Rapid Transit system
12. Only cars with even numbers on the license plates can use the roads
13. Daimler
14. Locomotive trials
15. Trans-Siberian Railway
16. Container carried by rail
17. Hovercraft
18. De Lorean
19. 1969
20. The first non-stop round-the-world flight without refuelling
21. G
22. From the Italian-Austrian border to the Greek frontier
23. Grand Central, New York
24. Magnetic levitation

Natural World   Nature's Wonders

1. Angel Falls
2. Galapagos
3. Mount Erebus
4. Greenland
5. 225 million
6. Limestone
7. Ayers Rock
8. The Nile
9. New Zealand
10. Chains of extinct volcanoes
11. James Hilton
12. Giant Panda
13. A spectacular display of meteors, which happens every August, burning up as they hit the Earth's atmosphere
14. Scandinavian countries
15. Great Barrier Reef
16. Peru
17. Giant sequoia
18. Komodo dragons
19. Mendelssohn
20. Lake Baikal
21. Painted Desert
22. Australia
23. Global warming: the greenhouse effect
24. The Ganges
25. Christopher Lee

Twentieth Century   Murders Most Foul

1. Bluebeard
2. Ethel le Neve
3. McDonalds
4. Lindy Chamberlain
5. Ruth Ellis
6. Sharon Tate
7. Dallas, Texas
8. Derek Bentley
9. Lord Lucan
10. Susan Hayward
11. The Scarsdale Diet
12. Savoy
13. 40
14. Myra Hindley
15. John Reginald Christie
16. Nazi war crimes
17. James Bulger
18. Truman Capote
19. The Boston Strangler
20. Sirhan Bishara Sirhan
21. Guillotine
22. Wayne Williams
23. The Black Panther
24. Airey Neave
25. Son of Sam

Pot Luck

1. Libraries
2. Films
3. One tenth
4. Australian
5. German measles
6. 1948
7. 103
8. Cyprus
9. Women's judo
10. Thanks for the Memory
11. Edward Heath
12. Odin
13. As the bell-tower of the cathedral
14. Don Vito Corleone
15. Hippies and flower children
16. Norway
17. Cats
18. 40 years
19. St. Paul's Cathedral
20. Ernest Hemingway
21. Florence
22. I came, I saw, I con-
quered
23. Monty Python
24. Blow it; it is a musical instrument
25. Sydney Carton

Quiz

11

1. What is the highest mountain in Africa?

2. Which mountains form the backbone of South America?

3. Where would you go to look for the Abominable Snowman?

4. Who wrote High Adventure, about a spectacular mountain climb?

5. On which mountain is it said that Noah's Ark came to rest?

6. They were once known as the 'mountains of the moon' and thought to be the source of the Nile. Their name means 'Rainmaker'; what are they?

7. In which country is Tongariro National Park with its three volcanoes, including Mt. Ruapahu?

8. What is the second highest mountain in the world?

9. What was the nationality of the party of climbers who scaled the world's second highest mountain in 1954?

10. The official country retreat of the President of the United States, Camp David, is in which mountains?

11. Which mountain range divides France and Spain?

12. What is Britain's highest mountain?

13 In which country are the Drakensberg mountains?

14 Name the highest mountain in the Alps.

15 Who was with Edmund Hillary when he reached the summit of Everest in 1953? ◀

16 How do the Dolomites get their name?

17 Which mountain, on the island of Honshu, was revered by the Japanese for centuries as a sacred mountain? ▲

18 Name the active volcano that stands above the Bay of Naples.

19 The highest mountain in North America is in Alaska. What is it called?

20 Which ancient civilization was nurtured in the Andes?

21 The world's third highest mountain is Kanchenjunga. What nationality were the climbers who first reached the mountain's summit in 1955?

22 Which mountains stretch from northern Canada to the southern United States?

23 How does Cotopaxi in the Andes of Ecuador earn its place in the record books?

24 How did climbers George Leigh Mallory and Andrew Irving find a place in mountaineering history?

25 Name the mountain named in the Bible on which Moses was given the Ten Commandments.

1. Who plays the incompetent proprietor of Fawlty Towers?

2. Golden Girls was a great success; which of the 'girls' is missing from the sequel, Golden Palace?

3. How were Gene Wilder and Richard Pryor dressed when they were arrested in the film Stir Crazy?

4. Who lived at Railway Cuttings, East Cheam?

5. Which comedienne, who starred with Lenny Henry in Three of a Kind, went to the United States in 1987 where, by the end of her first season, her show was nominated for five Emmy awards?

6. Who wrote the screenplay for Barefoot in the Park, based on his Broadway success?

7. I Love Lucy was the first American sit-com seen in Britain. Who was the star?

8. Which American comedian based much of his act on his meanness and incompetent violin playing?

9. Who does Paul Eddington play in Yes Minister?

10. Which comedian is the husband of Dawn French?

11. A Clown Too Many is the autobiography of which British comedian who died in 1993?

12. In which city is the bar in Cheers situated?

13. Who played the incompetent medium Madame Arcati in the 1954 film of Blithe Spirit?

14. In which film did Tony Curtis and Jack Lemmon dress in drag and join an all-girls band?

15. George Burns starred in a TV show with his wife for eight seasons before she retired. What was her name? ▶

16. In A Fish Called Wanda, what is the profession of the character played by John Cleese?

17. With whom did Penelope Keith star in To the Manor Born and Executive Stress?

18. Which sergeant was played by Phil Silvers?

19. What was John Inman's catchphrase as Mr. Humphries in Are You Being Served?

20. Which comedy quartet was made up of Spike Milligan, Harry Secombe, Peter Sellers and Michael Bentine?

21. Glenda Jackson won an Oscar for best actress when she starred opposite George Segal in a comedy in 1973. What was the film?

22. Who played the 'odd couple' in the 1968 film?

23. Which English comedian, famous for the bawdy humour of his shows, in which he created characters like Fred Skuttle and chased scantily-clad girls, had a great success on American TV?

24. Name the sit-com set in occupied France with stories involving resistance workers and stupid German officers.

25. Which actor, the first black actor to share equal billing with a white actor on American TV in I Spy, went on to star in a sit-com about a middle-class black family, and became the highest-paid sitcom star?

1 What is the Italian name for squid?

2 A 'smoothie' is a popular drink in Australia. Its ingredients are blended with ice until frothy; what are they?

3 Where was chop suey invented?

4 What food has a name that literally means 'on a skewer'?

5 Blinis are small, yeasted pancakes. With what are they traditionally served ?

6 Oysters are an expensive delicacy. What does it mean if they are 'shucked'? ◀ ▶

7 Where would you expect to eat paella?

8 If you ordered lassi as a drink with an Indian meal, it could be flavoured with salt and pepper, sugar or fruit. What is it made from?

9 What is the main ingredient of guacamole?

10 What type of food is gazpacho?

11 Which bread, sliced very thinly and crisped in the oven, is named after a famous opera singer?

12 What salad is made from chopped apple, celery, walnuts and creamy mayonnaise dressing?

13 What salad is made from diced cucumber, tomatoes, feta cheese and black olives, dressed with olive oil and lemon juice?

14 What type of food is pepperoni?

15 In a Japanese restaurant, diners might order a dish of thinly sliced beef and raw vegetables, which would be stir-fried at the table. What is it called?

16 At what stage of a meal would you eat rillette?

17 A vacherin may be filled with whipped cream or ice-cream and fruit. From what is the case made?

18 What type of food is Bombay duck?

19 On an American menu, what are home fries?

20 If you were looking at an American menu and wanted to order fried potatoes mashed in a pan and crisped on both sides, what would they be called?

21 What is the Swedish name for hot or cold dishes served as a buffet?

22 If you ordered gratin dauphinois, what would you expect to be served?

23 What is the name given to small cubes of bread, fried or toasted, that can be sprinkled on soups or salads?

24 What name is given to the type of coffee where steam is forced through very finely ground coffee, making a very strong brew?

25 Which type of meat usually goes into frankfurters?

1 Which side of a boat is port?

2 In what sport might you 'catch a crab'?

3 What is the name given to decompression sickness caused by ascending too fast from a deep dive?

4 Who was the first man to swim the English Channel in 1875?

5 In water polo, the game is divided into four quarters. How long is each quarter?

6 There are two main types of canoe: the kayak and the Canadian canoe. What is the difference between the paddles?

7 What do the letters SCUBA stand for?

8 What is a warp?

9 To what do the following rules apply: reach-throw-wade-row-swim/tow?

10 Roland Matthes,was probably one of the greatest ever backstrokers.He was Olympic champion in 1968 and 1972. Which country did this great swimmer represent?

11 Synchronized swimming is one of the newest Olympic sports. In the 1930s, 'water ballet' was a novelty in films. Which star was famous in this discipline?

12 A team in canoe polo consists of how many people?

13 What type of emergency drill is known as buddy breathing?

14 What is the name given to the short tube with a mouthpiece that enables a diver to breathe just below the surface of the water?

15 In sailing, what is turning the boat around through the wind called? ◀

16 Where does the Whitbread Round the World Race, organized by the Royal Naval Sailing Association, start and finish?

17 What are figure-of-eight, sheet bend, bowline and buntline hitch?

18 There are two types of diving competition. One is the highboard; what is the other?

19 When canoeing on rivers and canals, you may sometimes have to negotiate obstacles by portage. What is this?

20 In swimming, a 'pull buoy' is a shaped float held between the legs when practising what?

21 In sailing what is an MOB?

22 The Single-handed Transatlantic Race begins at Plymouth, England. Where does it finish?

23 In water-skiing, what are a cow-catcher and a side-curtain? ▼

24 What is a wake?

25 Which famous swimmer was suspended for 10 years by the Australian authorities for misbehaviour at the 1964 Olympics, when she led a midnight raid to steal a souvenir flag from the Emperor's palace in Tokyo?

1. Which European explorer discovered the Hawaiian islands?

2. Who beat Captain Robert Scott in the 'race' to the South Pole in 1911-12?

3. Mary Kingsley was one of the first women explorers. Where did she travel?

4. Which French naval officer and underwater explorer invented the aqualung?

5. What nationality was explorer Ferdinand Magellan?

6. Against which disease did Edward Jenner discover a vaccine?

7. Who introduced potatoes and tobacco to England after his voyage of exploration?

8. What was given the name the 'New World'?

9. When Abel Tasman discovered Tasmania, what did he call it?

10. Which United States President became an explorer at age 53 to trace the course of the South American Duvido River, now named after him?

11. Prince Henry of Portugal earned what nickname because he involved himself with so many voyages of exploration?

12. In 1947, Norwegian anthropologist Thor Heyerdahl crossed the Pacific on a raft. What was it called?

13. What name was given to the Spanish conquerors of large parts of south and central America in the 16th century?

14 Which explorer travelled in a ship called the Santa Maria?

15 David Livingstone disappeared while exploring Africa in the 1860s and Henry Stanley led an expedition to find him. What was Stanley's profession? ▼

16 What was crossed on foot for the first time in 1968-9?

17 Who led the expedition that set sail in five ships: the Pelican, the Marigold, the Elizabeth, the Swan and the Christopher?

18 In 1856 two Englishmen, Richard Burton and John Speke, set out through the African continent to find the source of which river?

19 Which part of the world was once known as the 'Dark Continent'?

20 What action did Lawrence Oates take in 1912, believing that he was holding up the exploration team?

21 Bartolomeu Dias called it the 'Cape of Storms'. What is it called now?

22 What was the name of Yuri Gagarin's spaceship in 1961?

23 In which land did Charles Doughty, T.E. Lawrence and Bertram Thomas travel and explore?

24 What nationality was Abel Tasman?

25 Terra Australia Incognita was the name given to the vast continent supposed, until the 18th century, to exist in the southern hemisphere. What does the name mean?

1. Budgerigars of all sorts of colours have been developed by breeders. What colour are they in the wild? ▲

2. What is the other name for a cavy?

3. Which cat has no tail?

4. What dog was once sacred in China?

5. Which breed of dog is the favourite of Queen Elizabeth II?

6. What would live in an apiary?

7. What is the family name of doves and pigeons?

8. From which country does the Korat cat come?

9. For what does the Bloodhound have a special reputation?

10. How many sets of teeth does a dog have in its lifetime?

11 What is the difference between the diet of the tortoise and the terrapin?

12 What type of animals are Cornish Rex and Devon Rex?

13 In which country did poodles originate?

14 Guinea pigs whose coats have two or more colours in a pattern are called 'Marked'. What are those with a single colour called? ▼

15 What is the world's smallest breed of dog?

16 What type of animal are Pinto, Haflinger and Waler?

17 To which bird family does the canary belong?

18 What is unusual about the Basenji dog?

19 Which pets can be Peruvian, Abyssinian or Himalayan?

20 What is distinctive about the coat of a piebald pony?

21 The Maine Coon cat gets part of its name from its native state of Maine, How does it get the second part?

22 Which country is the homeland of the Lhaso Apso dog?

23 What type of creature would lhave an aviary as a home?

24 Which particular domestic animal might be Netherland Dwarfs or New Zealand Whites?

25 Which well-loved breed of dog is known for its stalwart rescue work in the mountains of Europe?

1 What year did Adolf Hitler rise to power in Germany?

2 What was the name of the Italian dictator who had been in power since 1922?

3 Which treaty had concluded peace after World War I in 1919?

4 What was the name of the political police in Nazi Germany?

5 Why was the night when Jewish businesses and synagogues were attacked in November 1938 called Kristallnacht?

6 What was the Anschluss, which took place in March 1938?

7 What happened on 1 September, 1939 to precipitate the declaration of war by Britain and France?

8 The Maginot line was a defensive system constructed to protect the French border. How did it get its name?

9 Against which country did Hitler launch 'Operation Barbarossa'?

10 Who was the Desert Fox?

11 What mark did Jews under German rule have to wear on their clothing?

12 American conscripts called themselves GIs. What did the initials stand for?

13 Name the commander of the French armies in World War I who was appointed head of government after Hitler's invasion and was tried as a collaborator at the end of the war.

14 'Let nobody say it cannot be done. It must be done and we are prepared to do it.' Who said this about the 'victory programme' of his country?

15 In 1941 the Japanese attacked the American fleet in Pearl Harbor. Where is Pearl Harbor?

16 In 1943, the Red Army began to drive the Germans from Soviet territory. When they liberated Kiev, what horror did they find at Babi Yar?

17 What was remarkable about Japanese kamikaze pilots?

18 The codename 'Operation Overlord' was given to which military operation in 1944?

19 Where did Churchill and Roosevelt meet Stalin for a major conference in February 1945?

20 The first meeting of the United Nations Organization was scheduled for 25 April, 1945. What organization did it replace?

21 Which German city suffered the worst bombing of the war in February 1945?

22 The first atom bomb was dropped on Hiroshima. On which city was the second dropped? ◀

23 What trials began in November 1945 to bring war criminals to justice?

24 Which emperor ruled Japan at the time of the war?

25 Name the Jewish girl who kept a famous diary while in hiding from the Nazis in Amsterdam. ▼

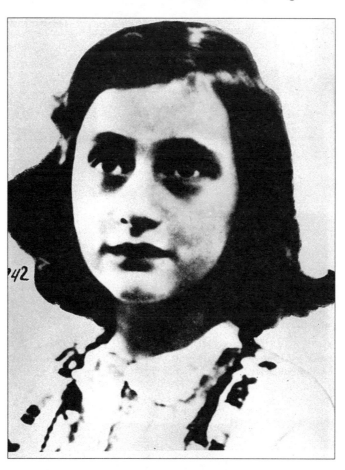

1. Which Commonwealth country celebrated its bicentennial in 1988?

2. What drink is made from vodka and tomato juice?

3. Who is Julie Andrews' director husband? ▲

4. How many points are awarded to the winning driver of a Formula I Grand Prix race?

5. Which zodiac sign is represented by the crab?

6. Which set of sporting rules are named after a 19th–century nobleman?

7. What film included the song Wandering Star?

8. By what name was the fictional Lord Greystoke better known?

9. What was the earliest type of antibiotic drug that was introduced in the 1940s?

10. Who was the Englishman who was saved from death by the Indian girl Pocahontas? ▶

11. Which North African city has a name meaning 'white house' in Spanish?

12. In the Bible, who buried Jesus in his own tomb?

13 Colonel Tom Parker was manager for which famous singer?

14 Under what name is the writer David Cornwell better known?

15 Which type of acid is usually found in car batteries?

16 What does 'C' stand for in film star George C. Scott's name?

17 To which country do the Molucca islands belong?

18 Which male singing voice comes below tenor?

19 In Paris, where is the Tomb of the Unknown Soldier?

20 Who is the world famous film star mother of Jason Gould?

21 What would you do with the Eastern device called a 'hookah'?

22 What type of paintings did artists of the Norwich school produce?

23 In 1943, a group of generals plotted to kill their leader with a bomb. Who was he?

24 Which ancient tribe of invaders gave the country of England and the English people their name?

25 The sea parrot is more usually known by another name. What is it?

People and Places Mountains and Climbers

1. Mt. Kilimanjaro
2. Andes
3. The Himalayas
4. Sir Edmund Hillary
5. Mt. Ararat
6. Ruwenzori
7. New Zealand
8. K2
9. Italian
10. Appalachians
11. Pyrenees
12. Ben Nevis
13. South Africa
14. Mont Blanc
15. Sherpa Tenzing Norgay
16. From the rock of which they are composed
17. Mt. Fuji
18. Vesuvius
19. Mt. McKinley
20. Incas
21. British
22. Rocky Mountains
23. The highest active volcano
24. They disappeared during an Everest climb in 1924; some people think they reached the summit
25. Mt. Sinai

Entertaining Arts A Good Laugh

1. John Cleese
2. Dorothy, played by Bea Arthur
3. As chickens
4. Tony Hancock
5. Tracy Ullman
6. Neil Simon
7. Lucille Ball
8. Jack Benny
9. Jim Hacker
10. Lenny Henry
11. Les Dawson
12. Boston
13. Margaret Rutherford
14. Some Like it Hot
15. Gracie Allen
16. Barrister
17. Peter Bowles
18. Bilko
19. 'I'm free'
20. The Goons
21. A Touch of Class
22. Walter Matthau and Jack Lemmon
23. Benny Hill
24. 'Allo 'Allo
25. Bill Cosby

Food and Drink A la Carte

1. Calamari
2. Milk, yogurt, fruit and honey
3. Chinatown, San Francisco
4. Kebab
5. Sour cream and caviar
6. Opened
7. Spain or a Spanish restaurant
8. Yogurt and ice water
9. Avocado pears
10. Cold soup
11. Melba toast
12. Waldorf salad
13. Greek salad
14. Spicy sausage
15. Sukiyaki
16. As a first course
17. Meringue
18. Fish
19. Sliced or cubed potatoes fried in bacon fat
20. Hash browns
21. Smorgasbord
22. Potatoes topped with cheese
23. Croûtons
24. Espresso
25. Pork

Sports and Pastimes On the Water

1. The left side
2. Rowing
3. The bends
4. Captain Matthew Webb
5. Seven minutes actual playing time
6. The kayak paddle has a blade at each end; the Canadian canoe paddle has one blade
7. Self-contained under water breathing
apparatus
8. A rope used to secure a boat
9. Life-saving
10. East Germany
11. Esther Williams
12. Five
13. Two or more divers share an aqualung
14. Snorkel
15. Tacking
16. Portsmouth, England
17. Nautical knots
18. Springboard
19. Carrying the canoe round the obstacle
20. Arm action
21. Man overboard
22. Newport, Rhode Island
23. A safety arrangement on the side of a jump
24. The pair of waves left by the boat
25. Dawn Fraser

History Exploration and Discovery

1. James Cook
2. Roald Amundsen
3. West Africa
4. Jacques Cousteau
5. Portuguese
6. Smallpox
7. Sir Walter Raleigh
8. The newly discovered American continent
9. Van Diemen's Land
10. Theodore Roosevelt
11. Henry the Navigator
12. Kon-Tiki
13. Conquistadors
14. Christopher Columbus
15. Journalist
16. North Pole
17. Sir Francis Drake
18. The Nile
19. Africa
20. Walked out into a blizzard and disappeared
21. Cape of Good Hope
22. Vostok I
23. Arabia
24. Dutch
25. Unknown southern land

Natural World Pets

1. Green
2. Guinea pig
3. Manx
4. Pekingese
5. Corgis
6. Bees
7. Columbidae
8. Thailand
9. Tracking
10. Two
11. The tortoise is vegetarian, the terrapin is
carnivorous
12. Cats
13. France
14. Selfs
15. Chihuahua
16. Horses
17. Finch
18. It does not bark
19. Guinea pigs
20. Large, definite and irregular patches of black and white
21. Its coat resembles that of a racoon
22. Tibet
23. Birds
24. Rabbits
25. St. Bernard

Twentieth Century World War II

1. 1933
2. Benito Mussolini
3. Treaty of Versailles
4. Gestapo
5. Because of the glass strewn across the streets; it means 'night of glass'
6. The annexation of Austria by Germany
7. Invasion of Poland
8. Maginot was the minister
of war who had it built
9. Russia
10. Field Marshall Rommel
11. Yellow star
12. Government Issue
13. Henri Pétain
14. President Roosevelt
15. Oahu, in the Hawaiian islands
16. Mass grave
17. They were suicide pilots, who died while
deliberately crashing their planes into enemy ships
18. Allied landings in Normandy
19. Yalta in the Crimea
20. League of Nations
21. Dresden
22. Nagasaki
23. Nuremberg trials
24. Hirohito
25. Anne Frank

Pot Luck

1. Australia
2. Bloody Mary
3. Blake Edwards
4. 10
5. Cancer
6. Queensbury rules
7. Paint Your Wagon
8. Tarzan
9. Penicillin
10. Captain John Smith
11. Casablanca
12. Joseph of Arimathea
13. Elvis Presley
14. John le Carré
15. Sulphuric acid
16. Campbell
17. Indonesia
18. Baritone
19. Arc de Triomphe
20. Barbra Streisand
21. Smoke it
22. Landscapes
23. Adolf Hitler
24. Angles
25. Puffin

Quiz

12

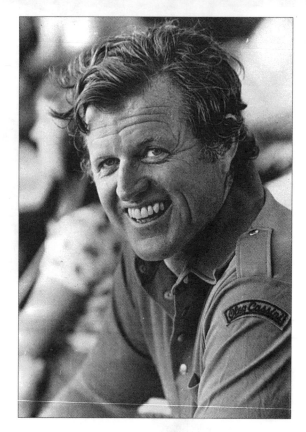

1. What was the name of William Wordsworth's sister.

2. What did Anne Sullivan teach Helen Keller to do?

3. In 1785 George IV of Britain married a Catholic widow, although the marriage was declared illegal by Parliament. What was her name?

4. What feat did Alcock and Brown accomplish in 1919?

5. Who was Ronald Reagan's first wife?

6. How were singers Karen and Richard Carpenter related?

7. Which loyal Highlander helped Prince Charles Edward Stuart to escape to France after the defeat at Culloden?

8. What was the name of Cesare Borgia's influential sister?

9. Which two leaders shared the Nobel Peace Prize in 1993?

10. Whom did both Debbie Reynolds and Elizabeth Taylor marry?

11. Richard III is suspected of having had the 'Princes in the Tower' murdered. What were the boys' names?

12. Which couple, working in France, pioneered research in radioactivity?

13. Sir Ranulph Fiennes set out on the first unassisted crossing of the Antarctic in 1992. Who was with him on this venture?

14. Torvill and Dean became famous as ice dancers. What was Christopher Dean's former profession?

15. Who led the mutiny against Captain Bligh of the Bounty?

16. Stephen, King of England from 1135 to 1154, usurped the crown that belonged to the daughter of Henry I. What was her name?

17. Clark Gable was married to an actress, who died in 1942. Who was she? ▶

18. Who was Shirley Williams' famous mother?

19. Which Russian dancer formed a famous partnership with Margot Fonteyn?

20. In what field did British husband and wife Sidney and Beatrice Webb make their name as pioneers in the last century?

21. Ellen Terry was most famous for her performance in plays by Shakespeare, when she played opposite which actor?

22. Who was Art Garfunkel's singing partner?

23. William III and Mary II were joint rulers of Britain. What relation were they?

24. What was the name of Senator Edward Kennedy's wife? ◀

25. Which tennis champion married John Lloyd?

5 What is Lovejoy's profession?

6 Lee Majors was the Six Million Dollar Man. Who was his female counterpart in Bionic Woman?

7 Which beautiful Bond girl is now a medicine woman?

8 In which series did Christopher Timothy star as a veterinary surgeon? ◄

9 Name the fiery pensioner played by Stephanie Cole in Waiting for God.

10 Who talks for Lamb Chop?

11 Two of the three original stars in Charlie's Angels were Kate Jackson and Jaclyn Smith. Who was the third?

12 Which television series began with a partially naked man playing an organ?

13 Which actress achieved success as Jane Tennison in Prime Suspect but was rejected for the film version?

14 Which actress plays head nurse Hot Lips in M*A*S*H?

15 Name the Cartwright ranch in Bonanza.

16 Which series was based on the real-life adventures of G-man Eliot Ness in prohibition Chicago?

17 In Open All Hours, Ronnie Barker plays a shopkeeper and David Jason also stars. What relation are the two characters?

1 Who plays Lieutenant Columbo in the TV series?

2 The American version of Till Death Us Do Part starred Carroll O'Connor as Archie Bunker. What was it called?

3 What is television's equivalent of the Oscar?

4 Which 1990s series coined the saying 'Who killed Laura Palmer'?

18 The Jewel in the Crown was set in the last days of the British Raj in India. It was based on four novels by Paul Scott. By what name are they known?

19 Who played the green monster in The Incredible Hulk? ▼

20 What was the first name of Grandpa Walton?

21 Which black woman hosts the No. 1 chat show in America, also shown on Britain's Channel 4?

22 Name the English actress who stars with Roy Scheider and Jonathan Brandis in Sea Quest.

23 Which American actor became famous as Lou Grant?

24 In which year was Coronation Street first televised in the United Kingdom?

25 In American soap opera Dallas, who was JR's alchoholic wife?

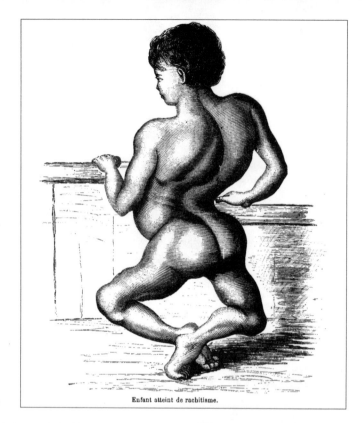

Enfant atteint de rachitisme.

1. In what foodstuff is gluten found?

2. Which vitamin do children with rickets lack? ▲

3. In 1897 a Swiss doctor invented a breakfast food which was a mixture of grains, fruit and nuts. What is it called?

4. TVP is a meat substitute. What do the initials stand for?

5. Babies are born with quite soft bones. What do we give them to provide calcium to harden the bones?

6. What is the name of the mild-flavoured bean curd which looks rather like white blancmange?

7. In which foods is vitamin C mainly found?

8. Why do we pasteurize milk? ▶

9. What are the names of the substances that make up proteins?

10. What name is given to a diet that cuts out all food known to cause allergic reaction or sensitivity?

11 Carrots supply carotene from which the body can make which vitamin?

12 What type of food is Quark?

13 The 'Zen' diet is based on foods divided into two basic groups, Yin and Yang, representing negative and positive elements. What is the other name for this diet?

14 Scurvy is caused by the lack of which vitamin to the body?

15 What is the name given to the eating disorder leading to dramatic weight loss?

16 Vegemite, especially popular in Australia, is one of the richest known sources of B complex vitamins. What is it?

17 Carob is used as a health-conscious substitute for what?

18 The additive tartrazine has been linked with hyperactivity in children. What is it?

19 Liver is high in which vitamin?

20 Which disease results from iron deficiency?

21 Cirrhosis of the liver is linked with what?

22 The 'Chinese Restaurant Syndrome' is the name given to dizziness and headaches caused by eating a lot of food with what additive?

23 Vegans are at risk of a shortage of which vitamin?

24 What enables the body to make vitamin D?

25 In healthy eating, what do the initials RDI stand for?

4 What was the Stumpjumper?

5 In photography, what is the name given to swinging the camera to follow a fast-moving subject so that the picture will be sharp?

6 In a game of chess, what are the limitations on the king's moves?

7 In the sport of skateboarding, what is the 'kick-tail'? ◄

8 What very simple game entails flicking plastic discs into a cup by pressing them sharply with other discs?

9 What is a 'coarse' fish?

10 If a stamp bears the words Deutsche Bundespost, from what country does it come?

11 What does to 'spook' a fish in fly fishing mean? ►

12 In golf, what is the traditional name for the No. 10 iron?

13 What fantasy game is known as D and D?

14 In bike-riding, what is a 'wheelie'?

15 Where would you play a game called Aunt Sally?

16 On a tent, what name is given to the extra layer of fabric over it, held away so that there is a gap between the two layers?

17 In mountain biking, what is often fixed to the pedals to help when climbing?

1 In photography, what does SLR mean?

2 How many squares are there along one side of a Scrabble board?

3 What does a deltiologist collect?

18 Which game has a name that means 'I play' in Latin?

19 What does a phillumenist collect?

20 What are the north, south, east and west points on a compass called?

21 Omar Sharif is a player of international standard in which games?

22 By what name is toxophily usually known?

23 In what game should you not knock down the skittles?

24 If a postage stamp bears the name Suomi, to which country does it belong?

25 What is the housing used for racing pigeons called?

1. What is the name given to the area of the Atlantic ocean where, since 1945, a number of ships and planes have disappeared without trace?

2. Which cloth, believed by some to be Christ's winding sheet, has been housed in an Italian Cathedral since the 16th century?

3. For what powers did Uri Geller become famous in the 1970s? ▲

4. What do the initials UFO stand for?

5. In the Christian tradition, what are stigmata?

6. What is formed in space when a huge star collapses inwards?

7. Some people believe that stone circles have special powers and are linked by lines of force carrying powerful psychic energy. What are they called?

8. Who might make a wax image of an enemy and stick pins in it?

9. For what did the ship the Marie Celeste become famous in 1872?

10. What name is given to the strange cases where a person bursts into flames for no apparent reason and is incinerated in a matter of minutes?

11. In the legend of The Flying Dutchman, a Dutch sea captain was condemned by God to sail the seas forever with a phantom crew. What was his crime?

12 A mysterious ape-man, similar to the Abominable Snowman, is sometimes sighted in North America. What is it called?

13 What name is given to the legendary creature who is half woman, half fish?

14 Nostradamus is the most famous prophet and forecaster of the future of all time. What was his home country? ▶

15 How were the white horses on the hillsides of Uffington, Pewsey and Cherhill in England made?

16 The Fox sisters of New York State became famous in the last century for their apparent ability to contact the spirit world, though they later confessed to fraud. What is the worldwide movement that started from their supposedly supernatural demonstrations?

17 Name the noisy spirit that causes loud disturbances, throwing things about, banging doors and so on.

18 Hampton Court Palace in England is supposedly haunted by three of Henry VIII's wives. Two of them are Catherine Howard and Jane Seymour. Who is the third?

19 What was the ideal kingdom described by Plato that was supposed to have vanished beneath the sea?

20 What name is given to the phenomenon by which a person or object rises into the air with no means of support?

21 What would you find at Carnac in Brittany, and in Britain at Avebury in Wiltshire and in 'Long Meg and her Daughters' in Cumbria?

22 Reports of vampires were widespread in Europe in the 18th century. According to tradition how must vampires be killed?

23 Several religious legends are associated with Glastonbury in southern England, one of them being that Joseph of Arimathea came here after the death of Christ. Which holy relic did he bring?

24 Which famous American clairvoyant from Washington predicted the deaths of both John and Robert Kennedy?

25 With which island is voodoo particularly associated?

1. Which is the heaviest insect?

2. Where do locusts lay their eggs?

3. What is the job of the soldier ant?

4. Give the other name for the shell of the tortoise or turtle.

5. Where is the rattlesnake's 'rattle'?

6. Why do glow-worms glow in the dark?

7. Bees store food and raise young in hexagonal cells made from what?

8. The earthworm has several pairs of tiny bristles called chaetae on its body. What are they used for?

9. How do a python and a boa kill their prey?

10. The body of an insect is divided into how many sections?

11. Where do dragonflies spend their early life?

12. The loud ticking sound produced by the death watch beetle as it knocks against timbers to attract a mate was once thought to herald what unhappy event?

13. What is an invertebrate?

14. Into what does the butterfly egg hatch?

15. What do the North American Gila monster and the Mexican beaded lizard have in common?

16 Where does the silk moth lay its eggs?

17 To which order do butterflies and moths belong? ◄

18 How does the stag beetle get its name?

19 There are three types of bee in a hive. What are they?

20 How do ants recognize one another?

21 Which are the largest living reptiles and the closest relatives of the dinosaurs?

22 The name of the 'atlas' moth, the largest moth, reflects its size. What is the smallest called?

23 What happens to the garden snail in winter?

24 What name is given to the change insects undergo as they change from larvae to adults?

25 When a snake has its tongue out, what is it likely to be doing? ▼

1 The daily newspaper of the Communist party was called Pravda. What does pravda mean?

2 In 1968 Soviet tanks invaded Czechoslovakia to crush the government's reforming regime. Who was the Czech leader?

3 In which year did the Berlin Wall come down? ▲

4 In which year was the Soviet Union officially dissolved?

5 Eleven of the 15 former Soviet republics formed an alliance known as the CIS. What do the initials stand for?

6 What is the main religion of Lithuania?

7 Which Soviet leader replaced Nikita Krushchev as the first secretary of the Communist party in 1964?

8 What was a gulag?

9 In which decade was the Cultural Revolution in China launched?

10 What is the given name of Mikhail Gorbachev's wife? ▶

11 In which year was the Russian revolution?

12 What is the capital of Latvia?

13 What was formed by ordinary people on 23 August, 1989 to mark the 50th anniversary of the Nazi-Soviet pact, which passed control of the Baltic States to the Soviets?

14 Which two republics dispute the rulership of Nagorno-Karabakh?

15 What is the Russian national drink?

16 Which American President made a historic tour of China in 1972, after the country had been ostracized by the West for some years?

17 What was the name of the most famous checkpoint between East and West Berlin?

18 Gorbachev was very popular abroad; why did he become so unpopular at home?

19 In 1987 Mathias Rust, from West Germany, arrived in Moscow and several military leaders were sacked. How did he arrive?

20 After the break-up of the U.S.S.R. the largest of the republics is the Russian Republic. What is the second largest?

21 By what initials were the Soviet secret police most recently known?

22 Of which republic did Eduard Shevardnadze become acting head in 1992?

23 Which high flying Soviet politician was closely associated with Krushchev, and made several foreign visits with him; then in 1957 was involved in an unsuccessful coup against Krushchev and lost power?

24 Part of the West's defences against the Eastern bloc was the stationing of nuclear missiles on European soil. What type of missiles were sited at Greenham Common in England ?

25 Which Polish politician was awarded the Nobel Peace Prize in 1983?

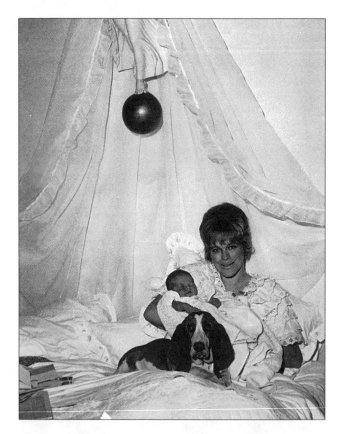

1. Which nocturnal bird known world-wide is the symbol of wisdom?

2. Which disease is the BCG vaccine used to combat?

3. Which famous playwright is the husband of historian Lady Antonia Fraser? ▲

4. Who performed the Dance of the Seven Veils?

5. In a rowing eight, what is the oarsman who sits nearest to the bow called?

6. Who was the Greek goddess of love, known to the Romans as Venus?

7. What medal, founded by George Washington, is awarded to American service personnel wounded in the course of duty?

8. Which hormone contributes to the development of male characteristics?

9. The Castle of Mey is the private residence of which member of the British royal family?

10. How did Princess Grace of Monaco die? ▶

11 What is a group of eight musicians called?

12 The British TV system uses 625 lines. How many does the American system use?

13 What would you do with a 'wandering sailor'?

14 In the financial world, what do the initials MLR stand for?

15 'Blood and Fire' is the motto of which organization?

16 The United Nations flag shows a map of the world. What is on either side of the map?

17 What popular Japanese meal is known as the 'friendship dish'?

18 In the television series, what was the name of Perry Mason's secretary?

19 Dachshunds were originally bred for hunting what?

20 What type of trees grew in the Garden of Gethsemane in Jerusalem?

21 Who played Private Benjamin?

22 Which film actress visited Hanoi to demonstrate her opposition to the Vietnam war?

23 At the summer Olympic Games, athletes from which country always lead the procession of competitors?

24 What do the initials UNESCO stand for?

25 When John F. Kennedy was assassinated, the Governor of Texas was seriously wounded. What was his name?

People and Places   Couples

1. Dorothy
2. Communicate
3. Maria Fitzherbert
4. They flew non-stop across the Atlantic
5. Jane Wyman
6. Brother and sister
7. Flora Macdonald
8. Lucrezia
9. Nelson Mandela and F.W. de Klerk
10. Eddie Fisher
11. Edward and Richard
12. Pierre and Marie Curie
13. Dr Michael Stroud
14. Policeman
15. Fletcher Christian
16. Matilda
17. Carole Lombard
18. Vera Brittain
19. Rudolf Nureyev
20. Socialist politics
21. Henry Irving
22. Paul Simon
23. Cousins and husband and wife
24. Joan
25. Chris Evert

Entertaining Arts   The Small Screen

1. Peter Falk
2. All in the Family
3. Emmy
4. Twin Peaks
5. Antique dealer
6. Lindsay Wagner
7. Jane Seymour
8. All Creatures Great and Small
9. Diana Trent
10. Shari Lewis
11. Farrah Fawcett-Majors
12. Monty Python's Flying Circus
13. Helen Mirren
14. Loretta Swit
15. Ponderosa
16. The Untouchables
17. Uncle and nephew
18. The Raj Quartet
19. Lou Ferrigno
20. Zeb
21. Oprah Winfrey
22. Stephanie Beacham
23. Edward Asner
24. 1960
25. Sue-Ellen, played by Linda Gray

Food and Drink   Healthy Eating

1. Wheat
2. Vitamin D
3. Muesli
4. Textured vegetable protein
5. Milk
6. Tofu
7. Fresh fruit and vegetables
8. To destroy harmful bacteria
9. Amino acids
10. Elimination diet
11. Vitamin A
12. Low-fat cheese
13. Macrobiotic
14. Vitamin C
15. Anorexia nervosa
16. Yeast extract
17. Chocolate
18. Yellow colouring
19. Vitamin A
20. Anaemia
21. Heavy drinking and
malnutrition
22. Monosodium glutamate
23. Vitamin B12
24. When sunlight falls on the skin
25. Recommended daily intake

Sports and Pastimes   Leisure Time

1. Single lens reflex
2. 15
3. Postcards
4. An early mountain bike
5. Panning
6. It may only move to an adjacent square
7. The curved back end of the board
8. Tiddlywinks
9. Any freshwater fish that is not a member of the
salmon family
10. Germany
11. You frighten it away
12. Wedge
13. Dungeons and Dragons
14. Pulling the front wheel into the air and balancing on the back one
15. At a funfair
16. Flysheet
17. Toe clips
18. Ludo
19. Match box labels
20. Cardinal points
21. Bridge and backgammon
22. Archery
23. Bar billiards
24. Finland
25. Loft

History   Mysteries

1. Bermuda Triangle
2. Turin Shroud
3. Metal-bending
4. Unidentified Flying Object
5. Bleeding from the sites of wounds suffered by Christ on the cross
6. A black hole
7. Ley lines
8. A witch or a practitioner of voodoo
9. It was found deserted; no trace of the crew was ever discovered
10. Spontaneous combustion
11. Blasphemy
12. Bigfoot
13. Mermaid
14. France
15. They were carved into the turf of chalk hillsides
16. Spiritualism
17. Poltergeist
18. Anne Boleyn
19. Atlantis
20. Levitation
21. Standing Stones
22. A stake through the heart
23. The Holy Grail
24. Jeanne Dixon
25. Haiti

Natural World   Insects and Reptiles

1. Beetle
2. In sand
3. To guard the colony
4. Carapace
5. The tip of the tail
6. To attract mates
7. Wax
8. Gripping the walls of its tunnel as it moves along
9. Coil around it and squeeze
10. Three
11. In water
12. Death in the house
13. A creature without a backbone
14. Caterpillar
15. Poisonous bite
16. On the leaves of mulberry trees
17. Lepidoptera
18. From its antler-like horns
19. Queen, workers and drones
20. By smell
21. Members of the crocodile family
22. Pygmy
23. It hibernates
24. Metamorphosis
25. 'Tasting' the air to smell out other animals

Twentieth Century   The Communist World

1. Truth
2. Alexander Dubcek
3. 1989
4. 1991
5. Commonwealth of Independent States
6. Catholicism
7. Leonid Brezhnev
8. Soviet labour camp
9. 1960s
10. Raisa
11. 1917
12. Riga
13. A human chain from Estonia through Latvia to Lithuania
14. Armenia and Azerbaijan
15. Vodka
16. Nixon
17. Checkpoint Charlie
18. His reforms did not improve the economic situation
19. He landed a small plane in Red Square
20. Ukraine
21. K.G.B
22. Georgia
23. Bulganin
24. Cruise
25. Lech Walesa

Pot Luck

1. The owl
2. Tuberculosis
3. Harold Pinter
4. Salome
5. Stroke
6. Aphrodite
7. The Purple Heart
8. Testosterone
9. The Queen Mother
10. In a car crash
11. Octet
12. 525
13. Plant it
14. Minimum Lending Rate
15. Salvation Army
16. An olive branch
17. Sukiyaki
18. Della Street
19. Badgers
20. Olive trees
21. Goldie Hawn
22. Jane Fonda
23. Greece
24. United Nations
Educational Scientific and Cultural Organization
25. John B. Connally

Quiz

13

1 In which century did Catherine the Great rule in Russia?

2 Which French Queen spent so wildly that she was known as 'Madame Deficit'?

3 Who succeeded Queen Juliana as ruler of the Netherlands in 1980?

4 Which British sovereign had the longest reign?

5 Prince Albert of Liège succeeded to which throne in 1993?

6 Which English Queen was nicknamed Brandy Nan?

7 Which Swedish Queen did Greta Garbo play on screen? ▲

8 Queen Salote reigned from 1918 to 1965 over which island kingdom?

9 In ancient times which country was ruled by the Moguls?

10 In 1931, when Communist forces were strong in his country, Alfonso XIII had to abdicate. What was his country?

11 To which powerful royal house did the Emperors Ferdinand I and Franz Joseph I of Austria belong?

12 Who followed King David as King of Israel?

13 Whom did Queen Elizabeth I succeed to the British throne? ▼

14 What happened to William II, Emperor of Germany, when he was defeated by the Allies in World War I?

15 Where was Napoleon born?

16 Which King of Prussia waged the Seven Years War in the 18th century?

17 How were the English King Richard I and his successor King John related?

18 Boris III was king of which country from 1918 to 1943?

19 Which French king was called Le Roi Soleil?

20 Who was the enlightened King of Sardinia who became King of Italy when the states united in 1861?

21 How many children did Queen Victoria and Prince Albert have?

22 To which royal house did Louis XIV, Henry IV and Louis Philippe of France belong?

23 Name the King of Jordan.

24 Which King of England was the first Prince of Wales?

25 King Umberto was deposed from the throne of which country in 1946?

1. The highest note can be reached by which female voice?

2. Which composer, from an Austrian family of musicians, was known as the 'Waltz King'?

3. In which country was the composer Debussy born?

4. What does the musical term fortissimo mean?

5. Arthur Sullivan wrote the music for the famous Savoy Operas? Who wrote the words?

6. Nijinsky was one of the greatest of all ballet dancers. Why did his career come to a premature end?

7. In which city did jazz have its origins?

8. Musical instruments are divided into four classes. Strings, wind instruments and keyboard are three of them. What is the fourth?

9. Which aria from Puccini's Madame Butterfly has become an 'opera pop song'?

10. At what age did Mozart die? ▲

11. What does the musical term lento mean?

12. Which composer wrote the Emperor Concerto and the Ninth Symphony?

13 Which Tchaikovsky ballet has Princess Aurora as a heroine?

14 A plectrum is used to play which musical instrument?

15 What is a paradiddle?

16 Who wrote the Enigma Variations and The Dream of Gerontius?

17 What were Bach's given names?

18 Which dancer was strangled by her own scarf?

19 Who wrote the opera Gloriana in honour of the coronation of Queen Elizabeth II in 1953?

20 Which ballet uses music by Chopin?

21 In which opera is the heroine a girl who works in a cigarette factory?

22 What nationality was the composer Delius, who died in 1934?

23 How many strings does a violin have?

24 Which ballerina was famous for her solo performance in The Dying Swan (La Cygne)? ▼

25 In which city is the famous opera house, La Scala?

1 What stimulant is found in tea and coffee?

2 Which drink is sometimes called Adam's Ale?

3 What are the ingredients of a Screwdriver? ▲

4 If a wine is described as brut, what does it say about the taste? ▶

5 What is a pre-prandial drink?

6 What is added to coffee to make Caribbean coffee?

7 What is added to coffee to make Kentucky coffee?

8 The organisation CAMRA has branches in many parts of the United Kingdom. What do the initials stand for?

9 For what type of drink was chicory a wartime substitute?

10 A Sidecar contains brandy, lemon juice and which liqueur?

11 Why are bottles that contain beer usually coloured brown?

12 From which fruit is perry made?

13 Malvern and Ashbourne are the best known of Britain's mineral waters. Which of these is sparkling?

14 A fortified wine has grape spirit added to increase the alcoholic strength – to what percentage?

15 What is a firkin?

16 What drink is associated with Holy Island, Northumberland, England?

17 A Piña Colada contains pineapple juice, coconut cream (or Malibu) and what else?

18 What type of wine usually accompanies game?

19 For what reason is yeast introduced into beer making?

20 What, in wine production, is another name for 'marrying'?

21 In which United States city was Coca-Cola originally made?

22 What is a posset?

23 Cradles are often used for serving wine, but what was the original use?

24 What does cuvée mean as a description of wine?

25 Planter's Punch has no set formula but on which spirit is it based?

1. What is the playing time of a Rugby League match?

2. How many intervals does an American football game have?

3. Walter Payton has been called the greatest-ever American football player. What is his nickname?

4. Which was the first British football club to win the European Cup?

5. What is the Argentinean soccer player Maradona's given name?

6. Which is larger, the Canadian or the American football field?

7. In 1990, West Germany won soccer's World Cup. Which team won in 1986?

8. Which country's rugby football team is called the All Blacks? ▼ ▶

9. When footballer Paul Gascoigne transferred from Tottenham Hotspur in 1991-2, the fee was £5.5 million. Where did he transfer to?

10. Which American football coach was known as Papa Bear?

11. Which major sporting event began on 17 June, 1994 at Soldier Field in Chicago?

12. In the sport of soccer, a yellow card shown to a player means a caution. What does a red card actually mean?

13. Where is the home of the American football team, the Cardinals?

14 In American football, how many players from each team join the scrimmage line?

15 Which two teams played the 1993 FA Cup at Wembley?

16 On what shape of pitch is Australian rules football played?

17 Arsenal is the team that has appeared most often in the FA Cup Final. How many times?

18 Which year was the first Olympic Games at which an official football tournament was played?

19 How many substitutes in American football?

20 Which country won the 6th European Football Championship for Women?

21 Mick Luckhurst joined a leading NFL club in the United States and became one of their star players; in 1984 he became their all-time leading scorer. Name his team.

22 Rugby Union has two teams of 15 players; how many players does each team in Rugby League have?

23 Name the German soccer star who led West Germany to victory over Holland in the World Cup, then managed the team that defeated Argentina in 1990.

24 Which country introduced Rugby League in 1990 and sent a 90-man squad on a three-month tour of Britain?

25 Which country kept the Jules Rimet Trophy, the first World Cup trophy, for good in 1970 after winning it three times out of four?

1. Whose autobiography is called Part of My Soul?

2. What is the estimate of the number of Jews who died in the Holocaust?

3. Which racist organization, whose members wear special outfits that conceal their identities, was founded in the South after the American Civil War?

4. The term 'prejudice' is derived from which word?

5. Which racial group did President Idi Amin of Uganda expel from his country in 1972?

6. In South Africa, people were assigned to one of four groups for the purpose of apartheid. They included Europeans, Asiatics and Black Africans. What was the fourth group?

7. What was the other name for 'Bantustans' in South Africa?

8. In what field did Miss Buss and Miss Beale become well-known in Britain in the last century?

9 The civil rights organization known as CORE was founded in the United States in 1942. What do the initials stand for?

10 In which area of London did the race riots of 1981 take place?

11 What name is given to the deliberate destruction of a specific social, national or racial group?

12 The Nazi party began in Germany in 1919. What was its full name?

13 The first slaves arrived in the United States in 1619 but they were imported in large numbers later in the century, mainly to work in what type of plantations?

14 In which decade were schools desegregated in the United States?

15 Who founded the first birth control clinic in England?

16 Nelson Mandela is President of which African organization? ◀

17 Which black woman writer is the author of I Know Why the Caged Bird Sings?

18 Who became the first Prime Minister of Israel in 1948?

19 How did woman's suffrage campaigner Emily Wilding Davison ensure a place in history on Derby Day in 1913? ▶

20 What item of clothing were supporters of Women's Lib supposed to burn?

21 Who was the first woman to run for Vice-President in the United States in 1984?

22 Which Australian author wrote The Female Eunuch?

23 Who was the political leader, later Prime Minister of South Africa, who said 'Natives will be taught from childhood to realize that equality with Europeans is not for them'?

24 In the United States, how many states had granted women the vote before World War I?

25 For which type of women did Erin Pizzey campaign in Britain?

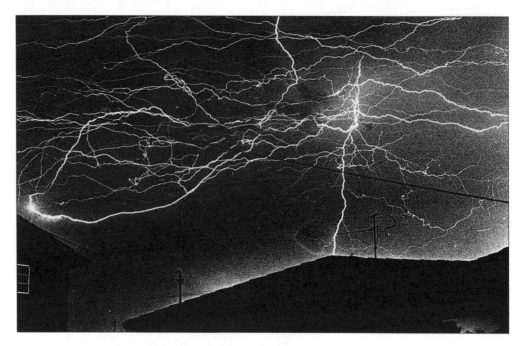

1 If cows are lying down in the field, what weather does this traditionally foretell?

2 What is the name given to a column of swirling dust or soil raised into the air by a small whirl-wind?

3 There are three bands of climate in the world: tropical, polar and which other?

4 What are the long curving lines on a weather map, designating areas of equal pressure, called?

5 What can be cumulus, stratus or lenticular?

6 Which weather system brings cloudy skies, winds and rain?

7 Who was the Norse god of thunder?

8 When there is a thunderstorm, why do you see the lightning before you hear the thunder? ▲

9 What name is given to the mixture of fog and smoke?

10 In which country is the hottest place in the world?

11 Why do metal pipes often burst when the water inside turns to ice?

12 The coasts of which countries experience the strong, dry and cold north westerly wind called the mistral?

13 What shape is a tornado?

14 What does an anemometer measure?

15 Pine cones are often used by amateur weather forecasters. What happens if the weather is about to turn wet?

16 What name is given to the white ice that forms on the branches of trees in very cold weather?

17 How many different patterns of snow flakes are there?

18 Hurricanes cause tremendous damage. What is the ring of low pressure at the centre of the storm called? ▼

19 What can be ribbon, rocket, streak or sheet?

20 An anticyclone brings what type of weather to the area it covers?

21 What name is given to the torrential rains experienced in India for six months beginning in May?

22 Weather occurs in the troposphere where most water vapour exists. Where do airliners fly to avoid too many bumps?

23 The special type of blue-green lightning that clings to the wing tips of most aircraft is known as what?

24 As the old saying goes a red sky at night means 'shepherd's delight', what does a red sky in the morning mean?

25 What do we call the refraction, reflection and dispersal of the suns rays caused by raindrops in the sky?

8. Who was the only man to become Vice President and President without being elected to either post?

9. Who said: 'Read my lips. No new taxes!'?

10. Two Presidents have been assassinated this century. One was Kennedy; who was the other?

11. The 27th President (1900-1913) was the heaviest President of all time. Who was he?

12. Where was Bill Clinton born?

1. Which President was crippled by polio? ▲

2. To what office did John F. Kennedy appoint his younger brother Robert? ▶

3. In 1961, what did Kennedy call on America to achieve in the next decade?

4. About which President did Dorothy Parker, when told of his death, say 'How could they tell?'?

5. Which President began his working life as a sports commentator?

6. Which President withdrew American troops from Vietnam?

7. What was Jimmy Carter's family business?

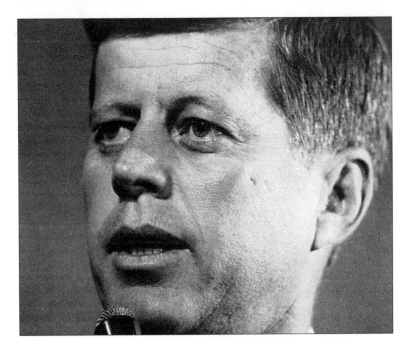

13 Which President renamed 'Shangri-la' as 'Camp David' after his grandson?

14 Who said in his inaugural speech 'The only thing we have to fear is fear itself'?

15 Which President was awarded the Nobel Peace Prize in 1919?

16 The 1981 attempted assassination of Ronald Reagan took place as he left which hotel?

17 'Ask not what your country can do for you...'. Complete this quotation from Kennedy's inaugural address. ▲

18 About what did President Bush say, 'A line has been drawn in the sand'?

19 What was the name given to the economics of the Reagan era?

20 Who was the independent candidate in the 1992 presidential campaign?

21 In a time of rising inflation, who called on Congress to 'bite the bullet'?

22 In Gerald R. Ford's name, what did the initial R. stand for?

23 Which President, early this century, was called the 'Great Engineer' and then later, when his policies failed to work, the 'President Reject'?

24 Which state did Harry S. Truman represent before his elevation?

25 What was the name of President Eisenhower's wife?

1 In which American state is Fort Knox?

2 What is the more usual name for the polygraph?

3 Who is singer Cleo Laine's husband?

4 What is the name for the organism on which a parasite lives and feeds?

5 Who was the first Roman Emperor to convert to Christianity?

6 What is the only movable bone in the human skull?

7 In which country is the Kimberley gold field?

8 What will never make a silk purse?

9 Which world famous poet lived at Dove Cottage ▶ in Grasmere?

10 In the 1993 film, Mrs Doubtfire, who plays the title role?

11 On what type of business was the fortune of John F. Kennedy's family built?

12 Greenland has two official languages. One is Greenlandic; what is the other?

13 What is the distaff side of the family?

14 When is Lammas day?

15 Which company launched the 'Walkman'?

16 What type of acid is in bee stings?

17 In the song, the House of the Rising Sun was in which city?

18 What sport would you be watching if the New York Knickerbockers were playing?

19 What word describes a doctor specializing in the medical problems of old age?

20 If you were making a wiener schnitzel, what meat would you buy?

21 'The Mindbenders' were the backing group for which pop singer?

22 In the Bible, whom did God tell, 'Escape to the mountain, lest thou be consumed'?

23 Where was Princess Elizabeth when she learned that she had become Queen Elizabeth II?

24 Which country's flag shows a white cross on a red background?

25 If your birthstone is turquoise, which is your birth month?

People and Places   Kings and Queens

1. 18th century
2. Marie Antoinette
3. Queen Beatrix
4. Queen Victoria
5. Belgium
6. Queen Anne
7. Queen Christina
8. Tonga
9. India
10. Spain
11. Hapsburg
12. Solomon
13. Mary I
14. He fled into exile in Holland
15. Corsica
16. Frederick the Great
17. Brothers
18. Bulgaria
19. Louis XIV
20. Victor Emmanuel
21. Nine
22. Bourbon
23. King Hussein
24. Edward II
25. Italy

Entertaining Arts   Music and Dance

1. Soprano
2. Johann Strauss
3. France
4. Very loud
5. W.S. Gilbert
6. He suffered from mental illness
7. New Orleans
8. Percussion
9. One Fine Day
10. 35
11. Slow
12. Ludwig van Beethoven
13. Sleeping Beauty
14. Guitar
15. A drum roll
16. Elgar
17. Johann Sebastian
18. Isadora Duncan
19. Benjamin Britten
20. Les Sylphides
21. Carmen
22. English
23. Four
24. Anna Pavlova
25. Milan

Food and Drink   Drink Up!

1. Caffeine
2. Water
3. Vodka and orange juice
4. It will be very dry
5. An aperitif
6. Rum
7. Southern Comfort
8. Campaign for Real Ale
9. Coffee
10. Cointreau
11. To protect the contents
from harmful sunlight
12. Pears
13. Ashbourne
14. 20 per cent
15. A small barrel or measure of ale
16. Lindisfarne mead
17. White rum
18. Robust red wine
19. To produce fermentation
20. Blending
21. Atlanta, Georgia
22. A drink of milk and ale
23. For bringing wines from the cellar without disturbing the sediment
24. Wine from the contents of a single vat
25. Rum

Sports and Pastimes   Football Facts

1. 80 minutes plus one interval
2. One long and two short
3. Sweetness
4. Celtic
5. Diego
6. Canadian
7. Argentina
8. New Zealand
9. Lazio, Italy
10. George Halas
11. Football World Cup
12. The player is sent off
13. Phoenix, Arizona
14. At least seven
15. Arsenal and Sheffield Wednesday
16. Oval
17. 12
18. 1908
19. An unlimited number
20. Norway
21. Atlanta Falcons
22. 13
23. Franz Beckenbauer
24. Russia
25. Brazil

History   Equal Rights

1. Winnie Mandela
2. 6 million
3. Ku Klux Klan
4. Prejudge
5. Asians
6. Coloureds
7. Homelands
8. Education for girls
9. Congress of Racial Equality
10. Brixton
11. Genocide
12. National Socialist Workers' Party
13. Tobacco and cotton
14. 1950s
15. Marie Stopes
16. African National Congress
17. Maya Angelou
18. David Ben-Gurion
19. She threw herself under the hooves of the leading horse
20. Bra
21. Geraldine Ferraro
22. Germaine Greer
23. Verwoerd
24. 11
25. Battered wives

Natural World   Weather

1. Rain
2. Dust devil
3. Temperate
4. Isobars
5. Clouds
6. Depression
7. Thor
8. Light travels faster than sound
9. Smog
10. Ethiopia
11. Water expands when it
freezes
12. Spain and France
13. Funnel-shaped
14. Wind speed
15. The scales close up
16. Rime or hoarfrost
17. Millions
18. Eye
19. Lightning
20. Settled weather
21. Monsoons
22. The stratosphere
23. St. Elmo's fire
24. Shepherd's warning
25. A rainbow

Twentieth Century   American Presidents

1. Roosevelt
2. Attorney General
3. Land the first man on the moon
4. Calvin Coolidge
5. Ronald Reagan
6. Richard Nixon
7. Wholesale peanut business
8. Gerald Ford
9. George Bush
10. William McKinley
11. William H. Taft
12. Hope, Arkansas
13. Dwight D. Eisenhower
14. Franklin D. Roosevelt
15. Woodrow Wilson
16. Washington Hilton
17. '... ask what you can do for your country'
18. Iraq's invasion of Kuwait
19. Reaganomics
20. Ross Perot
21. Lyndon Johnson
22. Rudolph
23. Herbert Hoover
24. Missouri
25. Mamie

Pot Luck

1. Kentucky
2. Lie detector
3. John Dankworth
4. Host
5. Constantine
6. Mandible or jawbone
7. Western Australia
8. A sow's ear
9. Wordsworth
10. Robin Williams
11. Real estate
12. Danish
13. The female side
14. August 1
15. Sony
16. Formic acid
17. New Orleans
18. Basketball
19. Geriatrician
20. Veal
21. Wayne Fontana
22. Lot
23. Kenya
24. Switzerland
25. December

Quiz

14

1. In which country would you find Legoland?

2. What is the Spanish name for a bullfighter? ▲

3. Which member of the British royal family favoured the holiday island of Mustique?

4. Spain's Costa Brava is a favourite destination of holidaymakers. What does 'Costa Brava' mean?

5. If you were reading Le Monde or Le Figaro with your morning coffee, where would you be?

6. In Israel, you will find that most shops shut during the Shabat or Sabbath. When is this?

7. For which festival, held in July, is the town of Bayreuth in Germany famous?

8. Where would you visit the Colossi of Memnon?

9. Which city was once known as Byzantium and later as Constantinople?

10. What is the name given to a lover of all things French?

11. Neuschwanstein is a romantic fairytale castle perched on a forested mountain in Bavaria. Who was the 'Mad King' who built it? ▶

12. In which country would you find the world's oldest brewery?

13. What is the special name given to an Arab market?

14. On which island is the Blue Grotto a major tourist attraction?

15. Where in the world would you find an eisteddfod?

16. Which Scandinavian country is famous for its fjords?

17. What unit of currency is used in India?

18 Where would you find gondoliers?

19 On which side of the road would you drive in Japan?

20 Which country was once known as Cathay?

21 If you wanted to follow in the footsteps of Count Dracula, you might visit Transylvania. In which country is it?

22 Where would you visit the Keys, Highland Hammocks and Everglades?

23 'The Emerald Isle' is the romantic name for which country?

24 Which great Moorish building in Spain includes the Court of Myrtles, Place of Cisterns, Hall of Ambassadors and the Hall of Secrets?

25 What is the French flag called?

1. Whose schoolmates were Bob Cherry, Frank Nugent and Harry Wharton?

2. In which novel does Catherine Earnshaw fall in love with Heathcliff?

3. What was the name of Long John Silver's parrot in Treasure Island?

4. Sweeney Todd was the demon barber who slit the throats of his customers. What did he do with the bodies?

5. 5. In which children's TV series did the Daleks threaten to 'exterminate' their enemies?

6. Which character did Joan Collins play in Dynasty? ▲

7. In which city does Bruce Wayne live and fight villains as Batman?

8. Gomez, Morticia and Uncle Fester belong to which family?

9. In The Wizard of Oz, which of the characters accompanying Dorothy to see the wizard was seeking a brain?

10. Which bird did the Ancient Mariner kill?

11. Jacob Marley was the partner of which famous miser in A Christmas Carol?

12. Who is constantly chased by Sylvester in cartoons?

13 What was the number of The Prisoner?

14 Which Japanese lady married Lieutenant Pinkerton and committed suicide when he deserted her?

15 Kunta Kinte was the leading figure in which book and TV mini-series?

16 What was the name of Frank Spencer's long-suffering wife in Some Mothers Do 'Ave 'Em?

17 Which American cops were played by Paul Michael Glaser and David Soul?

18 Who was a 'bear of very little brain'?

19 Whose friends are Obelix the muscle-man and Getafix the Druid?

20 Bunny Manders is the side-kick of which upper crust crook?

21 Who is the villain of the Star Wars trilogy?

22 Name M's secretary in the James Bond stories? ▼

23 Which famous frog puppet is the leader of the Muppets?

24 Which famous storyteller told the tales of Brer Rabbit and Brer Fox?

25 Who is the heroine of R.B. Blackmore's novel, the member of an outlaw family who falls in love with John Ridd?

1. Satay is an Asian dish with pieces of meat or fish grilled on bamboo skewers. What type of sauce is usually served with it? ▲

2. What are bratwurst, bockwurst and knackwurst?

3. What is the name given to savoury Indian pasties filled with meat or vegetables and seasoned with herbs and spices?

4. What is the name given to the yeasted bread containing yogurt that is served in Indian restaurants?

5. If you were in an American restaurant and you wanted your food grilled, what description would you look for? ▶

6. Also in an American restaurant, if you were offered 'grits', what would you expect to get?

7. Tahini is a paste used in Middle Eastern cooking. From what is it made?

8. In Japanese cooking, what are little parcels of raw fish and rice called?

9. What is salmagundi?

10. Gumbo is a Creole stew with meat, chicken or seafood, tomatoes and onions and what essential vegetable?

11. What is the main ingredient of the Russian soup bortsch?

12 Biltong originated in South Africa. What exactly is it?

13 Danish open sandwiches are usually called smorrebrod. What is the literal meaning of this word?

14 Couscous comes from North Africa. What is its base?

15 In China, what favourite drink is known as cha or ch'a?

16 Added to Indian dishes at the end of cooking time, what is garam masala?

17 From which country's cuisine does the thick soup called minestrone come?

18 In Spain, what are tapas?

19 What is the name of the dish made in the north of England from pig's blood, fat, oatmeal, onions and spices?

20 Goulash gets its name from the Hungarian word gulgas, meaning shepherd, as shepherds were supposed to have invented it. What is its main spice?

21 On a Russian menu, what is a coulibiac?

22 What are flapjacks?

23 In Italian cooking, what are gnocchi?

24 If pasta is cooked al dente, what does it mean?

25 In France, what is a baguette?

1 In skiing, what is the other name for cross country racing?

2 How many competitors form a team in bobsleigh racing?

3 Katarina Witt has been one of the world's brightest skating stars. Which country did she represent in competition?

4 In ice hockey, what is the 'sin bin'?

5 What is a piste?

6 The Summer Olympics have been held since 1896. In which year was the first Winter Olympics?

7 What name is given to a toboggan with metal runners but no steering or brakes, ridden in a sitting or face-up lying position?

8 In ice skating, what is 'tracing'?

9 What is the crouched position in downhill racing on smooth, straight slopes called?

10 In which country did ice hockey originate?

11 Which two sports make up the biathlon, introduced into the Winter Olympics in 1960?

12 In ski-jumping, what position must the skis maintain until just before landing?

13 Which ice or snow sport was the first to gain Olympic status?

14 What is the Super-G?

15 In skiing, what are aerials?

16 Which ice sport has leads, seconds, thirds and skips?

17 Ice hockey has teams with up to 20 players, but how many can be on the ice at one time?

18 What is the sport of the ski marathon called in the United States?

19 Which country hosted the 1992 Winter Olympics?

20 A slalom is a downhill race through a series of 'gates'.What are the gates represented by ? ◀ ▲

21 In snowboarding, boards are used instead of what?

22 Which country held the first recorded ski race in 1767?

23 What are moguls in skiing?

24 In ski-jumping, a 'large' jump is 85-90 metres. Jumps over 90 metres become a separate event called what?

25 What type of skiing is skijoring?

1 What do the initials VCR stand for?

2 Isaac Pitman published Stenographic Soundhand in 1837. What is his system now known as?

3 Before the telephone was invented, what electrical device was used to send messages?

4 The picture of a small dog listening to 'his master's voice' on a gramophone was the trade mark of which record company?

5 In a computer, what is the CPU?

6 What unit is used to measure the frequency of radio waves? ▲

7 For what are sandwich boards used?

8 What did John Logie Baird invent?

9 In which field of communication were Sir Humphrey Davy and Joseph Niepce involved?

10 Radar played an important part in the conduct of World War II, detecting the position of enemy planes. What does RADAR stand for?

11 What were 'cats' whiskers' used for in early 'crystal' radios?

12 In what year was the first flight around the world over both poles?

13 What was the name of the small box camera which became available early this century?

14 When was The Times first published?

15 What name is given to the decorated books made by monks in the Middle Ages?

16 Why are satellites necessary to send VHF signals around the world?

17 What year was the 'Telstar' satellite launched from Cape Canaveral?

18 Software is the name given to what?

19 Who printed the first book in English in 1474?

20 What is the name given to the method of sending signals by arrangement of flags or a post with movable arms? ▼

21 BASIC is an easy to learn computer language. What do the initials stand for?

22 When Thomas Edison invented the phonograph, the predecessor of the record player, what was the first recording he made?

23 The first records were played at 78 rpm. What does 'rpm' stand for?

24 What name is given to the spreading of opinions and ideas, often by giving one-sided information?

25 What was the first postage stamp called?

1. What name is given to a group of wolves? ▲

2. What do the Californian condor, the giant anteater and the Indian lion have in common?

3. In what position do adult horses normally sleep?

4. On what does the common mole normally feed?

5. What type of animals are eland, kudu and gazelles?

6. What is the collective name for a group of domestic cats?

7. Between which months do the hedgehog and dormouse hibernate?

8. If a rabbit thumps its back feet on the ground, what is it likely to be doing?

9 Why do thousands of Alaskan fur seals go to Pribilof Islands in the Bering Sea each year?

10 What is the fastest land mammal?

11 What is the main food of the aardvark?

12 The baby of which animal is called a joey?

13 The soles of Polar bears' feet differ from those of other bears. In what way?

14 Animals that eat grass are called grazers. What name is given to animals like elephants and giraffes, that eat leaves from trees and bushes?

15 The coypu is an aquatic rodent resembling the beaver. What is it sometimes called?

16 What name is given to the home of the beaver? ▼

17 Which is the largest mammal baby?

18 Which are the only mammals that can fly?

19 Nesting materials are in short supply in the Antarctic. Where do king and emperor penguins lay their eggs?

20 In ancient Egypt, the mongoose was a sacred animal. Families often kept one for what purpose?

21 What is the other name for a Russian wolfhound?

22 Lions live in family groups. What are they called?

23 What is the kangaroo's normal method of defence?

24 What type of animal is the caribou?

25 Which animal has a name that means 'river horse'?

1 1. From which country did the Soviet Union withdraw in 1988, ending a 10-year war?

2 Which engineering project, shared between Britain and France, was opened in December 1993?

3 Who was the first Prime Minister of an independent Zimbabwe?

4 4. In which country did Tamil guerrillas battle for political freedom?

5 5. Who is believed to be the wealthiest man in the world because of oil riches?

6 6. Which two young Australians made their names in Neighbours and then went on to great success on the pop scene?

7 The 1980s was the decade of the 'yuppie'. What does 'yuppie' stand for?

8 What disease killed film star Rock Hudson? ▶

9 Who became the first socialist President of France in 1981 and was re-elected in 1988?

10 The Brady Bill was much in the headlines in the United States in 1993. What did it concern?

11 Who was the President of Argentina when it invaded the Falklands?

12 Name the actor who played Crocodile Dundee.

13 After two years of drought and disorder, President Bush despatched American troops on a humanitarian mission in 'Operation Restore Hope' to which African country?

14 Whom did Neil Kinnock succeed as leader of the Labour party in Britain?

15 The sale of which Van Gogh painting trebled the previous auction price record for a work of art in 1987?

16 Who launched Virgin Airways in 1985?

17 Which American basketball star, reputed to be the world's highest paid sportsman, toured Britain in 1993?

18 Nicolae Ceaucescu, executed in 1989, was dictator of which country?

19 Which British character actor starred in Who Framed Roger Rabbit?

20 Prime Minister Kim Campbell faced a humiliating defeat in the Canadian elections of October 1993. Which party was thrown out of office?

21 Name the Greenpeace ship blown up in New Zealand by French agents on the eve of the protest against French nuclear tests in the Pacific. ◀

22 On which hand does Michael Jackson wear his famous glove?

23 In the attempted assassination of Ronald Reagan, how many people were shot?

24 Dictator Kim II Sung created a god-like status for himself in which country?

25 In 1993 Elton John won a large libel settlement against a British newspaper. What had the newspaper claimed about him?

1 What nationality is golfer Gary Player?

2 Who wrote the novel on which Benjamin Britten based his opera The Turn of the Screw?

3 How many wisdom teeth does the average adult have?

4 The United States has four mainland time zones. Three of them are Pacific, Mountain and Eastern. What is the fourth?

5 Which British racing driver has won most Grand Prix races?

6 What is the name given to the moon that follows the Harvest Moon?

7 On what date is Bastille day celebrated in France?

8 Which country gives a Christmas tree to Britain every year?

9 What race of nomadic people inhabit northern Scandinavia?

10 Which Paris club is famous for the can-can? ▲

11 Who is the patron saint of grave-diggers?

12 The nests from which type of birds are used in birds' nest soup?

13 What was the nickname of the German aviator Baron von Richthofen? ▼

14 British drivers call it a bumper. What do Americans call it?

15 What does white smoke coming from the Vatican chimney mean?

16 According to the proverb, what is nine-tenths of the law?

17 What do we call a chicken when it is under one year old?

18 Who sang Wake up Little Susie, Cathy's Clown and All I have to do is Dream?

19 Who is the young diary writer in the books by Sue Townsend?

20 What was nicknamed the 'Tin Lizzie'?

21 What name is given to the climate that would be produced by nuclear warfare?

22 Which American state was named for the wife of Charles I?

23 In mythology, which nymph was turned into a laurel bush to save her from Apollo?

24 In 1991 Slovenia declared its independence from which country?

25 Which artist angered Henry VIII by painting a flattering portrait of Anne of Cleves?

People and Places Travel and Tourism

1. Denmark
2. Matador
3. Princess Margaret
4. Rugged coast
5. France
6. From sunset on Friday to sunset on Saturday
7. Wagner festival
8. Near Luxor in Egypt
9. Istanbul
10. Francophile
11. Ludwig II
12. Germany
13. Souk
14. Capri
15. Wales
16. Norway
17. Rupee
18. Venice
19. Left
20. China
21. Romania
22. Florida
23. Ireland
24. The Alhambra, Granada
25. (Drapeau) tricolore

Entertaining Arts Imaginary Folk

1. Billy Bunter
2. Wuthering Heights
3. Captain Flint
4. Made them into meat pies
5. Dr Who
6. Alexis
7. Gotham City
8. Addams Family
9. Scarecrow
10. Albatross
11. Ebenezer Scrooge
12. Tweety Pie
13. Six
14. Madame Butterfly
15. Roots
16. Betty
17. Starsky and Hutch
18. Winnie-the-Pooh
19. Asterix the Gaul
20. Raffles
21. Darth Vader
22. Miss Moneypenny
23. Kermit
24. Uncle Remus
25. Lorna Doone

Food and Drink International Table

1. Peanut
2. Spicy German sausages
3. Samosas
4. Naan
5. Broiled
6. Coarsely ground grain or beans
7. Ground sesame seeds
8. Sushi
9. An elaborately arranged dish of minced, shredded and sliced salad ingredients, decoratively displayed in contrasting colours
10. Okra
11. Beetroot
12. Dried strips of beef
13. Buttered bread
14. Crushed semolina wheat
15. Tea
16. A mixture of herbs and spices
17. Italy
18. Savoury titbits served with drinks
19. Black pudding
20. Paprika
21. Hot fish pie
22. Pancakes
23. Pasta dumplings
24. Tender but still firm to the bite

Sports and Pastimes Ice and Snow Sports

1. Nordic
2. Two or four
3. East Germany
4. The penalty box where players infringing the rules must spend time
5. A downhill ski trail
6. 1924
7. Luge
8. The marks made on the ice by skate blades
9. Egg position
10. Canada
11. Cross-country skiing and rifle shooting
12. Horizontal and parallel
13. Figure skating
14. Super-giant slalom
15. Aerobatic jumps off a ramp
16. Curling
17. Six
18. Citizen racing
19. France
20. Pairs of flagpoles
21. Skis
22. Norway
23. Bumps on a steep slope
24. Ski flying
25. Skiing while being towed

History Communications

1. Video Cassette Recorder
2. Shorthand
3. Electric telegraph
4. HMV ('His Master's Voice')
5. Central Processing Unit
6. Hertz
7. Advertisements
8. Television
9. Photography
10. Radio Detection And Ranging
11. Tuning
12. 1965
13. Brownie
14. 1785
15. Illuminated manuscripts
16. High frequency radio waves travel in straight lines and cannot follow the curves of the Earth's surface
17. 1962
18. Computer programmes
19. William Caxton
20. Semaphore
21. Beginner's All-purpose Symbolic Instruction Code
22. Mary had a little lamb
23. Revolutions per minute
24. Propaganda

Natural World Animal Life

1. Pack
2. They are all endangered species
3. Standing up
4. Earthworms
5. Antelopes
6. Clowder
7. October and April
8. Warning its fellows of danger
9. To breed
10. Cheetah
11. Termites
12. Kangaroo
13. They are hairy; other bears have naked soles
14. Browsers
15. Swamp Beaver
16. Lodge
17. Blue whale calf
18. Bats
19. On bare ground or ice
20. Keeping down rodents
21. Borzoi
22. Prides
23. It kicks out with powerful back legs
24. Deer
25. Hippopotamus

Twentieth Century The 1980s and 1990s

1. Afghanistan
2. Channel Tunnel, Chunnel or Euro Tunnel
3. Robert Mugabe
4. Sri Lanka
5. Sultan of Brunei
6. Kylie Mynogue and Jason Donovan
7. Young urban professional
8. AIDS
9. François Mitterand
10. Gun control
11. General Galtieri
12. Paul Hogan
13. Somalia
14. Michael Foot
15. Sunflowers
16. Richard Branson
17. Shaquille O'Neal
18. Romania
19. Bob Hoskins
20. Conservative
21. Rainbow Warrior
22. Right
23. Four
24. North Korea
25. That he was on a bizarre diet

Pot Luck

1. South African
2. Henry James
3. Four
4. Central
5. Jackie Stewart
6. Hunter's Moon
7. July 14
8. Norway
9. Lapps
10. Moulin Rouge
11. St. Anthony
12. Chinese swallows
13. The Red Baron
14. Fender
15. A new pope has been elected
16. Possession
17. Pullet
18. Everley Brothers
19. Adrian Mole
20. Model T Ford
21. Nuclear winter
22. Maryland
23. Daphne
24. Yugoslavia
25. Hans Holbein

Index

Picture Credits:

(Abbreviations Key: r = Right, l = Left, t = Top, c = Centre, b = Below)

BFI: 11, 12, 13, 20, 64, 65, 82, 83, 103, 115, 120, 121, 123, 125, 138, 139, 156, 157, 168, 172, 173, 179, 186, 209, 210, 211, 223, 226, 246, 247, 257. **Mary Evans Picture Library:** 14, 25, 29L, 29R, 32T, 32B, 37, 38, 39, 42, 46, 50, 53, 54, 55, 56, 57BR, 57TL, 69, 71, 91, 92, 93, 105, 108, 109, 110, 111, 119, 122, 136, 141, 145, 155, 158, 159, 162, 165, 180, 181, 187, 191, 198, 199, 200, 201R, 212, 215, 218, 219, 231, 235, 253, 254. **Robert Harding Picture Library:** 15, 16, 17, 51, 132, 176, 177, 178, 213. **Hulton Deutsch Collection:** 10, 18, 19, 22T, 22B, 23, 24, 28, 30, 31, 33, 34, 35, 36, 40, 41, 43, 47, 48, 49, 52, 58, 59, 60, 61TL, 61BR, 68, 70, 74, 75, 76, 77, 78, 79, 84, 85, 86, 87, 88, 89, 90, 96L, 96R, 97, 100, 101, 102, 104, 106, 107, 112, 113, 114, 118, 124, 126, 127, 128, 129, 130, 131, 133, 137, 140, 142, 143, 144, 146, 147, 148, 149, 150, 151, 154, 160, 161, 163, 164; **Syndication International:** 166, 167L, 167R, 169, 174, 175, 182, 183, 184, 185, 190, 193, 194, 195, 196, 197, 201L, 202, 203; **Doug McKenzie:** 204, 205, 208, 214, 216, 217, 220, 221, 222, 227, 228, 229, 230, 232, 233, 234, 236, 237, 238TL, 238BR, 239, 241, 244, 245, 248, 249; **EMPICS LTD:** 250, 251, 251, 255, 256, 258, 259. **Kobal Collection:** 72BL. **Peter Newark's Pictures:** 72TR, 73. 94, 95.**Tate Gallery, London:** 67.

Every effort has been made to trace the copyright holders and we apologise in advance for any unintentional omissions. We would be pleased to insert the appropriate acknowledgement in any subsequent edition of this publication.

THE *Greatest* TRIVIA QUIZ BOOK

First published in Great Britain in 1996 by
Parragon.
Unit 13-17
Avonbridge Trading Estate
Atlantic Road
Avonmouth
Bristol BS11 9QD

This edition published in 1998

Edited, designed & produced by Haldane Mason, London
Printed in India

Acknowledgements:
Art Direction: Ron Samuels
Editors: Alexa Stace, Diana Vowles
Design: Anthony Limerick, Somewhere Creative
Picture Research: Jackum Brown & Vicky Walters

CONTENTS

INTROD

UCTION

The appetite for trivia, once acquired, can be insatiable, so here is a new bumper collection of nearly 3,000 questions to tease, torment and entertain. You can use them to test yourself, put your friends on the spot or organize your own quiz night.

The book is divided into several subject categories, which cover every aspect of life, whether ancient or modern, human or animal, spiritual or environmental. You can roam the world with Geography and Travel, delve into history with Past and Present or relax and enjoy yourself with Popular Culture or Sport and Leisure. Meet or re-meet Famous Folk and get practical with Indoors and Out. Some quizzes in Youth World will start you reminiscing, others are set to appeal to the kid in all of us. Pot Luck

aims to take you by surprise, so 'anything goes' with the subjects.

Each quiz has an assortment of questions, in random order. Some are dead easy, some will have you delving deep into your memory banks and others could stump you unless you have a working knowledge of the subject. Some will suit the older members of the family, while for others you may need help from the younger generation.

To meet the Greatest Trivia challenge you need quick reactions, a good store of general knowledge – and luck! Every trivia addict knows how maddening it is when they can answer their opponent's question but not their own. It's all in the game and who cares who wins, so long as everyone has fun!

How To

ULTIMATE TRIVIA GAMES

You can use the Greatest Trivia Quizzes just as you like, sitting alone, or with competitive teams. Here are three suggestions for games you might like to play, but try ringing the changes by making up your own rules.

Game 1

Single player

Pick your favourite from the seven subject categories (*not* including Pot Luck) and try to answer each question in order, scoring 1 point for each correct answer. Every time you fail to answer, take a question from Pot Luck 1. If you answer correctly, score 2 points, if not, deduct 1 point from your current score. When you have exhausted the questions in Pot Luck 1, the game is over. Next time you can begin again from where you left off, using Pot Luck 2, and competing against your last score.

Play

Game 2

2 or more players or teams

Each player or team picks a subject, which can include Pot Luck. You can cut cards or throw dice to decide who chooses first – or you can make the game more difficult by putting all the categories in a hat and making a random choice. Decide in advance how long you want the game to last, then go through the book with each player or team taking turns to answer question 1 in their chosen category, then question 2. Score 2 points for each correct answer. The winner is the person or team with most points when time is up. For the next round, start again where you left off.

Game 3

Several teams with 3 or more members, and a quiz master

Put numbers from 1 to 25 in a hat. Each team draws a number and tries to answer that number in one quiz after another each time their turn comes round. The questions are not graded for difficulty, so no team is at a disadvantage and team members can confer over their answers. Each correct answer in the subject categories earns 1 point, but each time a Pot Luck question is answered correctly, the team score is doubled. The game can be played over again with each team drawing a second number and proceeding through the book in the same way.

Q 9

3. Geneva stands at the tip of Lake Geneva. What do the Swiss call the lake?

4. In which city would you find elegant shopping streets called Via Morte, Via Napoleone, Via Manzoni and Via Spiga?

5. What do Les Halles in Paris and Covent Garden in London have in common?

6. Which city is known as the 'Venice of the North'?

7. From San Francisco, which prison, now closed, can be visited across the bay?

8. In which city is the house in which Anne Frank and her family hid from the Nazis?

9. In which part of Bangkok would you find the Temple of the Emerald Buddha?

10. Which German city has a chiming clock on its medieval town hall, with two tiers of dancing and jousting figures which emerge twice daily?

11. Name the square, called 'Heavenly Peace' in English, which lies at the heart of Beijing.

12. Which street is Dublin's main shopping centre?

13. What style of architecture is the Parthenon in Athens?

1. The Gran Teatre del Liceu is one of the world's finest opera houses. In which city is it located?

2. What was built in Berlin in 1788 as a victory arch for triumphant Prussian armies?

14. In which district in Paris would you find the Sacré-Coeur and the Place du Tertre, where painters gather?

15. Visitors who wish to return to Rome must throw a coin into which fountain?

16. The Taj Mahal can be visited in which Indian city?

17. Which city is sometimes called the 'Paris of the East' and sometimes 'the Whore of China'?

18. The Rockefeller Plaza in New York is used as an open-air cafe in summer. What is it in winter?

19. Where would you be if you could look out over the city from Victoria Peak?

20. In Brussels the small bronze statue of a boy urinating is called the 'Mannekin Pis'. What is the statue nicknamed?

21. In which city could you climb the Spanish Steps?

22. One of the great landmarks of Sydney was designed by Jorn Utzon and finished in 1973. What is it?

23. The Dome of the Rock was built in 691 by the caliph Abd-al-Malik. Where is it?

24. At the famous café in Venice's Piazza San Marco an orchestra plays to patrons. What is the name of the café?

25. Which is the only New York museum with architecture as famous as its collection?

1. Louis Armstrong's nickname was Satchmo. What does it stand for?

2. What was the name of King Oliver's famous jazz band?

3. What is Bix Beiderbecke's chief claim to fame?

4. What is the two-fisted style of piano playing built on ragtime emphasizing tenths in the bass called?

5. What is Jelly Roll Morton's real name?

6. Who was known as the 'King of Swing'?

7. What are the first names of the Marsalis brothers?

8. Who is famous for using the vibraphone in jazz?

9. With what style of jazz is US saxophonist Grover Washington associated?

10. Who was known as 'Lady Day'?

11. What was Glenn Miller's signature tune?

12. Gene Krupa is widely rated the greatest jazz musician on what instrument?

13. Which city is the home of jazz?

14. Who was the leader of the 'Hot Club of France'?

15. What instrument does Stephane Grappelli play?

16. What was the real name of Leadbelly, the great blues singer?

17. Dizzy Gillespie and Charlie Parker were the chief creators and exponents of what type of jazz?

18. Whose albums include *Birth of the Cool*, *Sketches of Spain* and *Bitches' Brew*?

19. The 1940s were the 'big band' era. How many players were needed for a 'big band'?

20. Which instrument did jazz musician John Coltrane play?

21. What name was given to the piano jazz that used a repeated motif for the left hand?

22. Whose numbers included 'Mood Indigo', 'Black and Tan Fantasy' and 'Sophisticated Lady'?

23. Which instruments were dominant in the Dixieland jazz style?

24. Who brought the tenor saxophone to prominence as a jazz instrument?

25. Which type of jazz did Lionel Hampton, Stan Getz and Miles Davis develop in reaction to hot bebop?

Q 16

1. What is the fruit of the hickory tree?

2. Who is supposed to have brought the sycamore tree to Britain?

3. How are maples and limes pollinated?

4. What type of flowers does the yucca have?

5. What is the wood at the centre of the tree stem called?

6. Japanese cedars have bright green leaves in summer. What colour are they in winter?

7. Are whitebeams and mountain ash deciduous or evergreen?

8. *Acer saccharum* produces large areas of bright colour in New England in the fall. What is its everyday name?

9. Arbutus is known as the 'strawberry tree'. Why?

10. To which family do gorse and broom belong?

11. For which flowering tree is Japan famous?

12. Why is it a poor idea to plant a rhus in a lawn?

13. The Judas tree, native to the Mediterranean region, has flowers which hang in clusters on twigs and branches. What colour are they?

14. Which trees have reached giant proportions in California and Oregon?

15. The leaves of the mulberry tree are the favourite food of which creature?

16. How do willow and poplar trees reproduce?

17. The kowhai has small yellow flowers grown in clusters. It is the national flower of which country?

18. Basswood is a lime tree with white flowers. What shape are the leaves?

19. When growing fruit trees, cordons are one of the best types for a small garden. What shape is a cordon?

20. What is the popular name of the pyracantha?

21. Rhododendrons and azaleas belong to the same genus. Which of them is deciduous?

22. Gum-trees are mainly natives of Australia. What is their proper name?

23. Which family of trees do junipers belong to?

24. The flower of which tree is called May blossom?

25. What is the national tree of Lebanon?

8. Name the satellite launched into space in July 1962 and used to send live TV programmes across the Atlantic.

9. What are FORTRAN, PASCAL and COBOL?

10. In which decade was the compact disc developed?

11. At the moment, phone calls travel as electricity along copper cables but they can be sent as light along thin strands of glass. What are these called?

12. Modern computers operate at a speed of up to 400 megaflops. What is a megaflop?

13. The film Star Wars featured two lovable robots. What were their names?

14. When using a bank card in a cash dispenser, customers use a PIN. What do the initials stand for?

15. What is the usual term for an input device used to move an on-screen pointer or cursor to select commands?

16. Name the device that takes information from the computer and modifies it so that it can be transmitted along ordinary phone lines.

17. What do the initials ROM stand for?

18. In which decade did the first minature TV sets appear?

1. How many bits make a byte?

2. What do the letters RAM stand for?

3. In which decade did pocket calculators first make their appearance?

4. In the computer world, what is nicknamed Big Blue?

5. What name is given to the type of printer which makes up each character from a pattern of dots?

6. Goods in shops are often marked with a pattern of black and white stripes. What is this called?

7. The earliest type of robot was a water-clock invented in 250BC. In which country?

19. A fax machine is used to send or receive documents. What is fax short for?

20. Synthesizers are complex pieces of electronic equipment. What do they combine with a computer?

21. As part of a computer, what does a clock chip do?

22. Robot is a word coined by Czech playwright Karel Capek from the word 'robota'. What does it mean?

23. What does interactive cable TV enable viewers to do?

24. What is CAD?

25. A microwriter is an electronic word processor but it lacks one major feature of a standard word processor. What is it?

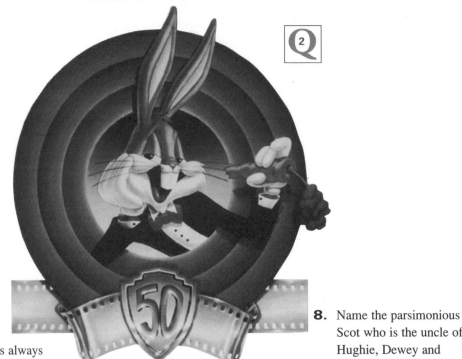

1. Who is always in pursuit of the canary Tweety Pie, though he is always outwitted in the end?

2. What is Bugs Bunny's catchphrase?

3. Why are the popular Tom and Jerry cartoons often criticized?

4. Name the cartoon cat who 'kept on walking'.

5. Where do the Flintstones live?

6. What breed of dog is Snoopy from the Peanuts cartoon?

7. Who has a girl-friend named Olive Oyl?

8. Name the parsimonious Scot who is the uncle of Hughie, Dewey and Louie.

9. Who created the girls of St Trinians?

10. In the TV series *Star Trek*, Mr Spock is played by Leonard Nimoy. Who is Spock's voice in the cartoon series?

11. Mickey Mouse first appeared in 1928, in a short silent film. What was it called?

12. What is Mr Magoo's handicap?

13. Name the sexy cartoon character with a squeaky voice and big eyes who appeared in short films like *Red Hot Mama* and *Zula Hula* in the 1930s.

14. Who created Scooby Doo?

15. Who has the reputation as the fastest mouse in Mexico?

16. Which ancient Gaul, originally featured in strip cartoons, became the star of several French animated films?

17. Which bird, found in the North American deserts, has become a cartoon character who zooms along like a car at full speed?

18. Chip 'n' Dale are two lively, clever chipmunks. What is the difference in appearance between them?

19. What breed of dog is Pluto?

20. Where is Popeye's home?

21. On whose adventures is the cartoon Willy Fog based?

22. How old was Donald Duck in 1994?

23. In *Who Framed Roger Rabbit?*, what is the name of Roger's curvaceous wife?

24. In which cartoon would you find Elmer Fudd?

25. Whose neighbours are Barney and Betty Rubble?

1. Who was the 'Iron Chancellor' who united Germany?

2. Which Roman emperor sentenced St Peter to crucifixion?

3. Name the German mayor of West Berlin who became internationally known during the Berlin Wall crisis.

4. Which Ugandan president deposed Milton Obote and expelled the Asian community?

5. Norman Manley was Prime Minister of Jamaica from 1959 to 1962. His son became Prime Minister in 1972. What was his name?

6. As dictator of Haiti he was known as 'Papa Doc'. What was his name?

7. Who was Secretary General of the United Nations from 1962 to 1971?

8. As leader of the Nationalist Congress Party of India, he was imprisoned by the British nine times. Name him.

9. How did Heinrich Himmler meet his death?

10. What was British Prime Minister Gladstone's middle name?

11. Ivan IV united Russia but in the later years of his reign his actions earned him a nickname. What was it?

12. Mohandas Gandhi was born in India and studied law in England. Where did he practise law before returning to India in 1914?

13. Why did Vorster resign from the presidency of South Africa?

14. What was formally announced by George Bush and Mikhail Gorbachev on 3 December 1989?

15. Which Christian democrat politician was imprisoned by Hitler but later became Chancellor of Germany?

16. Who successfully led North Vietnam in the Vietnam War?

17. Which king ordered the construction of the Tower of London?

18. Name the Chinese leader who organized the Long March beginning in 1934.

19. Lech Walesa founded Solidarity in Poland and later became President. Originally he was a trade union leader but what was his trade?

20. Who was given the title 'Emperor of the West' at his coronation in Rome in AD800?

21. Where was US diplomat Henry Kissinger born?

22. Where was British Prime Minister Winston Churchill born?

23. Who became President of Romania in 1990?

24. Hastings Banda became the first President of which country in 1966?

25. Who succeeded Juan Perón in Argentina in 1974?

Q 13

1. To which family of fish does the char belong?

2. In fishing, lines, hooks, floats and weights are known collectively as what?

3. Where would you find clownfish, boxfish and lion fish?

4. Which TV private eye enjoyed fishing with his father?

5. For what type of fishing are waggler floats used?

6. What are spade end, tucked half blood and dropper loop?

7. Are fish equipped with eyelids?

8. Why should tunny fish be cooked soon after capture?

9. What tool would an angler use to lift a hooked fish from the water?

10. How would an angler keep his catch alive?

11. Salmon return to the river where they were spawned to lay their eggs in fresh water. How do they identify the right river?

12. What type of fish is a jack?

13. What are 'Thunder & Lightning', 'Wycombe's Fancy' and 'Greenwell's Glory'?

14. Which fish has black spots which are said to represent the finger marks of St Peter?

15. For fishing from the beach you need a powerful rod which can cast long distances. What is it called?

16. Name the type of bait which fishermen dig up on sand or mud beaches, where it can be identified by casts.

17. At what time of year does the rainbow trout spawn?

18. Flying fish swim just below the surface then when danger approaches they fly over the water using outspread pectorals as wings. What gives them the power for flight?

19. Which are the only fish in which the head forms a right-angle with the body?

20. Where does the sturgeon breed?

21. Barbels are essential to catfish. What are they?

22. What are large whites, pinkies and squatts?

23. Which type of fishing was featured in the film *A River Runs Through It*?

24. What is the largest of the flatfish?

25. Which fish camouflage themselves on the seabed by remaining still and trusting to their sandy colouring?

1. What is the plural of mongoose?

2. Which Jerusalem church marks the spot where Joseph of Arimathea buried Jesus?

3. Which river flows through the city of Limerick in Ireland?

4. Why do seals appear to cry?

5. Which game was named after the Duke of Beaufort's house in Gloucestershire, England?

6. Who made the song 'My Old Dutch' famous?

7. What is pumpernickel?

8. If you were visiting the 'Met' in New York, where would you be going?

9. What mysterious trade was carried on at Jamaica Inn?

10. Which European country's flag is a yellow cross on a blue field?

11. During which two centuries did Queen Elizabeth I reign?

12. In falconry, what is a stoop?

13. Where would a troglodyte live?

14. In what would a cryptologist specialize?

15. What is the capital of Venezuela?

16. Which planet is closest to the sun?

17. Who wrote the 'New World' symphony?

18. In the television series *Mission Impossible*, what did the initials IMF stand for?

19. What would you be doing if you were wearing a tutu?

20. Which legendary character has been portrayed by both Sean Connery and his son Jason?

21. Who asked for the head of John the Baptist, according to the Bible story?

22. In what field is the Brazilian Jorge Amado well known?

23. Which words appear on the George Cross?

24. What song became a hit single after Lee Marvin sang it in *Paint Your Wagon*?

25. Are dates, pomegranates and avocados tropical or subtropical fruits?

Geography and Travel • City Sites

1. Barcelona
2. Brandenburg Gate
3. Lac Léman
4. Milan
5. Both used to be markets
6. Stockholm
7. Alcatraz
8. Amsterdam
9. In the complex of the Grand Palace
10. Munich
11. Tiananmen Square
12. O'Connell Street
13. Doric
14. Montmartre
15. Trevi
16. Agra
17. Shanghai
18. A skating rink
19. Hong Kong
20. Brussels' oldest citizen
21. Rome
22. Sydney Opera house
23. Jerusalem
24. Florian
25. Guggenheim

Youth World • Cartoons

1. Sylvester
2. 'What's up Doc?'
3. For their violence
4. Felix
5. Bedrock
6. Beagle
7. Popeye
8. Scrooge McDuck
9. Ronald Searle
10. Leonard Nimoy
11. *Plane crazy*
12. He is short-sighted
13. Betty Boop
14. William Hanna and Joseph Barbera
15. Speedy Gonzales
16. Asterix
17. Roadrunner
18. Chip has one tooth, Dale has two
19. Bloodhound
20. The Island of Sweetwater
21. Phileas Fogg
22. 60
23. Jessica
24. Bugs Bunny
25. Fred and Wilma

Popular Culture • Jazz

1. Satchelmouth
2. The Creole Jazz Band
3. The first white jazz musician
4. Stride piano
5. Ferdinand Joseph Lemott
6. Benny Goodman
7. Wynton and Branford
8. Lionel Hampton
9. Jazz funk
10. Billie Holiday
11. Moonlight Serenade
12. Drums
13. New Orleans
14. Django Reinhardt
15. Violin
16. Huddie Ledbetter
17. Bebop
18. Miles Davis
19. 13 or more
20. Saxophone
21. Boogie woogie
22. Duke Ellington
23. Cornet, trombone and clarinet
24. Coleman Hawkins
25. Cool jazz

Famous Folk • Statesmen and Tyrants

1. Bismarck
2. Nero
3. Willy Brandt
4. Idi Amin
5. Michael Manley
6. François Duvalier
7. U Thant
8. Jawaharla Nehru
9. Suicide
10. Ewart
11. Ivan the Terrible
12. South Africa
13. Financial scandal
14. End of the Cold War
15. Konrad Adenauer
16. Ho Chi Minh
17. William the Conqueror
18. Mao Tse-tung
19. Electrician
20. Charlemagne
21. Bavaria, Germany
22. Blenheim Palace
23. Ion Iliescu
24. Malawi
25. Isabel Perón

Indoors and Out • Trees and Shrubs

1. A small, edible nut
2. The Romans
3. The flowers attract bees and insects
4. Creamy-white, bell-shaped flowers
5. Heart wood
6. Purple and bronze
7. Deciduous
8. Sugar maple
9. It has strawberry-like, but tasteless fruits
10. The pea family
    (*Leguminosae*)
11. The cherry
12. It throws up suckers
13. Pinkish-purple
14. Californian redwood (*Sequoia sempervirens*)
15. The silkworm
16. The seeds are spread by the wind
17. New Zealand
18. Heart-shaped
19. They have a single stem, grown at an angle to form a hedge, with no large spreading branches
20. Firethorn
21. Azaleas
22. Eucalyptus
23. Cypress
24. Hawthorn
25. Cedar

Sport and Leisure • Fish and Fishing

1. Salmonidae
2. Tackle
3. On a coral reef
4. James Rockford
5. Stillwater fishing
6. Types of knot
7. No, their eyes do not close
8. They are prone to a type of bacterial decay which can render them poisonous
9. A landing net
10. By using a keep-net
11. By smell
12. Pike
13. Flies used in Fly-fishing
14. John Dory
15. Beachcaster
16. Lugworms
17. Spring
18. The action of the tail
19. Seahorses
20. Rivers
21. Whiskers
22. Maggots
23. Fly fishing
24. Halibut
25. Rays

Past and Present • Modern Technology

1. Eight
2. Random Access Memory
3. 1970s
4. IBM
5. Dot-matrix printer
6. Bar code
7. Egypt
8. Telstar
9. Computer languages
10. 1970s
11. Optical fibres
12. One million floating operations per second
13. C-3PO and R2-D2
14. Personal identity number
15. A mouse
16. Modem
17. Read-only memory
18. 1980s
19. Facsimile
20. Musical keyboard
21. Produces a regular timing signal
22. Slave labour
23. Send messages back to the TV station
24. Computer aided design
25. A standard keyboard

Pot Luck

1. Mongooses
2. Church of the Holy Sepulchre
3. River Shannon
4. They produce tears to keep their eyes moist
5. Badminton
6. Albert Chevalier
7. A type of black bread
8. Metropolitan Opera House
9. Smuggling
10. Sweden
11. 16th and 17th
12. The falcon's dive on its prey
13. In a cave
14. Cracking codes
15. Caracas
16. Mercury
17. Dvořák
18. Impossible Missions Force
19. Ballet dancing
20. Robin Hood
21. Salome
22. Novel writing
23. 'For gallantry'
24. Wandrin' Star
25. Subtropical

1. At what age does a baby kangaroo, or joey, leave its mother's pouch because it has grown too big?

2. Which animals have species known as Burchell's and Grevy's?

3. Where is the calf of the hippopotamus born?

4. Gorillas and chimpanzees are found in Africa. In which continent would you find gibbons and orang-utans?

5. From which country did the pheasant originate?

6. The kinkajou has acquired a popular name because of its fondness for a certain type of food. What is the name?

7. How does the skunk keep enemies at bay?

8. Which is the only type of deer to have been domesticated, so that it supplies meat, milk and skins?

9. How many chambers has the stomach of a giraffe?

10. What is unusual about the incubation of the emu's eggs?

11. Some porcupines nest in trees. True or false?

12. Why are bush-babies so called?

13. What type of animal is an impala?

14. The feet of the puffin are red in summer. What colour are they in winter?

15. What does the raccoon seem to do with its food before it eats?

16. Which is the only mammal able to kneel on all fours?

17. What is the name given to the nesting site of penguins?

18. Whales live in groups of 20 to 50. What are the groups called?

19. In which country can wild budgerigars be found?

20. Name the animals popularly thought to commit mass suicide by hurling themselves into the sea.

21. Which is the largest of the American big cats?

22. What is stored in the camel's hump?

23. The roadrunner, found in the stony deserts of North America, is a member of which bird family?

24. Which animal has species called elephant, crabeater and fur?

25. Why do desert-living gerbils never need to drink?

Q9

1. Which newspaper was nicknamed 'The Thunderer'?

2. Spiderman's alter ego was newspaper photographer Peter Parker. For which paper did he work?

3. Newspaper reporters now put their copy straight onto a VDU. What do the initials stand for?

4. *Le Figaro* is published in Paris. Is it daily or weekly?

5. Which magazine was launched by Helen Gurley Brown?

6. Canada's first newspaper was the *Halifax Gazette*. In which century was the earliest edition published?

7. The film *Citizen Kane*, starring Orson Welles, was loosely based on the life of which newspaper magnate?

8. Which is larger, a tabloid or a broadsheet newspaper?

9. Name the Australian businessman who has made a fortune in the newspaper industry.

10. Was *Vogue* first published in America in 1892, 1905 or 1921?

11. Which is Britain's oldest Sunday newspaper?

12. What newspaper do the Flintstones read?

13. In a newspaper, what is a 'splash'?

14. Reporter Clark Kent worked for the *Daily Planet*. By what name was he better known?

15. New York's penny paper was launched in 1833 and had the same name as a current British tabloid. What was it?

16. Which magazine has a yellow border on the front cover?

17. In which decade was *Marie Claire* first published in France?

18. For which newspaper did TV's Lou Grant work?

19. *Der Spiegel* is a famous German publication. What does the name mean in English?

20. Which newspaper had almost 950 pages one morning in October 1965?

21. Woodward and Bernstein wrote for which newspaper?

22. How often is *Life* magazine published?

23. Newspaper proprietor Max Aitken was born in Canada in 1879. By what name is he better known?

24. *Barrons* is a well-respected weekly publication in the US. What field does it cover?

25. The wife of disgraced tycoon Robert Maxwell published her autobiography in 1994. What is her name?

Q18

6. What is added to stock to make Venetian soup?

7. Which type of meat is traditionally used in moussaka?

8. When barbecuing meat, how would you flavour and tenderize it in advance?

9. What is the traditional material used for a wok?

10. In a freezer kept at −18°C (0°F), how long can you store sausages?

11. In a freezer kept at −18°C (0°F), which could you keep longer, beef or pork?

12. Which type of cheeses are Liptauer, Feta and Munster?

13. What would you add to béchamel sauce to make aurore sauce?

14. At a meal with several courses, when would you serve Welsh rarebit?

15. American recipes give quantities of ingredients in standard cups. How much sugar (caster or granulated) does one cup hold?

16. When making cappuccino you would use a fine ground coffee. What kind would you use in a percolator?

17. What are riccini, bucatini and ziti?

1. What is the substance that gels in water and enables jam to set?

2. Goulash takes its name from the Hungarian word for shepherd. What spice gives goulash its distinctive flavour?

3. In microwave cooking, what is the other name for standing time, when the food can continue cooking after it leaves the oven?

4. What name is given to bread dipped in beaten egg and fried?

5. The Italian pasta called tagliatelle comes in what shape?

18. In what type of oven are pizzas traditionally made?

19. If you were serving an Indian 'thali', how would you present it?

20. Which of these materials would be suitable for use in microwaves: glass, ceramics, metal, paper?

21. If you were making a bisque, what main ingredient would you use?

22. What is 'beurre fondu'?

23. What is the zest of an orange or lemon?

24. What is the traditional herbal accompaniment for lamb?

25. If a recipe called for 450g (1lb) butter, what would be the equivalent in American cups?

Q 11

1. When the state of Israel was first formed, which country occupied the West Bank?

2. Lawrence of Arabia helped to organize Arab revolt against whose rule?

3. In which war did Israel defeat the Arab nations in June 1967?

4. Which Egyptian leader nationalized the Suez Canal in 1956?

5. After World War II a million Jews were in DP camps across Europe. What did DP stand for?

6. Which Egyptian king was forced to abdicate after the army coup in 1952?

7. Where did Black September terrorists kill 11 Israeli athletes in 1972?

8. Who was Israel's leader at the time of the Yom Kippur war?

9. The Gulf War between Iran and Iraq began in 1980. When did it end?

10. Which was the only Arab state to support Iran against Iraq?

11. What did Saddam Hussein abolish in Iraq in 1977?

12. When Iraqi forces invaded Kuwait in 1990 the ruler and the Crown Prince fled. Where did they take refuge?

13. At the beginning of the Gulf War, Saddam Hussein detained western hostages in Iraq, keeping many of them at military targets. What was this policy called?

14. Against which nations did Saddam Hussein fire Scud missiles when the Allies attacked in the Gulf war?

15. Who has been leader of the PLO since 1969?

16. What percentage of the world's oil reserves is owned by Saudi Arabia?

17. Who was the first prime minister of the independent state of Israel?

18. What name was given to the operation to liberate Kuwait from Iraqi invaders?

19. The Kurds in the north of Iraq openly rebelled against Saddam Hussein. When government troops hit back, where did Kurdish refugees gather?

20. What council was formed by Iraq, Jordan, North Yemen and Egypt in 1989?

21. Since 1984 there has been guerilla fighting in what part of Turkey?

22. The Palestinian Al Fatah was formed as an illicit organization in 1956. Al Fatah is Arabic for what?

23. Hafiz Al-Assad has been president of which country since 1971?

24. What was the name given to the popular Palestinian uprising against Israeli occupation?

25. At the 1991 Madrid peace conference Hanan Ashrawi, a professor of English literature and a Christian, was the unlikely spokesperson for which organisation?

7. In Italy, who would study at the Instituto Magistrale?

8. What is the French baccalauréat?

9. Many Australian children live in the outback, too isolated to attend school. They talk to teachers by two-way radio and submit work by post. What is the 'school' called?

10. Which school did Billy Bunter attend?

11. Arnold Schwarzenegger plays a policeman masquerading as a teacher in which film?

1. To which creature does Shakespeare compare the schoolboy in the famous 'Ages of Man' speech?

2. In America, what is a sophomore?

3. What is a magnet school?

4. How many key stages are there in the British national curriculum?

5. Which schoolboy did Flashman bully in a famous novel?

6. A fraternity is a society of male college students in America. What is the female equivalent?

12. In Germany, what are Fachschulen?

13. What is TEFL teaching?

14. Plato was the pupil of which famous teacher?

15. Plato was the teacher of which famous pupil?

16. What is the main difference between British and American public schools?

17. The University of Paris is normally known by the name of one of its departments. What is it?

18. Which teacher taught Helen Keller to communicate?

19. King Hussein of Jordan was educated at which British public school?

20. *Blackboard Jungle* is a classic film of a tough urban school, based on a novel by which author?

21. What is the name of the school in Charles Dickens' *Nicholas Nickelby*?

22. The word education is based on the Latin educo. What does it mean?

23. In which field of education did Maria Montessori introduce revolutionary ideas?

24. What is the name usually given to the older, more traditional universities of the north-eastern US?

25. Bel Kaufman's bestseller about a New York public school was filmed as *Up the Down Staircase*. Who starred as the new teacher?

1. Who was known as the 'King of Marches'?

2. Sir Thomas Beecham founded two orchestras. The first was the London Philharmonic in 1932. What was the other?

3. Which modern American musician wrote the ballets *Billy the Kid*, *Rodeo* and *Appalachian Spring*?

4. Who wrote the score for the film *Lawrence of Arabia*?

5. Before James Galway embarked on a freelance career, he was a flautist with which orchestra?

6. What name is given to the music associated with Debussy, Ravel and Delius?

7. How old was Johann Strauss when he wrote his first waltz?

8. Which opera, the story of ill-fated love, was written by George Gershwin for a black cast in 1935?

9. What nationality was Anton Bruckner?

10. From what handicap did J. S. Bach suffer in later life?

11. What forced Rachmaninov to leave his native country?

12. The oratorio *The Dream of Gerontius* was first performed in Germany in 1901. Who was the composer?

13. What nationality was Gustav Holst?

14. Name the Beatles' manager who died in 1967.

15. Which composer always began his score with the words 'In nomine Domini' and ended it with 'Laus Deo'?

16. Whose musical shows include *Kiss me Kate* and *The Gay Divorcee*?

17. Rimsky-Korsakov was a leading member of a Russian group called what?

18. At the age of six Mozart was touring Europe as a performer with his talented older sister. What was her name?

19. Which composer founded the Festival Theatre in Bayreuth?

20. Who was the first great master of the string quartet?

21. For which English king did Handel write his *Water Music* in 1717?

22. What nationality was Jean Sibelius?

23. At what age did Chopin make his debut as a pianist?

24. Frederick Delius was born in England but in 1884 he went to Florida. What business was he engaged in?

25. Wagner's *Ring of the Nibelung* consists of four epic music dramas. Which is the first?

1. What does the Jewish festival of the Passover commemorate?

2. During Ramadan, in the ninth month of the Muslim year, what is observed during daylight hours?

3. When does the famous Mardi Gras carnival in New Orleans take place?

4. In the Christian calendar, advent is a period of preparation for which festival?

5. Wesak is an important festival for Buddhists. What does it mark?

6. Which country has a Boys' Festival, or Childrens' Day, on 5 May, when paper carp are hoisted on to poles?

7. Holi is a harvest time festival for Hindus when people light bonfires and throw coloured water over one another. Which deity does it honour?

8. During the pilgrimage to Mecca, male pilgrims don what type of dress?

9. Which celebration, once linked with dancing and flowers and now associated with socialism, was forbidden in England in the time of Oliver Cromwell?

10. In Thailand Songkrar Day is also New Year. What is the main feature of the celebrations, held on 31 December?

11. The Muslim Hijrat commemorates whose journey from Mecca to Medina?

12. The Jewish Hanukkah celebrates the recapture and rededication of the Temple of Jerusalem in 165BC. It lasts eight days; what happens on each day?

13. When is Thanksgiving celebrated in the US?

14. At the Chinese New Year, people honour the kitchen god, who will then report back to heaven on their conduct. What kind of dance is associated with the festivities?

15. For Christians, Lent means the 40 days leading up to Easter. What day marks the beginning of Lent?

16. What does the Jewish feast Shavout celebrate?

17. The first Christians did not observe Christmas, but it was being celebrated by which century?

18. Which Hindu festival of lights, when lights stand in every window, honours Lakshmi, the goddess of fortune?

19. Who do the Chinese particularly remember at Ching Ming?

20. Which saint's feast day falls on 26 December in the Christian calendar?

21. In many European and Asian countries, on which day do people play tricks on one another?

22. What does Rosh Hashanah mark for the Jews?

23. Which religion celebrates Baisakhi?

24. In which German town does the famous Oktoberfest, where beer flows freely, take place?

25. Name the ancient Celtic celebration, particularly popular in the US, which marks the time when witches and evil spirits were supposed to be driven away before the beginning of the new year.

1. What are baby squirrels called?

2. Which chain of shops was originally called the Great Five Cent Store?

3. What is measured by a chronometer?

4. Which aviator made the first solo Trans-Atlantic flight?

5. In the nursery rhyme, what did the dish run away with?

6. Name the capital of New Zealand.

7. What is gymnophobia?

8. Who painted *The Rake's Progress*?

9. In the TV series *Dempsey and Makepeace*, was Dempsey or Makepeace the man?

10. What kind of creature is a flying dragon?

11. Whose life is portrayed in the musical *Evita*?

12. Which is the world's largest freshwater lake?

13. What is the main ingredient of taramasalata?

14. In which film did Charlie Chaplin first speak on screen?

15. If you were suffering from gingivitis, what part of your body would be affected?

16. What is the main explosive ingredient of dynamite?

17. If a golfer loses a ball, what is the penalty?

18. In Shakespeare's *Macbeth*, which king is killed in his sleep?

19. What is the meaning of the word 'karate'?

20. Three of the four largest deserts in the world are the Sahara, Arabian and Australian. What is the fourth?

21. According to George Orwell, who is watching us?

22. How many dimes are there in one American dollar?

23. Name the character who sings 'I Feel Pretty' in *West Side Story*.

24. In which operetta would you find Yum-Yum and Nanki-Poo?

25. What did the nickname 'dinkies' describe when applied to a couple?

Answers to Quiz 2

Geography and Travel • Wildlife

1. Six months
2. The zebra
3. Under water
4. Asia
5. China
6. Honey bear
7. It sprays a smelly liquid which can cause a predator temporary blindness
8. Reindeer
9. Four
10. The male sits on the eggs, not the female
11. True
12. Because their cry sounds like a wailing baby
13. Antelope
14. Yellow
15. It washes the food
16. The elephant
17. Rookery
18. Pods
19. Australia
20. Lemmings
21. The jaguar
22. Fat
23. Cuckoo
24. Seal
25. They obtain the moisture they need from the overnight dew on their food

Popular Culture • Newspapers and Magazines

1. The Times
2. The Daily Bugle
3. Visual display unit
4. Daily
5. Cosmopolitan
6. 18th century
7. William Randolph Hearst
8. Broadsheet
9. Rupert Murdoch
10. 1892
11. The Observer
12. The Daily Slate
13. A front-page lead story
14. Superman
15. The Sun
16. National Geographic
17. 1950s
18. Los Angeles Tribune
19. The Mirror
20. New York Times
21. The Washington Post
22. Monthly
23. Lord Beaverbrook
24. Finance
25. Elizabeth

Indoors and Out • Cookery Course

1. Pectin
2. Paprika
3. Carry over cooking
4. French toast or 'eggy bread'
5. Long ribbons
6. Egg and lemon
7. Lamb
8. Marinade
9. Iron
10. Three months
11. Beef
12. Soft cheeses
13. Tomato
14. The end of the meal
15. 200g (7oz)
16. Medium grind
17. Types of pasta
18. Brick
19. With each dish in a separate small bowl
20. Glass, ceramics, paper
21. Shellfish
22. Butter melted with lemon juice, salt and white pepper
23. The very outside of the peel
24. Mint
25. Two cups

Past and Present • Middle East

1. Jordan
2. Turks
3. Six Day War
4. Nasser
5. Displaced Persons
6. King Farouk
7. Munich Olympics
8. Golda Meir
9. 1988
10. Syria
11. The use of surnames
12. Saudi Arabia
13. The 'human shield policy'
14. Israel and Saudi Arabia
15. Yasser Arafat
16. 40%
17. David Ben-Gurion
18. Operation Desert Storm
19. On the Turkish border
20. Arab Co-operation Council
21. Kurdistan
22. Victory
23. Syria
24. Intifada
25. PLO

Youth World • Education

1. A snail
2. A second-year student in high school or college
3. It specializes in a particular area of the curriculum
4. Four
5. Tom Brown
6. Sorority
7. Teachers
8. School leaving certificate
9. School of the Air
10. Greyfriars
11. Kindergarten Cop
12. Technical colleges
13. Teaching English as a foreign language
14. Socrates
15. Aristotle
16. In the US they are free: in Britain they are fee-paying
17. Sorbonne
18. Anne Sullivan
19. Harrow
20. Evan Hunter
21. Dotheboys Hall
22. To draw out
23. Infant teaching
24. Ivy League
25. Sandy Dennis

Famous Folk • Musicians and Composers

1. John Philip Sousa
2. Royal Philharmonic, 1947
3. Aaron Copland
4. Maurice Jarre
5. Berlin Philharmonic
6. Impressionist
7. Six
8. Porgy and Bess
9. Austrian
10. Blindness
11. The Russian Revolution
12. Elgar
13. English
14. Brian Epstein
15. Haydn
16. Cole Porter
17. The Five
18. Anna or Nannerl
19. Wagner
20. Haydn
21. George I
22. Finnish
23. Eight
24. Orange-growing
25. The Rhinegold (Das Rheingold)

Sport and Leisure • Religious Festivals

1. The escape from slavery in Egypt
2. A strict fast
3. Shrove Tuesday
4. Christmas
5. Buddha's birth, enlightenment and death
6. Japan
7. Krishna
8. A white sheet
9. May Day
10. A water festival
11. Muhammad
12. A new candle is lit on the menorah
13. The fourth Thursday of November
14. Lion dance
15. Ash Wednesday
16. The giving of the Ten Commandments on Mount Sinai
17. Fourth century
18. Diwali
19. The dead
20. St Stephen
21. 1st April, All Fools Day
22. New Year
23. Sikh
24. Munich
25. Hallowe'en

Pot Luck

1. Kittens
2. Woolworths
3. Time
4. Charles Lindbergh
5. Spoon
6. Wellington
7. Fear of nakedness
8. Hogarth
9. Dempsey
10. Lizard
11. Eva Perón
12. Lake Superior
13. Cod's roe
14. The Great Dictator
15. Gums
16. Nitro-glycerine
17. One stroke added to the score
18. Duncan
19. Empty hand
20. Gobi
21. Big Brother
22. Ten
23. Maria
24. The Mikado
25. Dual income and no kids

3

1. In which area of the US would you find a multitude of covered bridges?

2. Lake Tahoe, the largest alpine lake in North America, is half in California and half in which other state?

3. Which is the largest Indian reservation in America?

4. What is the legal drinking age in all American states?

5. In which Canadian town, nicknamed Cowtown, does a famous 'stampede' take place in July each year?

6. Which American city has the largest cruise ship port in the world?

7. A quarter of the world's geysers are found in which national park in Wyoming ?

8. Name the string of islands at the southern tip of Florida.

9. What is the state bird of Texas?

10. In Washington DC, which park is overlooked by the White House?

11. Which mountain range stretches from Alaska to New Mexico?

12. The Golden Gate Bridge is one of the longest suspension bridges in the world. Which US city does it connect with Marin County?

13. Which capital city stands on Vancouver Island in Canada?

14. In which American state would you find the world's most active volcano?

15. Nearly half the population of Alaska lives in one town. What is its name?

16. Canada's most popular resort stands in its oldest national park. What is its name?

17. The Yukon Territory is named after the Yukon River ('yukon' means 'clear water'). Is it in Canada or the USA?

18. Which American state is known as the Lone Star state?

19. The Pennsylvanian Dutch Country is home to the Amish and Mennonite people, who turn their back on much of the modern world. What nationality were the original immigrants?

20. In which state would you find Carlsbad Caverns, El Morro National Monument and Taos?

21. Which country gave the Statue of Liberty to America?

22. The famous two-week siege of the Alamo, Texas, took place in 1836 when its 187 defenders died. Which country's army besieged the fort?

23. What notable feature would you expect to find at the Mesa Verde National Park in Colorado?

24. Which is the only Canadian province where the urban population is more than 80% of the total?

25. How long is the Grand Canyon?

BOND BOOKS AND FILMS

1. How did James Bond like his martini?

2. Which was the first book to feature James Bond?

3. Who sang the theme song to *A View to a Kill*?

4. Name the producer of the Bond films.

5. Which Bond film features the Carnival at Rio?

6. Who is the villain in *Diamonds are Forever*?

7. In 1973 Roger Moore took over as Bond, but one film tempted Sean Connery back to the role. Which was it?

8. Ursula Andress collects shells on the beach in which film?

9. 'M' is Bond's boss, but who supplies him with his high-tech gadgetry?

10. Which film used Phang Nga Bay, in southern Thailand, as the location for the villain's private island?

11. In the 17th Bond film, *Goldeneye*, who plays Bond's female boss?

12. Which villain likes to bite his victim to death?

13. Which of the Bond girls shares a surname with the secret agent?

14. Who wrote the Bond novels?

15. The film *Casino Royale*, made in 1967, is a spoof. Who plays Bond?

16. Following the death of Bond's creator, who wrote sequels called *Icebreaker*, *Roll of Honour* and *Scorpius*?

17. Pussy Galore runs a 'flying circus' in which film?

18. Who is Mr Big's sidekick in *Live and Let Die*?

19. In which film does George Lazenby play Bond?

20. Which well-known novelist wrote *The James Bond Dossier* in 1965?

21. Who plays the tarot-reading Solitaire in *Live and Let Die*?

22. Matt Munro sang the title song for which film?

23. Which actor appears as Bond for the first time in *The Living Daylights*?

24. In which film does a Lotus car convert into an underwater craft?

25. In *Goldfinger*, what does Oddjob use as a lethal weapon?

1. Apricots are native to which country?

2. The boysenberry was raised in California in the 1930s by Rudolph Boysen. It is thought to come from a mixture of which fruits?

3. What is a 'maiden' fruit tree?

4. Morello is a sour type of which fruit?

5. A date palm has a life of about 80 years. What is the world's most popular variety of date?

6. Which 15th-century explorer brought the pineapple, a native of Brazil, to Spain?

7. Viticulture is the name given to the growing of which fruit?

8. The French are not great gooseberry eaters, except as a basis for a sauce for a fish dish named *groseille à maquereau*. Which fish does it complement?

9. The commercial cultivation of grapefruit began in the 1880s. Where was this?

10. Which type of melon has a yellow-orange skin with green rib markings in a network pattern?

11. What is another name for the papaya or tree melon?

12. Pectin is essential for jam-making. Which will contain more pectin: slightly under-ripe, ripe or slightly over-ripe fruit?

13. Which fruit has the botanical name *Ribes nigrum*?

14. Apples were cultivated by the ancient Greeks. True or false?

15. Which fruit did a companion of Captain Cook, in north Queensland, describe as a 'kind of wild Plantain, whose fruit was so full of stones that it was scarcely eatable'?

16. When thawing fruit, is it best to thaw it in the fridge or at room temperature?

17. Which Spanish city is thought to have been named after the pomegranate?

18. The durian fruit, native to Malaysia, is notorious for what?

19. Seckle, Jargonelle and Doyenne du Comice are varieties of what type of fruit?

20. The name 'strawberry' is often thought to come from the growers' habit of laying straw round the plants. In fact, it probably comes from what habit of the plant itself?

21. Where was the kiwi fruit first grown and harvested?

22. Which country grows the largest number of mangoes?

23. The carob, a member of the pea family, can be used to replace which substance in cooking?

24. The blackberry, or bramble, belongs to which family of plants?

25. Cranberries are cultivated on a large scale in the eastern US. In what kind of ground are they grown?

Q 3

1. Which European country was the first to start building its overseas empire?

2. In 1454 the German Johann Gutenberg set up his printing press. Later, he used metal type, but what material did he use to begin with?

3. Which ocean was named by navigator Ferdinand Magellan?

4. Christopher Columbus set out to find a route to Asia in 1492. Where did he land?

5. Who created the Moghul empire in India in the 16th century?

6. Which all-male theatre with a highly stylized form was established in Japan in 1586 and can still be seen today?

7. The Spanish adventurer Cortés landed in Mexico in 1518 and by 1521 had conquered the country. Which empire did he destroy in the process?

8. Sebastian Cabot was supported by King Henry VII of England in his explorations and in 1497 discovered Newfoundland. What nationality was he?

9. Europeans who tried to trade with China in the 16th century were not welcomed. Which famous dynasty was at the height of its power?

10. The Julian calendar was used in Europe until the 1580s. Which calendar was adopted after 1582 in Roman Catholic countries and later in Protestant countries?

11. The Renaissance was a great cultural revival in Europe after the Middle Ages. What does 'renaissance' mean?

12. Which Renaissance artist painted the ceiling of the Sistine Chapel and designed the dome of St Peter's in Rome?

13. In which decade of the 16th century did John Hawkins begin the slave trade by shipping Africans to the West Indies?

14. Which country was discovered by Abel Tasman in 1662 and surveyed by Captain Cook in 1769?

15. What important navigational aid did Flemish geographer Gerardus Mercator produce in 1569?

16. The 16th century was Spain's golden age. Philip II made which city Spain's capital?

17. In 1608 Samuel de Champlain founded the city that was to become Quebec. What trade did he organize between France and Canada?

18. In 1587 Sir Francis Drake destroyed Spanish ships in Cadiz harbour. What did he call this enterprise?

19. The defeat of the Spanish Armada began Spain's decline. What is Drake popularly supposed to have been doing when the Armada was sighted?

20. Which vegetable did Sir Walter Raleigh bring back from his journey to America?

21. In 1488 Bartholomeu Diaz sailed to the southern tip of the African continent and turned back because of bad weather. He called the area the 'Cape of Storms'. What cheery name does it bear today?

22. Which empire was destroyed by Francisco Pizzaro and his forces in the mountains of South America in the 1530s?

23. What name was given to the movement whereby half Europe broke away from the Roman Catholic church and Protestantism flourished?

24. Who succeeded Queen Elizabeth I to the throne of England in 1603?

25. America's first university was founded in 1636 in Cambridge, Massachusetts. Name it.

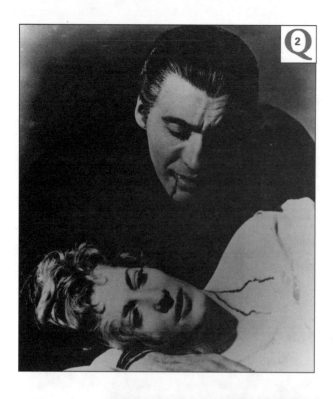

1. The Sherpas of the Himalayas have always believed that which creature lives beyond the snowline?

2. Which historical figure is supposed to have been the prototype of Bram Stoker's creation *Dracula*?

3. Which ugly, misshapen creatures, in the form of men, are said to lurk in the northern forests of Scandinavia?

4. What type of monsters were defeated by Ragnar of Denmark, Beowulf and St George?

5. Name the imaginary creature described by Lewis Carroll as having 'jaws that bite and claws that catch'.

6. The Marvel comics introduced many monsters, among them the fearsome King of the Negative Zone. What was he aptly named?

7. A werewolf could only be killed by what type of bullet?

8. Which monster appears as Harry in *Harry and the Hendersons*?

9. In the film *Jason and the Argonauts* monsters such as winged harpies and fighting skeletons were produced by a process called 'dynamism' by their creator. Who is he?

10. A lake demon called Ogapogo is said to inhabit Okanagan Lake in Canada. In which province is the lake?

11. Which people believe that 'whowies' and 'bunyips' existed in the Dreamtime?

12. Who was Dr Jekyll's alter ego?

13. Name the dragon who guarded treasure in *The Hobbit*.

14. Modern sightings of the Loch Ness monster began in the 1930s, but which saint and his followers first saw 'Nessie' in AD 565?

15. 'Nessie' is thought by some people to be the survivor of a species of dinosaur believed extinct for 70 million years. What is the species?

16. In *The Hound of the Baskervilles*, a Dartmoor family is plagued by a phantom hound. Name the author of the novel.

17. The giant Goliath was slain by the boy David in the Bible story. Goliath was a member of which army?

18. The Kraken was a legendary monster, said to be big enough to drag down ships. What type of creature is the Kraken now believed to have been?

19. In the film *Ghostbusters*, a pagan deity calls up a monster who appears in a surprisingly cuddly form. What is it?

20. How was King Kong killed?

21. In Canada, the monster Cadborasaurus has been sighted regularly off the coast of Vancouver. What is its nickname?

22. The Bigfoot is often known by its Native American name. What is it?

23. In Bram Stoker's *Lair of the White Worm*, which lady is the worm's human manifestation?

24. Name the home of the giants visited in *Gulliver's Travels*.

25. In James Herbert's *The Rats*, how did the monster rat differ in appearance from the other monster mutants?

5. Jonas Salk's research into viruses produced the first effective vaccine against which crippling disease?

6. James Watson, Frances Crick and Maurice Wilkins were awarded the Nobel Prize for their work in which modern field?

7. Who revolutionized surgery by his discovery of anaesthetics in the 1860s?

8. The German physicist who first used mercury in a thermometer also fixed a scale of temperature that still bears his name. What is it?

9. Which Italian astronomer and physicist invented the astronomical telescope and put forward the Law of Accelerated Motion?

10. In 1903 Russian Konstantin Tsiolkovsky drew up designs for a spaceship powered by what?

11. Marie Curie is one of the few people to be awarded two Nobel prizes. The first was the prize for physics in 1903. Who shared this award with her?

12. A lamp used by miners for the detection of gas still bears the name of its inventor. What is it?

13. Edward Jenner developed a vaccination to prevent which disease?

14. Alfred Nobel left the lion's share of his fortune to found the prize that bears his name. He had made his money from which invention?

1. Stephen Hawking, who is confined to a wheelchair and talks with the aid of computers, is best known for his study of what?

2. The fall of an apple spurred Newton into considering what?

3. Who is known as the 'father of nuclear physics'?

4. Wallace Carothers invented a strong, light synthetic fibre. What is it called?

15. In the 19th century Michael Faraday was a pioneer in which field?

16. Work on the atomic bomb was carried on in New Mexico under the direction of J. Robert Oppenheimer. What was the project called?

17. Alexander Fleming discovered penicillin. What type of drug is penicillin?

18. Wernher von Braun worked on rocket development in Germany during World War II. What did he work on in America after the war?

19. Archimedes discovered the principle that when a body is immersed in water, the displaced volume of liquid is equal to the weight of the body. Legend has it that he jumped from his bath and ran naked down the street. What was he shouting?

20. In what field are Louis Daguerre, Karl Kleitsch and George Eastman famous names?

21. Name the Scottish engineer who constructed the Caledonian Canal and the Menai Suspension Bridge.

22. What process takes its name from its inventor, Louis Pasteur?

23. In 1927 Le Maître was the first to advance the theory that the universe began with an explosion. What is this theory called?

24. What 'first' did John Logie Baird achieve in 1925?

25. Name the engineer who produced bouncing bombs to breach German dams and 'Tall Boy' and 'Grand Slam' penetration bombs in World War II.

Q 16

4. There are two basic types of organ pipe. What are they?

5. What was the early name for the pianoforte?

6. Which artist painted *The Beggar's Opera* several times in the 18th century?

7. In which part of the world would you find an orchestra called a gamelan?

8. What is a koto?

9. From which family of instruments does the cittern come?

10. Give the common name for aerophones.

11. Give the common name for chordophones.

12. What was founded in 1876 for the purpose of performing Gilbert and Sullivan operettas?

13. A cappella, 'in church style', is what type of song?

14. In whose memory was the Royal Albert Hall opened in 1871?

1. What is the name given to a boating song, especially the type sung by gondoliers in Venice?

15. What is the science of sound called?

2. Which simple tune, often played by children, is known as 'cutlets waltz' in France and Germany?

16. With which instrument was George Formby associated?

3. What instrument did Sir Charles Wheatstone invent in 1824?

17. Bagpipes were known in Roman times. True or false?

18. What name, meaning 'fellowship' in Italian, was given to a society of musicians and poets in Florence around 1600?

19. In which century was the recorder, or English flute, first used?

20. To which family of musical instruments do the cor anglais and bassoon belong?

21. If a chord is played with the notes individually sounded, how is it described?

22. What name is given to a choir that can be divided in two, so that they can 'answer' one another when singing?

23. In what style would a barbershop quartet sing?

24. Which country's music would be played by a sarangi, a tabla or a shanai?

25. In which century were the operas *Norma*, *Otello* and *Lucia di Lammermoor* written?

1. One-upmanship was invented by which author?

2. What is the chemical symbol for lead?

3. Which country is the original home of the balalaika?

4. Who 'packed her trunk and said goodbye to the circus'?

5. What does the Latin term *tempus fugit* mean?

6. *The Naked Civil Servant* was the story of whose life?

7. Which party did Abraham Lincoln lead?

8. If you were prognathous, what facial feature would you have?

9. What would you do with a toque?

10. The four gospels of the *New Testament* appear in which order?

11. What is the capital of New South Wales in Australia?

12. In legend, King Midas had a gift that sounded valuable, but made life impossible. What was it?

13. Which top model did Richard Gere marry?

14. Which partnership wrote the music and lyrics for *The Sound of Music*?

15. Which element has the lowest boiling point?

16. Give the previous name of the country now called Malawi.

17. In what subjects did artist George Stubbs specialize?

18. Who said: 'Patriotism is the last refuge of a scoundrel'?

19. Which is the correct spelling of the following word: accomodate, acommodate or accommodate?

20. What is the name of the frog in *The Muppet Show*?

21. Hermit, spider and blue are types of which creature?

22. In Scotland, in which room of the house would you find a spurtle?

23. Which nation put the 'gang of four' on trial in the 1970s?

24. Doris Day sang *Secret Love* and *The Black Hills of Dakota* in which film?

25. What name is given to a show involving satirical and topical sketches and songs?

Answers to Quiz 3

Geography and Travel • North America

1. New England
2. Nevada
3. Navajo
4. 21
5. Calgary
6. Miami
7. Yellowstone
8. Florida Keys
9. Mockingbird
10. Lafayette Park
11. Rocky Mountains
12. San Francisco
13. Victoria
14. Hawaii
15. Anchorage
16. Banff
17. Canada
18. Texas
19. German
20. New Mexico
21. France
22. Mexico's
23. Ancient cliff dwellings
24. Ontario
25. 349 km (217 miles)

Popular Culture • Bond Books and Films

1. Shaken, not stirred
2. *Casino Royale*
3. Duran Duran
4. Cubby Broccoli
5. *Moonraker*
6. Blofeld
7. *Never Say Never Again*
8. *Dr No*
9. 'Q'
10. *The Man with the Golden Gun*
11. Dame Judi Dench
12. Jaws
13. Samantha Bond
14. Ian Fleming
15. David Niven
16. John Gardner
17. *Goldfinger*
18. Tee Hee
19. *On Her Majesty's Secret Service*
20. Kingsley Amis
21. Jane Seymour
22. *From Russia with Love*
23. Timothy Dalton
24. *The Spy Who Loved Me*
25. His hat

Indoors and Out • Fruit Harvest

1. China
2. Blackberry, loganberry and raspberry
3. One-year-old
4. Cherry
5. Deglet Noor
6. Columbus
7. Grapes
8. Mackerel
9. Florida
10. Ogen
11. Pawpaw
12. Slightly under-ripe
13. Blackcurrant
14. True
15. Banana
16. In the fridge
17. Granada
18. Its pungent smell
19. Pear
20. Its runners are inclined to 'stray'
21. New Zealand
22. India
23. Chocolate
24. Rose
25. Wet, peaty bogs

Past and Present • The Age of Expansion and Discovery

1. Portugal
2. Wood
3. Pacific
4. West Indies
5. Akbar
6. Kabuki
7. Aztec
8. Italian
9. Ming
10. Gregorian
11. Rebirth
12. Michelangelo
13. 1560s
14. New Zealand
15. A new system of map-making
16. Madrid
17. Fur
18. Singeing the King of Spain's beard
19. Playing bowls
20. Potato
21. Cape of Good Hope
22. Inca
23. The Reformation
24. James I
25. Harvard

Youth World • Monsters

1. Yeti
2. Vlad the Impaler
3. Trolls
4. Dragons
5. The Jabberwocky
6. Annihilus
7. Silver
8. Bigfoot
9. Ray Harryhausen
10. British Columbia
11. The Aborigines of Australia
12. Mr Hyde
13. Smaug
14. St Columba
15. Plesiosaur
16. Conan Doyle
17. Philistines
18. A giant squid
19. A giant marshmallow man
20. He was shot down by aircraft from the Empire State Building
21. Caddy
22. Sasquatch
23. Lady Arabella March
24. Brobdingnag
25. It was white with two heads

Famous Folk • Scientists

1. Black holes
2. The force of gravity
3. Ernest Rutherford
4. Nylon
5. Polio
6. DNA
7. Joseph Lister
8. Fahrenheit
9. Galileo
10. Liquid oxygen and liquid hydrogen
11. She shared it with her brother Pierre
12. Davy
13. Smallpox
14. Gelignite
15. Electricity and magnetism
16. Manhattan Project
17. Antibiotic
18. Space rockets
19. Eureka!
20. Photography
21. Thomas Telford
22. Pasteurization
23. The 'big bang' theory
24. The first television transmitter
25. Barnes Wallis

Sport and Leisure • Making Music

1. Barcarolle
2. Chopsticks
3. Concertina
4. Flue and Reed
5. Fortepiano
6. William Hogarth
7. Indonesia
8. A Japanese form of zither
9. Guitar
10. Wind instruments
11. Stringed instruments
12. D'Oyly Carte Opera Company
13. Unaccompanied
14. Queen Victoria's husband, Prince Albert
15. Acoustics
16. Ukelele
17. True
18. Camerata
19. 12th century
20. The oboe
21. Arpeggio
22. Double choir
23. Close harmony
24. India
25. 19th century

Pot Luck

1. Stephen Potter
2. Pb
3. Russia
4. Nellie the elephant
5. Time flies
6. Quentin Crisp
7. Republican
8. You would have a projecting jaw
9. Wear it
10. Matthew, Mark, Luke, John
11. Sydney
12. Everything he touched turned to gold
13. Cindy Crawford
14. Rogers and Hammerstein
15. Helium
16. Nyasaland
17. Horses
18. Dr Samuel Johnson
19. Accommodate
20. Kermit
21. Crab
22. Kitchen
23. China
24. Calamity Jane
25. Revue

4

1. Where in the world does the largest car and passenger ferry operate?

2. Steam locomotives need fuel, which is kept in a wagon next to the engine. What is the wagon called?

3. Where was the first elevated railway in the world, in the late 19th century?

4. In London it is the underground, in New York it is the subway. What is it in Paris?

5. Every cargo ship has a Plimsoll line. What is indicated when the water reaches that line?

6. When was the first Channel tunnel begun?

7. In the language of aircraft and flying, what is 'drag'?

8. In which country would you find the high-speed, tilting train called the Pendolino?

9. What is the world's largest airliner?

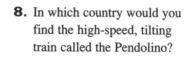

10. What 'first' in flight did Richard Branson and Per Lindstrand achieve in 1987?

11. Which country opened its first underground railway in 1904?

12. What was invented by Kirkpatrick MacMillan, a Scot, in about 1840?

13. The Blue Riband of the Atlantic, awarded to the liner making the fastest crossing of the Atlantic, was won by the *Queen Mary* on her maiden voyage in 1936. How fast was the crossing?

14. The Isle of Man TT motor-cycle race was established in 1907. What does TT stand for?

15. 'Big Boys', the largest and heaviest locomotives in the world, first appeared in 1941 on which railroad?

16. The *Cutty Sark*, one of the most famous tea clippers, was built in 1869. Where can it now be seen as a museum?

17. The Japanese underground employs burly, uniformed officials with white gloves. What is their job?

18. Murder on the *Orient Express*, the 1974 film starring Albert Finney, was based on whose novel?

19. Who designed the locomotive *Rocket* in 1829?

20. Where did the diesel engine get its name?

21. Which type of boat has underwater wings that develop lift in the water?

22. What was the name of the first nuclear-powered submarine launched by the USA in 1955?

23. Where is the world's steepest 'rack' railway?

24. When were wheeled vehicles first invented?

25. Which English 'character' played the publisher interested in the race to promote aviation in *Those Magnificent Men in their Flying Machines*?

Q 1

1. The modern illustration of Sagittarius is a bowman. How was this sign depicted in early forms of astrology?

2. What is the birthstone for those born under the sign of Leo?

3. Which are the fire signs?

4. According to the Chinese horoscope, 1996 is the year of what animal?

5. If you were born at the end of May, which sign would you belong to?

6. There is a beautiful set of 15th-century images on a famous clocktower in Venice. Where is the clocktower situated?

7. Which element governs the sign of Libra?

8. What zodiacal age are we about to enter, or have just entered?

9. Which sign has amethyst as a birthstone?

10. In early 1995 the Royal Astronomical Society announced that there should be 13 signs rather than 12. What did they call the extra sign?

11. Name the only sign not represented by a living creature.

12. If you were the strong, silent type, solid and steady, sometimes downright obstinate, what sign is most likely to be yours?

13. What are sigils?

14. Which sign do those born on 1 April belong to?

15. The emerald is the birthstone of which sign?

16. The sign of Virgo belongs to which element?

17. Today, Cancer is usually represented by the crab. How was it represented in early astrology?

18. How many signs does the Chinese horoscope have?

19. Pisces is usually represented by two fishes swimming in opposite directions. What is unusual about the fishes in the basilica church of San Miniato al Monte in Florence?

20. Which sign is represented by the goat?

21. Two of the water signs are Cancer and Scorpio. What is the third?

22. In which cathedral is the oldest zodiac in England to be found?

23. In reading the zodiac, what is the 'cusp'?

24. If you are versatile, changeable and impatient, with two sides to

your personality and able to do two things at once, you were probably born under what sign?

25. The 12 divisions of the Zodiac in current use were established by about 500BC. How many signs did the old Babylonian zodiac have?

1. Which type of fat can increase the cholesterol level in blood?

2. How many amino acids is it essential for adults to obtain from food?

3. How many amino acids is it essential for children to obtain from food?

4. Insulin controls the amount of sugar in the blood. Which organ produces insulin?

5. What name is given to the use of essential oils on the skin for a wide range of therapeutic effects?

6. Mesomorphs are well-muscled athletic people. What are ectomorphs?

7. What word describes plump people with round heads and pear-shaped bodies?

8. Which organ would a doctor examine with an otoscope?

9. Many people are allergic to tartrazine. What is it?

10. NPT is the length of time skin can stay in the sun without burning. What do the initials stand for?

11. What diet, which triples the average protein intake and cuts fat and carbohydrates, was invented by New York specialist Dr H. Tarnower?

12. Which gland produces the hormones that control the body's metabolism?

13. What would an exfoliating face pack do to your skin?

14. What name is given to the fungus infection that affects the skin between the toes?

15. Ketosis would result from what inadequacy in the diet?

16. When making up, at what stage should you apply blusher?

17. What is the normal body temperature?

18. The Beverly Hills diet was developed by Judy Mazel in California. What is it based on?

19. Haematology is concerned with which area of medicine?

20. Why is it important that a pregnant woman should not catch rubella?

21. What treatment is based on the idea that there are energy channels in the feet that relate to every organ and function of the body?

22. Many people suffer from dry or oily hair. What is combination hair?

23. A dialysis machine replaces the functioning of which organs?

24. What is the Alexander technique famous for improving as a result of its therapies?

25. Ophthalmology is concerned with which area of the body?

1. Which religious leader looked over the Salt Lake Valley in 1847 and announced 'this is the place'?

2. The Maronites are the largest religious group in the Lebanon. Which religion do they belong to?

3. Who was the religious leader who returned to Iran from exile in 1979 and described the USA as the 'great Satan'?

4. The Guru Granth Sahib, or Adi Granth, is the holy book of which religion?

5. In which country did Buddhism originate?

6. How did Protestantism get its name?

7. For Hindus who is the Supreme Being?

8. Who is the spiritual leader of Tibet, enthroned at the age of five and forced to leave the country after the Chinese invaded?

9. Desmond Tutu is the Anglican archbishop of which South African town?

10. What are the two main Muslim sects?

11. Which faith was founded in the late 1850s by Baha'u'Ullah and is characterized by the absence of priests or public rituals?

12. In what language was the New Testament of the Bible originally written?

13. In which decade were women priests authorized in the USA?

14. Which country did Pope John Paul II visit in early 1995 to receive a rapturous welcome?

15. Which religious group was founded by George Fox in the 17th century?

16. The followers of which religion believe that Haile Selassie of Ethiopia was the Messiah?

17. In Buddhism what is the name given to the final goal of human endeavour?

18. What type of churches are the Elim Church and the Assemblies of God?

19. In Confucianism, the origin of things is seen as the union of which principles?

20. Who was the first Archbishop of Canterbury?

21. Where did the Prophet Muhammad live and die after he fled from Mecca, making it a holy city second only to Mecca?

22. The first five books of the Hebrew Bible are contained in what Jewish holy book?

23. Where did John Bunyan write *Pilgrim's Progress*, about a religious journey through life?

24. William Booth founded the Salvation Army in 1865. To which religious sect did he originally belong?

25. Liberal Judaism goes further than Reform Judaism in trying to adapt the faith to the modern world. What is the other name given to this movement?

1. In what year did Morris and Rose Michtom sell the first teddy bears, named after President Theodore Roosevelt?

2. In which decade of the 20th century did machine-washable teddies appear?

3. Which bear is called 'the Lord of the Arctic'?

4. The name 'koala' comes from the Aboriginal 'no drink'. Why is the koala so called?

5. Where does the koala bear usually sleep?

6. Who wrote about the 'bear of little brain'?

7. Name the teddy bear who is Sebastian Flyte's constant companion in Evelyn Waugh's *Brideshead Revisited*?

8. The only South American bear is the Andean bear, which has white circles round its eyes. What is its popular name?

9. How do bears differ in their eating habits from other carnivores?

10. Name the bear from *The Muppet Show*.

11. The first teddy bear in space orbited the earth in Salyut 6. What was its name?

12. What is the favourite food of the sloth bear, or Indian bear?

13. According to the song, which American hero 'killed him a bear when he was only three'?

14. Who stole the porridge belonging to the three bears?

15. The commonest type of bear is the brown bear. How long do the brown bear cubs stay with their mother?

16. What sport did 'Bear' Bryant coach?

17. Brer Bear is a character in the stories of Uncle Remus, the old cotton-plantation slave. Who wrote the stories?

18. Archibald Ormsby Gore was the much-loved bear of which famous poet?

19. *Bear Island* was a 1980 film starring Donald Sutherland and Vanessa Redgrave. On which author's adventure novel was it based?

20. The sun bear, or Malayan bear, feeds at night. How and where does it spend its days?

21. The grizzly bear, now found mainly in northern Canada, is the north American race of which type of bear?

22. Which fictional bear lived in a bear pit in Berne, Switzerland?

23. What name is given to the hobby of collecting teddy bears?

24. The American black bear is the best known of the black bears. In which month are the cubs usually born?

25. Where did Paddington Bear come from?

Q 21

3. Which American chat show hostess appeared in the movie *The Color Purple*?

4. Who became minister and then prime minister?

5. Which English actress stars as a 'medicine woman'?

6. Name the character played by David Hasselhof in *Baywatch*.

7. Who played JFK in *Kennedy*?

8. Kevin Whately plays Sergeant Lewis. Whose trusty sidekick is he?

9. At the beginning of each episode of *Fame*, which actress said: 'You want fame. Well, fame costs and right here's where you start paying'?

10. What type of show is presented by Sally Jessy Raphael, Vanessa and Donahue?

11. Which character is played by Corbin Bernsen in *LA Law*?

12. Name the son of an actor father who patrolled the streets of San Francisco with Karl Malden.

13. In which series does David Jason play an unconventional policeman?

14. Name the first Dr Who.

1. Who are Sky, Hawk, Nightshade, Jet and Sabre?

2. Alan Alda won three awards in different categories for *MASH*. What were the categories?

15. Who has been investigating the private life of plants?

16. Which irascible pensioner is played by Richard Wilson in *One Foot in the Grave*?

17. In *The Buccaneers*, who played the governess, Miss Testvalley?

18. Which actor from *LA Law* joined the precinct in *NYPD Blue* as David Caruso left?

19. Who plays Dr Mark Greene in *ER*?

20. In which store did Miss Brahms, played by Wendy Richard, work?

21. Who starred with Bill Cosby in *I Spy*?

22. In which classic series did Clint Eastwood play Rowdy Yates?

23. Who wrote *Only Victims*, about the activities of the Un-American Activities Committee?

24. Name the playwright husband of actress Maureen Lippman.

25. Which actor played Orry Main in the mini-series *North and South*?

75

1. In what year did Steve Davis win his first world title in snooker?

2. Anthony Nesty of Surinam was in 1988 the first Olympic gold medallist from his country. What other distinction did he have at this Olympics?

3. Who knocked out Mike Tyson to take the world heavyweight crown in 1990, causing a major upset in boxing history?

4. Red Rum won the Grand National three times. Who was his trainer?

5. At the Berlin Olympics in 1936, black athlete Jesse Owens won the 100 metres, 200 metres and long jump. Who stormed out of the stadium in disgust?

6. What forced Nigel Mansell out of the 1986 Australian Grand Prix, robbing him of the world title?

7. What was remarkable about the men's 100 metre final at the World Championships in Tokyo in 1991?

8. What tragedy overtook 'Busby's Babies' in 1978?

9. Who scored a World Cup Final record of five goals in one game when Russia beat Cameroons 6-1 in June 1994?

10. After the 1904 Olympic marathon the winner, Fred Lorz, was banned for life by the US Amateur Athletic Union. Why?

11. When was the first England v Australia Test match played?

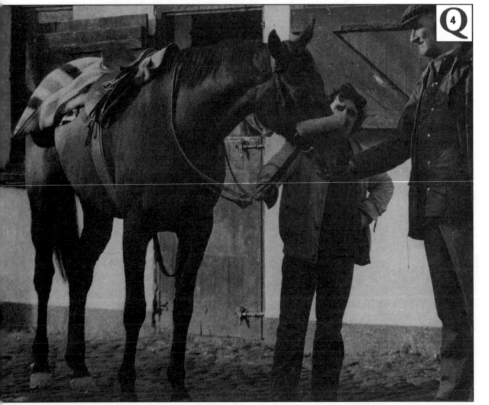

12. Who was the first gymnast in Olympic history to be awarded a perfect score, in the 1976 Games?

13. In the 1986 World Cup, Maradonna scored with what appeared to be a handball. What did he call this?

14. Who was the first footballer to be knighted?

15. In which year was the Olympic flame introduced to the modern games?

16. Who regained the World Heavyweight Boxing Championship twice?

17. Which motor racing star won the World Drivers' Championship five times in the 1950s?

18. Which pop-star raced a yacht named *Drum*?

19. In which event did Britain's Linford Christie win an Olympic gold in Barcelona?

20. In 1983, who scored a touchdown after the longest run from scrimmage in American football?

21. Who won the 5,000 metres, the 10,000 metres and also the Marathon in the 1952 Olympics?

22. Which Russian gymnast won many hearts in the 1972 Olympics with her charismatic performance on balance beam and floor exercise?

23. In 1988 the tallest gold medallist yet recorded competed in the Olympic Games in what sport?

24. In which sport did Gert Fredriksson win six Olympic gold medals?

25. Vitaly Scherbo won six golds at the 1992 Olympics representing the Commonwealth of Independent States in which sport?

Q16

1. In which American state is the Grand Canyon?

2. What would you do with grissini?

3. Noah's ark came to rest on which mountain?

4. By what name is dyspepia usually known?

5. Which is the world's warmest sea?

6. To which group of painters do Monet, Sisley and Pisarro belong?

7. In which Orwell novel were some of the characters 'more equal than others'?

8. According to the saying, who makes the best gamekeeper?

9. What does an anti-coagulant drug do?

10. Who killed Martin Luther King in 1968?

11. Name the dramatist who wrote *Entertaining Mr Sloane* and *Loot*?

12. What type of wine is Asti Spumante?

13. In which sport would you hear of roundhouse, knuckler and outcurve?

14. What do the letters MGM stand for?

15. The songs 'You'll Never Walk Alone' and 'If I Loved You' come from which musical?

Q 18

16. Who designed Madonna's famous pointed corset?

17. Bibliomania is a compulsive desire for what?

18. Which film first teamed Ginger Rogers and Fred Astaire?

19. Dachshunds were bred as hunting dogs in Germany. What did they hunt?

20. In Australia, you might have the opportunity of seeing a corroboree. What is it?

21. Two of the types of particle present in an atom are proton and neutron. What is the third?

22. Cochise and Geronimo were chiefs of which Native American tribe?

23. What name was given to the Hindu custom whereby a widow would throw herself on the funeral pyre?

24. Inflammable means easily set on fire. What does flammable mean?

25. If you were reading Nagel and Baedeker what would you be planning?

Geography and Travel • Air, Land and Sea

1. Between Stockholm in Sweden and Helsinki in Finland
2. A tender
3. New York
4. Metro
5. The ship is fully loaded
6. 1877
7. Air resistance
8. Italy
9. Boeing 747
10. The first transatlantic crossing by hot-air balloon
11. USA
12. The first pedal-bicycle
13. Four days
14. Tourist Trophy
15. Union Pacific
16. Greenwich, London
17. To push passengers into crowded trains
18. Agatha Christie's
19. George Stephenson
20. From its pioneer, Dr Rudolf Diesel
21. Hydrofoil
22. Nautilus
23. Switzerland
24. About 3000BC
25. Robert Morley

Popular Culture • Signs of the Zodiac

1. A centaur drawing a bow
2. Sapphire
3. Aries, Leo and Sagittarius
4. The rat
5. Gemini
6. St Mark's Square
7. Air
8. Aquarius
9. Sagittarius
10. Ophiuchus
11. Libra
12. Taurus
13. The graphic symbols used to represent the signs
14. Aries
15. Cancer
16. Earth
17. The crayfish
18. 12
19. They swim in parallel
20. Capricorn
21. Pisces
22. Canterbury
23. The first and last days of the sign period
24. Gemini
25. 18

Indoors and Out • Health and Beauty

1. Saturated fat
2. Eight
3. 10
4. Pancreas
5. Aromatherapy
6. Naturally slender people
7. Endomorphs
8. Ear
9. A dye that produces a yellow colour
10. Natural Protection Time
11. Scarsdale diet
12. Thyroid
13. Remove the dead skin cells
14. Athlete's foot
15. Too low carbohydrate
16. After foundation and powder
17. 37°C (98.5°F)
18. Fruit
19. Diseases of the blood
20. It can cause defects in the unborn child
21. Reflexology
22. Oily at the scalp and dry at the ends
23. Kidneys
24. Posture
25. Eyes

Past and Present • Religious Affairs

1. Brigham Young
2. Christian
3. Ayatollah Khomeini
4. Sikh
5. India
6. From the protest of Luther and other church reformers
7. Brahma
8. Dalai Lama
9. Cape Town
10. Sunni and Shi'ite
11. Baha'i
12. Greek
13. 1970s
14. Philippines
15. Society of Friends or Quakers
16. Rastafarian
17. Nirvana
18. Pentecostal
19. Yin and yang; passive and active
20. St Augustine
21. Medina
22. Torah
23. In prison
24. Methodist
25. Reconstructionism

Youth World • Bears

1. 1903
2. 1950s
3. Polar bear
4. It gets all the moisture it needs from its diet of eucalyptus leaves
5. In the fork of a tree
6. A. A. Milne
7. Aloysius
8. Spectacled bear
9. They eat fruit and honey as well as meat and fish
10. Fozzie
11. Mishka
12. Termites
13. Davy Crockett
14. Goldilocks
15. Three years
16. American football
17. Joel Chandler Harris
18. John Betjeman
19. Alistair McLean
20. Sleeping high in a nest of twigs and branches
21. Brown bear
22. Mary Plain
23. Arctophily
24. January
25. Darkest Peru

Famous Folk • TV Stars

1. *Gladiators*
2. Actor, director, writer
3. Oprah Winfrey
4. Paul Eddington as Jim Hacker
5. Jane Seymour
6. Mitch Buchannon
7. Martin Sheen
8. Inspector Morse
9. Debbie Allen
10. Chat shows
11. Arnie Becker
12. Michael Douglas
13. *A Touch of Frost*
14. William Hartnell
15. David Attenborough
16. Victor Meldrew
17. Cherie Lunghi
18. Jimmy Smits
19. Anthony Edwards
20. Grace Bros
21. Robert Culp
22. *Rawhide*
23. Robert Vaughn
24. Jack Rosenthal
25. Patrick Swayze

Sport and Leisure • Sporting Moments

1. 1981
2. He was the first black swimmer to win an Olympic event
3. James 'Buster' Douglas
4. Donald 'Ginger' McCain
5. Adolf Hitler
6. An exploding tyre
7. It produced four of the fastest times ever recorded in the event
8. The Munich air crash
9. Oleg Salenko
10. He was taken part of the way by car
11. 1877
12. Nadia Comaneci
13. 'The hand of God'
14. Stanley Matthews
15. 1928
16. Muhammad Ali
17. Juan Fangio
18. Simon Le Bon
19. Men's 100 metres
20. Tony Dorsett
21. Emil Zatopek
22. Olga Korbut
23. Basketball
24. Canoe racing
25. Gymnastics

Pot Luck

1. Arizona
2. Eat them
3. Ararat
4. Indigestion
5. Red Sea
6. Impressionist
7. *Animal Farm*
8. An old poacher
9. It stops blood clotting
10. James Earl Ray
11. Joe Orton
12. Sparkling
13. Baseball
14. Metro-Goldwyn-Mayer
15. *Carousel*
16. Jean Paul Gaultier
17. Books
18. *Flying Down To Rio*
19. Badgers
20. An Aboriginal dance ceremony
21. Electron
22. Apache
23. Suttee
24. The same: easily set on fire
25. Travel

1. Which Russian fortress, incorporating palaces and churches, became the seat of modern government?

2. Where would you find the Palace of Nurturing the Heart, the Palace of Heavenly Purity and the Palace of Peaceful Longevity?

3. The Palace of Versailles was built by which French king?

4. Which 15th-century palace in Florence houses the Palatine Gallery, with its collections of paintings made by the Medici princes in the 17th and 18th centuries?

5. Name the romantic poet who lived in Dove Cottage and Rydal Mount in the English Lake District.

6. On which famous river would you find the Cat and Mouse Castles?

7. Many plantation homes survive in the deep south of the US. What was the name of the O'Hara family home in *Gone with the Wind*?

8. The palace of Schönbrunn, built between 1696 and 1713, was the summer home of which royal house?

9. What English name is usually given to the Palazzo Ducale in Venice?

10. The Treaty House on the shore of the Bay of Islands is important in the history of New Zealand. Whose representatives signed the Treaty of Waitangi in 1840?

11. Whitehall, once the opulent home of Henry Morrison Flagler, is in Palm Beach, Florida. In what business did Flagler make his millions?

12. Neuschwanstein, the fairytale castle built by King Ludwig II, is one of Germany's top tourist attractions. In which part of Germany is it located?

13. Which castle, belonging to the English Crown for over 900 years, is open to the public again, following a disastrous fire?

14. The Winter Palace in St Petersburg, now Russia's Hermitage Museum, was built in the mid-18th century in what architectural style?

15. A 1964 film starring Peter Ustinov and Melina Mercouri told the story of jewel thieves planning a robbery at Istanbul's 15th-century palace. What is its name?

16. In which eastern European city would you find the Palais Palffy, Palais Kolovrat and Palais Furstenburg, all with elegant 18th-century facades?

17. Vita Sackville-West and Sir Harold Nicholson made a famous garden in the grounds of Sissinghurst Castle. In which English county is Sissinghurst?

18. Switzerland's Chateau de Chillon, the 13th-century castle with grim dungeons, inspired which poet to write *The Prison of Chillon*?

19. The Palazzo Vecchio, once the ducal palace and new city hall, is the symbol of Florence. What is its other name?

20. Cairo's sumptuous Manial Palace, built in 1901 by a royal prince, is in which part of the city?

21. Anna Leonowens, an English governess whose story inspired a musical show and two films, was a governess to royal children in the Grand Palace in which city?

22. Spain's Alhambra has a grove of great elms, called the Alameda, in the grounds. Which British statesman had them planted during the Peninsular War?

23. Colonial Williamsburg is America's unique restoration project, re-creating an 18th-century town. In which state is Williamsburg?

24. Holyrood House, in Edinburgh, is the official Scottish residence of Queen Elizabeth II. What does the name mean?

25. In which country is the Sacred Valley of the Incas, with its terraced fortress of Ollantytambo?

1. Which band was named after a character in the film *Barbarella*?

2. How did Buddy Holly die?

3. Matt Sorum joined Guns 'n' Roses from which group?

4. Which Michael Jackson album sold 41 million copies?

5. George Michael went on to a number of solo hits after splitting from Andrew Ridgeley in 1986. What was the duo called?

6. Who won Grammy awards for 'Saving All My Love For You' and 'I Wanna Dance with Somebody' and was chosen to sing America's Olympic anthem 'One Moment in Time' in 1988?

7. Soca is Caribbean music. How does it get its name?

8. *Dark Side of the Moon* sold 10 million copies worldwide. Which group recorded the album?

9. Which rock band, among the earliest fronted by a woman, recorded the albums *Brigade*, *Bad Animals* and *Dreamboat Annie*?

10. Whose only hit was 'Shaddup Your Face'?

11. Which group had a hit with 'Love is All Around' in 1994?

12. Name the pop star who played the leader of a teenage gang in the film *Quadrophenia*?

13. What was the debut single for Take That, securing them a major record contract with RCA?

14. 'Touch Me in the Morning' was a hit for which singer?

15. Who is nicknamed 'His Royal Badness'?

16. Which rock star, one of the highest paid performers of the 1980s, married top model Christie Brinkley?

17. Whose first album was *Are You Experienced*?

18. What type of music is salsa, made popular by Puerto Ricans in New York in the 1980s?

19. Who won the 1990 BRITS award for Top British Group and returned it, saying that the awards show was used to promote Margaret Thatcher?

20. The Pet Shop Boys were formed in 1981. Name them.

21. What was the former name of the group Led Zeppelin?

22. Which teen pop group had seven top 10 singles in the UK in 1990, the first time an American group had achieved this?

23. Who created the 'wall of sound' in the mid-1960s?

24. How many albums does an artist have to sell to go platinum?

25. What type of music would headbangers listen to?

Q 8

1. Which country has the largest area under vine?

2. On a German wine label, what would 'trocken' mean?

3. In one method of red winemaking, the grapes are fermented in bunches under a layer of carbon dioxide instead of being crushed. What is this method called?

4. If grapes are harvested slightly late, what happens to their flavour?

5. Which country is the largest wine producer in South America?

6. From 1920 to 1933 alcohol was banned in America. What was this era called?

7. Where does Marsala come from?

8. What colour wine is produced by Merlot and Syrah grapes?

9. Is better wine produced if it is aged in new oak barrels or old?

10. Which is the lightest style of sherry?

11. Which is the fullest and richest style of sherry?

12. Besides gin, what are the ingredients of a White Lady cocktail?

13. An old enemy of the vine is phylloxera. What is it?

14. A new enemy of the vine is eutypia dieback. What is it?

15. What name is given to the German wine made from grapes that have been left on the vine over winter?

16. Where are the Sonoma and Napa Valley wine-growing areas?

17. If a wine was described as aggressive, what would it be?

18. Where does the name whisky come from?

19. The south of France, because of its willingness to experiment, is known as what?

20. Hungary has the oldest wine tradition in Eastern Europe. Which is its most famous wine?

21. What did the Rev. Elijah Craig start distilling in Georgetown, Virginia in 1789?

22. In Germany, what is supposed to be the equivalent of the French 'vin de pays'?

23. What is the equivalent of the French 'vin de pays' in Spanish wine?

24. In which decade did the white wine boom begin for Australian producers?

25. The cocktail Yankee Invigorator contains brandy, port, sugar, egg and what else?

Q16

4. What was unusual about the crowning of Hatshepsut, who reigned Egypt for 20 years?

5. Who was the Egyptian god of the dead?

6. The main measurement in Egypt was the cubit. How long was a cubit?

7. Which king built the great temple of Karnak, still to be seen near Luxor in Egypt?

8. Which of the seven wonders of the ancient world was at Ephesus?

9. What ancient civilization flourished in Crete?

10. In 1500 BC there was a volcanic eruption on an island near Crete. Some historians believe that it did so much damage that the great civilization never recovered. Name the island.

11. Into how many tribes were the Israelites divided?

12. Which race dominated the Israelites in Palestine for nearly 200 years?

13. After the death of King Solomon the Israelite kingdom was split in two. Israel had its capital at Shechem. Where was Judah's capital?

14. What is an ankh?

15. Which Greek poet told the story of the Trojan war?

1. Between which two rivers was the land of Mesopotamia?

2. Among which people do we find the first evidence of the use of wheels?

3. Where did the Vikings believe their warriors were taken after death?

16. The sight of a Viking ship would have struck fear into the hearts of the Scots or English in early days. How were these ships propelled?

17. Where did the Greeks believe the souls of the wicked would go to suffer eternal punishment?

18. Which empire was conquered by Alexander the Great between 334 BC and 331 BC?

19. Who was the most important god of the Vikings?

20. Which of the seven wonders of the ancient world stood at Rhodes?

21. The ancient Olypmpic Games were started in 776 BC. How often did they take place?

22. Why did the ancient Olympic Games end in 395 BC?

23. Civil war in the Roman Republic culminated in 63 BC in the First Triumvirate under Caesar, Crassus and which third leader?

24. Egyptian gods were often identified with animals – for instance, Anubis with the jackal and Sekmet with the lioness. With which animal was Horus identified?

25. In the centre of a Roman town there was an open area, surrounded by the buildings of government. What was it called?

Q18

5. In the Roald Dahl book, who runs a chocolate factory?

6. Which boys' hero has friends called Algy Lacy and Ginger Hebblethwaite?

7. What is the real name of super heroine Wonder Woman?

8. Who wrote the children's novel *Chitty Chitty Bang Bang*?

9. In *Alice in Wonderland*, what did the Queen of Hearts yell at those who annoyed her?

10. Which little girl would get her own way by threatening to scream and scream until she was sick?

11. *National Velvet* was originally a novel by Enid Bagnold. Who played Velvet in the 1944 film?

1. Robin Williams plays Mrs Doubtfire in the film of that name. Who wrote the book on which it is based?

2. In which book does Bilbo Baggins first appear?

3. What nationality was Little Lord Fauntleroy?

4. Which character, with friends including Mole and Rat, has a passion for fast cars?

12. Which elephant first appeared in a book by Jean de Brunhoff, published in France in 1931?

13. In *The Jungle Book*, who is the boy raised in the Indian forests?

14. The lead strip of the British *Eagle* comic featured which heroic space pilot?

15. What word does Billy Batson need to say to transform himself into Captain Marvel?

16. Which doctor lives in Puddleby-on-the-Marsh and talks to animals?

17. Name the novel in which Mary Lennox becomes friends with Dickon and Colin.

18. Which comic strip heroine did Jane Fonda play in a 1964 film?

19. Who wrote about Noddy and Big-Ears?

20. In which American state did Tom Sawyer and Huckleberry Finn have their adventures?

21. Tintin, red-haired cub reporter, first appeared in comic strips in the 1920s and later in an animated TV series and two films. In which country was he invented?

22. A race of pixie-like creatures became popular throughout Europe from the 1960s onwards after they appeared in a Belgian comic-strip and were used to sell a wide variety of merchandise. In French they were 'Les Schtroumpfs'. Who are they in English?

23. In an American novel by Jean Webster, orphaned Judy Abbott writes a series of letters to an unknown benefactor and eventually meets and falls in love with him. What is her nickname for him?

24. Who is the young narrator of Robert Louis Stevenson's novel *Treasure Island*?

25. Who are Homily, Pod and little Arriety?

1. When T. E. Lawrence returned from Arabia, he tried to become anonymous. Give either of the false names he used.

2. The French motor racing champion of 1985, 1986 and 1989 was nicknamed 'The Professor'. Who was he?

3. What is Madonna's real first name?

4. Eric and Ernie took the names Morecambe and Wise because their own surnames were too long for the billboards. What were they?

5. Which boxer was known as Smokin' Joe?

6. The novels of Mary Ann Evans became famous in the 19th century and are classics today. What name did Mary Ann Evans write under?

7. What is pop star Sting's real name?

8. By what name is Peter Sutcliffe better known?

9. Big Daddy and Giant Haystacks are both wrestlers. Which one's real name is Shirley Crabtree?

10. Zsa Zsa Gabor changed only her first name. What was it originally?

11. Under what name is sportsman Edson Arantes do Nascimento better known?

Q 3

14. Give the real name of rock star Adam Ant.

15. Nikolai Poliakov became which well-known circus performer?

16. What name does Stephen Judkins use?

17. Which prolific Victorian novelist was known as 'Boz'?

18. US singer, songwriter and record producer William Robinson exchanged his first name for what nickname?

19. Born in 1914 as Joseph Barrow, he became known as the 'Brown Bomber'. Who was he?

20. Doris Kappelhoff changed only her last name. What did she choose?

21. Which boxer was known as the Manassa Mauler?

22. In 1925 MGM ran a contest to find a new name for Lucille Le Sueur. What did they decide on?

23. John Wayne Gacy was one of America's most sadistic mass murderers. What was he often called?

24. Which US baseball player was known as the Georgia Peach?

25. During World War II, how was William Joyce better known?

12. Singer Arnold Dorsey changed his name and never looked back. What name does he use now?

13. What are the first names of novelist P. D. James?

1. When petrol-powered vehicles first replaced those drawn by horses, what were they called?

2. The body of a car is now built in one unit. The body used to be mounted on a wood or metal structure. What was it called?

3. Which famous film star is the joint owner of an Indy car racing team?

4. Where is the Italian Grand Prix held?

5. Cars usually race with 'slicks'. What are they?

6. In drag racing a series of lamps flash a countdown sequence to the start. What are the lamps called?

7. What colour were all Model T Fords?

8. What type of car is the Impact, produced by General Motors?

9. Ayrton Senna had his first Brazilian Grand Prix win in 1985. What nationality was he?

10. Which country do you associate with the production of Renault cars?

11. In the Belgian Grand Prix of 1994 which driver was disqualified, giving Damon Hill the victory?

12. Thorpe and Salter made the first car speedometer in 1910. What speeds did it cover?

13. At a race meeting, what does a white flag mean?

14. At a race meeting, what warning does a red and yellow striped flag give?

15. Which British father and son both held the land speed record?

16. Championship Auto Racing Teams (CART) make the rules for which type of racing?

17. Which driver's racing career ended with a serious accident in Indianapolis in 1992, when he suffered multiple leg injuries?

18. The first Grand Prix World Championship was held in 1950. Who won?

19. What does a differential gear enable the wheels of a car to do?

20. Formula One cars must weigh a minimum of 500 kg. What is the minimum for Indy cars?

21. Name the father of Formula One star Damon Hill.

22. Which country do you associate with the manufacture of Nissan cars?

23. Who was the first posthumous world champion?

24. Who won the 1995 Formula One driver's title?

25. On a wet road, a tyre may lose its grip and ride on a film of water so that the driver loses control. What is this called?

1. In the Bible, who is turned into a pillar of salt?

2. How many sides has a prism?

3. In Britain it is called a truncheon. What is it called in America?

4. With which song did Abba win the European Song Contest?

5. Pastrami is a highly seasoned type of what?

6. In which English county are Winston Graham's Poldark novels set?

7. What is another name for the linden tree?

8. Who was shot as he left the Washington Hilton in 1981?

9. Which TV series had a character called Potsie?

10. What do the author Thackeray's initials, W. M., stand for?

11. In which country did Father's Day first become a day for cards and presents?

12. Which painter portrayed the life of 19th-century Paris bars and music halls?

13. Imran Khan is a famous cricketer. Which country does he come from?

14. Who went to sea in a beautiful pea-green boat?

15. What blood relation was Prince Albert to Queen Victoria?

16. If a Native American tribe used 'wampum' as currency, what would they be paying with?

17. The following are three American Presidents assassinated while in office: Lincoln, McKinley and Kennedy. Name the fourth.

18. What did the 'lolly ladies' do in English theatres?

19. Soyuz is a name given to Russian spacecraft. What does it mean?

20. The largest lake in Africa is Lake Victoria. Which countries is it bounded by?

21. In the song, how long is Campdown race track?

22. Give the common name for the trachea.

23. What is the highest British decoration for bravery?

24. In the 18th century, what sort of young man would be called a 'macaroni'?

25. The film *Midnight Express* was about a young American's experiences in prison in which country?

Geography and Travel • Houses and Palaces

1. The Kremlin
2. The Forbidden City, Beijing
3. Louis XIV
4. Pitti Palace
5. William Wordsworth
6. Rhine
7. Tara
8. Hapsburgs
9. Doge's Palace
10. Representatives of the Maoris and the British government
11. Railroads
12. Bavarian Alps
13. Windsor Castle
14. Baroque
15. *Topkapi*
16. Prague
17. Kent
18. Lord Byron
19. Palazzo della Signoria
20. Roda Island
21. Bangkok
22. Duke of Wellington
23. Virginia
24. Holy Cross
25. Peru

Popular Culture • Rock and Pop

1. Duran Duran
2. Air crash
3. The Cult
4. *Thriller*
5. Wham!
6. Whitney Houston
7. It is a mixture of soul and calypso
8. Pink Floyd
9. Heart
10. Joe Dolce
11. Wet Wet Wet
12. Sting
13. 'Do What You Like'
14. Diana Ross
15. Prince
16. Billy Joel
17. Jimi Hendrix
18. Latin big band dance music
19. Five Young Cannibals
20. Neil Tennant and Chris Lowe
21. The Yarbirds
22. New Kids on the Block
23. Phil Spector
24. One million
25. Heavy metal

Indoors and Out • Wines and Spirits

1. Spain
2. Dry
3. Carbonic maceration
4. The acidity will drop
5. Argentina
6. Prohibition
7. Sicily
8. Red
9. New
10. Manzanilla
11. Olorosa
12. Lemon juice and Cointreau
13. An aphid
14. A fungus
15. Eiswein
16. California
17. Young, or unmellowed older wine
18. The Gaelic, uisge beatha
19. The new California
20. Tokay
21. Bourbon
22. Landwein
23. Vino de la tierra
24. 1970s
25. Coffee

Past and Present • Early Civilizations

1. Tigris and Euphrates
2. Sumerians
3. Valhalla
4. She was crowned king, not queen; rulers had to be considered male
5. Osiris
6. The distance from elbow to fingertip
7. Rameses II
8. Temple of Artemis
9. Minoan
10. Thíra or Santoríni
11. Twelve
12. Philistines
13. Jerusalem
14. An Egyptian amulet worn as a charm
15. Homer
16. By both oars and sails
17. Tartarus
18. Persian
19. Odin
20. Colossus
21. Every four years
22. Olympia was destroyed by earthquake
23. Pompey
24. Falcon
25. Forum

Youth World • Books and Comics

1. Anne Fine
2. *The Hobbit*
3. American
4. Toad
5. Willie Wonka
6. Biggles
7. Diana Prince
8. Ian Fleming
9. 'Off with his head!'
10. Violet Elizabeth Bott
11. Elizabeth Taylor
12. Barbar
13. Mowgli
14. Dan Dare
15. Shazam
16. Dr Dolittle
17. *The Secret Garden*
18. Barbarella
19. Enid Blyton
20. Mississippi
21. Belgium
22. Smurfs
23. Daddy Long-Legs
24. Jim Hawkins
25. The Borrowers

Famous Folk • True Identity

1. Ross and Shaw
2. Alain Prost
3. Madonna
4. Bartholomew and Wiseman
5. Joe Frazier
6. George Eliot
7. Gordon Sumner
8. The Yorkshire Ripper
9. Big Daddy
10. Sari
11. Pelé
12. Engelbert Humperdinck
13. Phyllis Dorothy
14. Stuart Goddard
15. Coco the Clown
16. Stevie Wonder
17. Charles Dickens
18. Smokey
19. Joe Louis
20. Day
21. Jack Dempsey
22. Joan Crawford
23. The Killer Clown
24. Ty Cobb
25. Lord Haw-Haw

Sport and Leisure • Cars and Driving

1. Horseless carriages
2. Chassis
3. Paul Newman
4. Monza
5. Smooth tyres with no tread
6. Christmas tree
7. Black
8. It runs on electricity
9. Brazilian
10. France
11. Michael Schumacher
12. 0–35 mph
13. Ambulance or rescue vehicles on the track
14. Slippery surface
15. Michael and Donald Campbell
16. Indy car
17. Nelson Picquet
18. Guiseppe Farina
19. Rotate at different speeds round corners
20. 703 kg
21. Graham Hill
22. Japan
23. Jochen Rindt
24. Michael Schumacher
25. Aquaplaning

Pot Luck

1. Lot's wife
2. Five
3. Night-stick
4. 'Waterloo'
5. Beef
6. Cornwall
7. Lime
8. President Reagan
9. *Happy Days*
10. William Makepeace
11. USA
12. Toulouse-Lautrec
13. Pakistan
14. The owl and the pussycat
15. First cousin
16. Beads made of shells
17. Garfield
18. They sold oranges
19. Union
20. Kenya, Uganda, Tanzania
21. Five miles
22. Windpipe
23. Victoria Cross
24. He would be a dandy, wearing fashionable clothes from the continent
25. Turkey

QUIZ

6

1. If a volcano is neither active nor extinct, what is it?

2. Rock made of coarse sand is called sandstone. What is rock made from layers of thin mud and clay called?

3. Where would you find a delta?

4. What type of mountains are the Himalayas?

5. The Richter scale measures the magnitude of an earthquake. What does the Mercalli scale measure?

6. What is another name for a limestone landscape?

7. The bulk of the island of Tenerife is one volcanic mountain. Name the mountain.

8. On the ground of the rainforest, there is a layer of rotting leaves and vegetation. What is it called?

9. Which is the world's largest volcanic crater?

10. How much of an iceberg is submerged?

11. What name is given to rocks formed from other rocks changed in some way, usually by heat or pressure?

12. Which is the longest mountain range in North America?

13. What are the world's three main fossil fuels?

14. In the tundra regions, the soil and often the bedrock is permanently frozen. What is this called?

15. What type of valleys are those formed by land subsiding between two parallel faults?

16. The chain of volcanic activity around the Pacific Ocean is called what?

17. What name is given to the continuous action of waves on the shore whereby sand and shingle are moved along the beach?

18. In 1883 Krakatoa was the greatest volcanic explosion in modern times. Where was Krakatoa?

19. What is the tallest type of grass?

20. The Vinson Massif is the highest mountain in which continent?

21. The removal of salt from water which is then used for irrigation or drinking is known as what?

22. What is a honeypot area?

23. What is the name for rocks which water cannot pass through?

24. What name is given to the point on the earth's surface directly above the focus of an earthquake?

25. Which part of the earth's structure, rich in silica, lies between the core and the crust?

1. Which Australian sometimes appears as the 'cultural attaché to the Court of St James'?

2. What is Sergeant Bilko's first name?

3. Which film stars Anthony Hopkins and is billed as 'a comedy of the heart and other organs'?

4. What was the profession of Cliff Huxtable, Bill Cosby's character in *The Cosby Show*?

5. Which member of the comedy duo Laurel and Hardy was born in England?

6. Who plays the dim member of *The Golden Girls*?

7. What was the name of the piano-playing dog in *The Muppet Show*?

8. Which successful fat comic starred in *The Great Outdoors* and *Uncle Buck*?

9. What did Mork in *Mork and Mindy* mean when he said 'Nanoo, nanoo' in his own language?

10. Name the film in which Arnold Schwarzenegger becomes pregnant.

11. Which American actress and comedienne created Ernestine the telephone operator and Trudy the bag-lady?

12. Who was George Burns' wife and comedy partner?

13. Denis Norden hosts *It'll be Alright on the Night* on British TV, showing clips of all sorts of mistakes made during filming. What do Americans call these shows?

14. Which was the first of the *Carry On* films?

15. In *Roseanne*, who plays the star's husband?

16. Who took over from Johnny Carson in *The Tonight Show* on American television?

17. Name the play by Victoria Wood in which two sisters are unwillingly reunited by a TV show.

18. In which TV sit-com did Mollie Sugden play Mrs Slocombe?

19. In which film do Jack Lemmon and Tony Curtis dress in drag?

20. Which British TV comic had his contract cancelled in 1988 and went on to become a big star on American TV?

21. Who stars as a self-confessed serial-monogamist in *Four Weddings and a Funeral*?

22. Which character is played by Ted Danson in *Cheers*?

23. Name the gentle, accident-prone French eccentric portrayed by Jacques Tati.

24. Lucille Ball and Desi Arnaz starred in *I Love Lucy*, which was made by their own production company. What was the company called?

25. Which British comedy magician collapsed on stage and died during a televised theatre show, *Live at Her Majesty's*?

Q19

1. What is the largest carnivore in the African savannah?

2. What gives the bald eagle its name?

3. How does the boa constrictor kill its prey?

4. The survival of some Arctic species of predator depends on the availability of which animals?

5. What habit gives the praying mantis its name?

6. Which predator was accused of taking and killing the Chamberlain baby in Australia?

7. The cheetah is the fastest land animal. Roughly what speed can it reach?

8. How do puff adders disable their prey?

9. The peregrine, highly prized by falconers, is found on every continent but one. Which is it?

10. At what age are tigers fully grown?

11. Which predator often follows the polar bear, feeding on the abandoned carcass of its kill?

12. What type of animal is a meerkat?

13. Which is larger, the grey or red wolf?

14. What family of animals does the serval belong to?

15. In the polar lands, which type of seal is the main enemy of penguins?

16. What is the other name for the beluga whale?

17. Which type of predators can be pygmy, scops and eagle?

18. Coyotes, found all over America, pair for life. True or false?

19. How does the crocodile prepare to lay its eggs?

20. Piranha fish have a fearsome reputation for their attacks on animals and humans, reducing them to skeletons in a matter of minutes. In what part of the world are they found?

21. What is a female walrus called?

22. Which is the largest and most aggressive of the three hyena species?

23. Spiders spin silk webs to catch insects. The silk is spun from organs at the end of the abdomen. What are they called?

24. What do leopards do with a kill, to protect the meat from other predators?

25. What is the name of the African cat whose anal glands secrete a strong smelling substance used in perfume manufacture?

1. Where did Edwin Drake drill the first production oil well in 1819?

2. What valuable resource was discovered in South Africa's Orange Free State in 1867?

3. In what year did the Great Exhibition open at Crystal Palace in London?

4. Who was known as the father of the factory system because of his invention of a spinning machine?

5. What did Jethro Tull invent in the early 1700s, making better harvesting possible?

6. In which decade of the 19th century was the refrigerator first successfully developed?

7. The world's first iron bridge was erected in which English county in 1779?

8. What name was given to the factory-hands whose objective was to destroy the new factory machinery?

9. Benjamin Franklin proved that lightning is a form of electricity by flying a kite in a thunderstorm. What did he go on to invent?

10. Which poet wrote about the 'dark satanic mills' of the Industrial Revolution?

11. The Suez Canal was opened in 1869. Which seas did it link?

12. What kind of British settlers started arriving in Australia by the shipload in 1788?

13. The musical show *Les Miserables* was based on a novel about the plight of the poor, written in 1862. Who was the author?

14. Which American mail order firm was established in 1886, growing very quickly over the next decade?

15. The Caribbean and the Pacific Ocean were linked by which canal in 1914?

16. Who was the world's first oil billionaire?

17. Who wrote the *Communist Manifesto* in 1848, stating that workers were wage slaves?

18. Which reformer's Abolition Bill ended the British slave trade in 1801?

19. The first successful revolver was patented by which American gunsmith in 1835?

20. Which railway was completed in 1886, linking the Pacific and the Atlantic?

21. For what event was the Eiffel Tower erected in 1889?

22. Brunel was responsible for building three of the greatest 19th-century ships and was the chief engineer of the Great Western Railway. What was his full name?

23. Charles Dickens exposed many of the evils of Victorian England in his books. In which novel did he write about half-starved workhouse children?

24. Canals came later to America than Europe. In 1825, which canal linked the Great Lakes to the Atlantic Ocean?

Q21

25. A machine gun capable of firing 600 rounds a minute was invented in 1862 and named after its inventor. Who was he?

Q 12

Q 25

1. Which was Disney's first full-length feature?

2. In *Fantasia*, who was the sorcerer's apprentice?

3. In *Fantasia*, what task does the sorcerer's apprentice try to dodge by using magic?

4. Who played Captain Nemo in the 1954 film *20,000 Leagues Under the Sea*?

5. *One Hundred and One Dalmatians* was based on a novel by which author?

6. Name the villainess in *One Hundred and One Dalmatians*.

7. What unique ability does Dumbo have?

8. Which nanny could slide up banisters and fly with the help of an umbrella?

9. Disney's film *Pinocchio* was released in 1939. It was based on a children's classic from which country?

10. Who is Pinocchio's conscience?

11. In *Bambi*, what was the unlikely name given to the skunk?

12. *Swiss Family Robinson* was adapted from Johann Wyss's novel. Who was the star?

13. What was the name of the Volkswagen car that featured in several slapstick comedies?

14. What is the name of the Lion King?

15. Which film tells the story of a pedigree cat called Duchess who falls on hard times and meets up with an alley-cat called O'Malley?

16. In *Bedknobs and Broomsticks*, who played the amateur witch Eglantine Price?

17. What type of dog is Nana in *Peter Pan*?

18. *The Sword in the Stone* tells the story of whose boyhood?

19. In which film do the aristocratic Siamese Si and Am make their appearance?

20. Hayley Mills played Pollyanna in the 1960 film. What was Pollyanna's way of tackling setbacks and disappointments?

21. In *Robin Hood*, the title character was portrayed as which animal?

22. Which comic actor starred in several films, including *The Absent-Minded Professor* and *The Shaggy Dog*?

23. Who is the teller of tales in *Song of the South*?

24. What did absent-minded scientist Moranis do in his 1989 adventure?

25. *In Search of the Castaways* was an adaptation of which author's novel?

1. 'Seasons of mists and mellow fruitfulness, Close bosom-friend of the maturing sun'. Who wrote this description of autumn?

2. In which novel does Ernest Hemingway write about a Cuban fisherman fighting nature in pursuit of a marlin?

3. Patrick White was born in London but in which country did he live and set novels like *The Happy Valley* and *The Tree of Man*?

4. Who was the angry young man of the 1950s who wrote *Look Back in Anger*?

5. Which poet wrote about a sailor who was punished for killing an albatross?

6. *Lady Chatterley's Lover* was the subject of an obscenity trial in Britain in 1959. Who was the author?

7. Rudyard Kipling wrote a famous novel about his childhood in India. What was it called?

8. Name the New Zealand writer, famed for her short stories, who married critic and editor John Middleton Murry and suffered from tuberculosis?

9. Which poet wrote the story of the Lady of Shalott?

10. What narrative technique do James Joyce and William Faulkner use in their novels?

11. Who wrote about the feuding inhabitants of Wuthering Heights?

12. The musical *Cats* was based on the poems of T. S. Eliot. Whose *Book of Practical Cats* did he write?

13. In which play did Shakespeare write about Claudius, Ophelia and Polonius?

14. Alexander Solzhenitsyn suffered prison and exile in the USSR for his anti-Stalinist views between 1945 and 1957. In which famous book did he expose the reality of the Soviet labour camps?

15. Name the American 19th-century poetess who was a recluse by the age of 30, dressing in white and carrying on friendships through correspondence.

16. Henry Fonda starred in the film based on John Steinbeck's novel about farm workers who were refugees from the dust bowl region. Name it.

17. What type of books does modern novelist Ramsey Campbell write?

18. Which poet wrote to a skylark: 'Hail to thee, blithe Spirit'?

19. Name the Norwegian dramatist who wrote *The Wild Duck* and *Hedda Gabler*.

20. What were Lord Byron's first names?

21. US writer James Baldwin wrote about what contemporary issue?

22. Charles Dickens wrote about Charles Darney, Madame Defarge and Dr Manette in which novel?

23. Which 19th-century playwright spent two years in Reading prison and wrote a ballad about his experiences?

24. Name the author of *Tender is the Night* and *The Last Tycoon*.

25. Shakespeare wrote the following opening lines for which play: 'If music be the food of love, play on'?

1. What is the name given to one stroke over par for a hole?

2. The early type of ball was a leather case full of feathers. True or false?

3. The four biggest championships in golf are the Masters, the British Open, the US Open and which other?

4. What name is given to all four championships together?

5. In what way does the Masters differ from the other major championships?

6. Tom Morris was the youngest golfer ever to win the British Open. How old was he?

7. What is another name for a bunker?

8. A shot that starts straight and curves slightly to the right is called what?

9. In which year did America lose the Ryder Cup for the first time ever?

10. What is shouted to warn players ahead of an approaching ball?

11. Which are the medium irons?

12. What is an albatross?

13. What do Americans call an albatross?

14. Who holds the record for the most wins in a US season?

15. St Andrews is the oldest golf course in Britain. True or false?

16. What is called the 'game within a game'?

17. Who is the biggest-ever money winner among women golfers?

18. What is another name for the flagstick?

19. Which are the short irons?

20. In 1994 Nick Price won the US PGA Championship. Which country does he come from?

21. Arnold Palmer is known for his 'come from behind' victories. What are they called?

22. What is a birdie?

23. Who is the world's best-paid golfer?

24. What does a 'shag bag' hold?

25. A player who regularly plays below his current handicap is called what?

1. In which English county is Blenheim Palace?

2. What are Nahum, Haggai and Malachi?

3. The Kiel canal links the Baltic Sea with which other sea?

4. Which TV series was based on *The Raj Quartet* by Paul Scott?

5. What was Steve McQueen's last film?

6. In an orchestra, what is a tam-tam?

7. Which famous composer wrote the music which 'Twinkle, twinkle little star' is sung to?

8. Name the English painter who was exposed as a prolific art forger, having produced more than 2,000 fakes. He died in 1984.

9. Which author created Tarzan?

10. What breed of dog is Scooby Doo?

11. In the Black Forest area in Germany, religious families lay an extra place at the Christmas table. Who is it for?

12. Which city is the capital of Iceland?

13. Name the US playwright who wrote *Barefoot in the Park* and *The Odd Couple*.

14. In which disaster film is an ocean liner overturned by a massive wave?

15. The British call them estate agents. What do Americans call them?

16. What was the name of Evelyn Waugh's elder brother, who was also a well-known novelist?

17. The Pope wears a signet ring which portrays St Peter in a boat. What is this ring often called?

18. What type of creature is an ale-wife?

19. If a horse is golden in colour with cream or white mane and tail, what is it called?

20. What name is given to the 'halo' of gas that surrounds the sun?

21. In music, what is a pastiche?

22. What name is given to a piece of rock from space that reaches the surface of the earth?

23. Which airport serves the city of Venice?

24. 'Apples and pears' is Cockney rhyming slang for what?

25. The Beatles were awarded which honour in 1965?

Answers to Quiz 6

Geography and Travel • Features of the Land

1. Dormant
2. Shale
3. Where a river enters the sea
4. Fold mountains
5. The intensity of an earthquake
6. Karst
7. Mount Teide
8. Leaf litter
9. Mount Aso, Japan
10. About 80%
11. Metamorphic rocks
12. Rockies
13. Coal, oil and natural gas
14. Permafrost
15. Rift
16. Ring of fire
17. Longshore drift
18. Between Java and Sumatra
19. Bamboo
20. Antarctica
21. Desalination
22. A tourist area, more luxurious and therefore more popular than the surrounding area or country
23. Impermeable
24. Epicentre
25. Mantle

Youth World • Disney Films

1. *Snow White and the Seven Dwarfs*
2. Mickey Mouse
3. Filling a vat of water
4. James Mason
5. Dodie Smith
6. Cruella de Vil
7. He can fly
8. Mary Poppins
9. Italy
10. Jiminy Cricket
11. Flower
12. John Mills
13. Herbie
14. Simba
15. *The Aristocats*
16. Angela Lansbury
17. St Bernard
18. King Arthur's
19. *Lady and the Tramp*
20. She always found something to be 'glad' about
21. A fox
22. Fred MacMurray
23. Uncle Remus
24. Shrank the kids
25. Jules Verne

Popular Culture • Comedy

1. Barry Humphries
2. Ernest
3. *The Road to Wellville*
4. Obstetrician
5. Stan Laurel
6. Betty White
7. Rowlf
8. John Candy
9. Hello
10. *Junior*
11. Lily Tomlin
12. Gracie Allen
13. Blooper shows
14. *Carry on Sergeant*
15. John Goodman
16. Jay Leno
17. *Pat and Margaret*
18. *Are You Being Served?*
19. *Some Like It Hot*
20. Benny Hill
21. Hugh Grant
22. Sam Malone
23. Monsieur Hulot
24. Desilu Productions
25. Tommy Cooper

Famous Folk • Writers and Poets

1. Keats
2. *The Old Man and the Sea*
3. Australia
4. John Osborne
5. Coleridge
6. D.H. Lawrence
7. *Kim*
8. Katherine Mansfield
9. Tennyson
10. Stream of consciousness
11. Emily Brontë
12. *Old Possum's*
13. *Hamlet*
14. *The Gulag Archipelago*
15. Emily Dickinson
16. *The Grapes of Wrath*
17. Horror
18. Shelley
19. Henrik Ibsen
20. George Gordon
21. Civil Rights
22. *A Tale of Two Cities*
23. Oscar Wilde
24. F. Scott Fitzgerald
25. *Twelfth Night*

Indoors and Out • Predators

1. Lion
2. White feathers on the head
3. By squeezing it, causing suffocation
4. Lemmings
5. When it is awaiting its prey, its fore legs are held out in front of its body
6. Dingo
7. 100 km/h (62 mph)
8. With a venomous bite
9. Antarctica
10. Three
11. Arctic fox
12. Mongoose
13. Grey
14. Cat family
15. Leopard seal
16. White whale
17. Owls
18. True
19. It digs a pit
20. South and Central America
21. Cow
22. Spotted or laughing hyena
23. Spinnerets
24. Carry it into a tree
25. Civet

Sport and Leisure • Golf

1. Bogey
2. True
3. US Professional Golfers Association Championship
4. Grand Slam
5. It is by invitation only
6. 17
7. Trap
8. Fade
9. 1986
10. Fore
11. Four, five and six
12. Three strokes below par on a hole
13. A double eagle
14. Byron Nelson
15. False
16. Putting on the green
17. Patricia Bradley
18. Pin
19. Seven, eight and nine
20. Zimbabwe
21. Palmer's charges
22. One stroke below par on a hole
23. Jack Nicklaus
24. Practice balls
25. A bandit

Past and Present • Age of Industry

1. Titusville, Pennsylvania
2. Diamonds
3. 1851
4. Richard Arkwright
5. Seed drill
6. 1860s
7. Shropshire
8. Luddites
9. Lightning conductor
10. William Blake
11. Mediterranean Sea and Indian Ocean via the Red Sea
12. Convicts
13. Victor Hugo
14. Sears Roebuck
15. Panama Canal
16. John D. Rockefeller
17. Karl Marx and Friedrich Engels
18. William Wilberforce
19. Samuel Colt
20. Canadian Pacific
21. Paris International Exposition
22. Isambard Kingdom Brunel
23. *Oliver Twist*
24. Erie Canal
25. Richard Gatling

Pot Luck

1. Oxfordshire
2. Books of the Bible
3. North Sea
4. *The Jewel in the Crown*
5. *The Hunter*
6. A large gong
7. Mozart
8. Tom Keating
9. Edgar Rice Burroughs
10. Great Dane
11. Virgin Mary
12. Reykjavik
13. Neil Simon
14. *The Poseidon Adventure*
15. Realtors
16. Alec Waugh
17. The fisherman's ring
18. A fish
19. Palomino
20. Corona
21. A piece of music imitating another composer's style
22. Meteorite
23. Marco Polo
24. Stairs
25. MBE

7

1. The Costa Dorada is a well-known Spanish holiday destination. What does the name mean?

2. Barbados is a volcanic island. True or false?

3. Which fashionable US town appointed Bob Hope as honorary mayor?

4. On which Greek island would you find the late Minoan palace of Knossos?

5. Where would you find the resorts of Albufeira, Praia da Rocha and Lagos?

6. Which English county, popular with holidaymakers, was the setting for the novels of Daphne du Maurier?

7. Name the US state famous for its surfing and its volcanoes.

8. The Canary Islands were once known by what pretty name?

9. Fjordland National Park is an area of great beauty on New Zealand's South Island. What is the jewel of the park, called the 'eighth wonder of the world' by Rudyard Kipling?

10. Niagara Falls has always been a favourite honeymoon spot. Which actress starred in the 1953 film *Niagara*?

11. In 1974 the Turkish invasion divided the island of Cyprus. Which half of the island is Greek?

12. The beautiful French resort of Nice holds a large-scale and very colourful carnival each year. When does it take place?

13. Bali is a favourite holiday destination for Australians and many other nationalities. When is the dry season?

14. The island of Elephantine, so called because it was once an ivory trading post, stands in the Nile opposite which Egyptian city?

15. Ibiza is part of which island group?

16. In which part of France would you find the cathedrals of Rouen and Bayeux?

17. The modern name for Ceylon means 'resplendent land'. What is it?

18. Which Brazilian city is overlooked by Christ the Redeemer at Corcovado?

19. One of Queensland's major tourist attractions gives visitors the opportunity to explore coral reefs by scuba-diving, snorkelling and glass-bottomed boats. What is this attraction called?

20. To which island did Gracie Fields retire?

21. The Maldives is an independent republic of almost 2000 tiny coral islands in which ocean?

22. In Disneyworld's Magic Kingdom in Florida, which of the park's 'lands' is entered through Cinderella's Castle?

23. In which country would you find the Masai Mara game reserve?

24. In which US state would you visit national parks called the Arches, Canyonlands and Bryce Canyon?

25. The ski resort of St Moritz stands on the southern side of which mountain range?

1. What was Kojak's first name?

2. Name the author played by Angela Lansbury in *Murder She Wrote*.

3. Who wrote about the pipe-smoking detective Maigret?

4. Lord Peter Wimsey was created by Dorothy L. Sayers. Whom did he marry?

5. What type of car did Columbo drive?

6. Which instrument did Sherlock Holmes play?

7. Amateur sleuth Brother Cadfael was a 12th-century Welsh monk. Who played him in the TV series?

8. Where did Rockford keep his gun?

9. Sharon Gless was the third actress to play Christine Cagney in *Cagney and Lacey*. Who was the first?

10. Who is the San Franciscan private eye in Dashiell Hammett's *The Maltese Falcon*?

11. Adam Dalgleish is a Scotland Yard detective in whose crime novels?

12. Which girl detective whose father was a former district attorney was created by Edward Stratemeyer?

13. Name the actor, later a star of *Dynasty*, who was the voice of the unseen Charlie in *Charlie's Angels*.

14. What was the nationality of Ngaio Marsh, who often set her work in an English country house?

15. Who was Sexton Blake's boy assistant?

16. What is Miss Marple's first name?

17. In which village does Miss Marple live?

18. Name the author who first wrote about detective Philip Marlowe in *The Big Sleep*.

19. Which actor was the most famous screen Marlowe in *The Big Sleep* in 1946?

20. Agatha Christie created which detective with waxed moustache and 'patent-leather hair'?

21. Name the bumbling detective played by Peter Sellers in *The Pink Panther*.

22 Which fat detective did William Conrad play in the TV series?

23. Who is the modest Roman Catholic priest created by G. K. Chesterton and now the star of a TV series?

24. Barry Foster played Van der Valk in the TV series of that name. In which city did Van der Valk operate?

25. The exploits of comic strip hero Dick Tracy were brought to the screen in the 1990 film. Who played Tracy?

Q 1

5. In a Spanish bar, what are tapas?

6. Zuppa pavese is an Italian consommé. What would it contain in addition to the basic soup?

7. What is hummus?

8. If a dish you order contains tofu, what would you expect to be eating?

9. Paupiettes are slices of meat or fish prepared in what way?

10. The Japanese call it kanten, other eastern countries call it agar-agar. What is it?

11. What type of beef or lamb is used in keema curry?

12. On a French menu, what name would be given to poached eggs in individual flat dishes with Hollandaise sauce?

13. Calamari are eaten in large quantities in Italy. What is the English name?

14. In Greece or Turkey, rolls of savoury rice wrapped in vine leaves are a popular starter. What are they called?

15. You might finish a meal in Turkey with a cup of sweet coffee and delicious loucoumi. What would you be eating?

16. In an American restaurant, if you asked for a dish to be cooked 'over easy', what would the dish be?

1. In a Mexican restaurant, what name is given to crisp maize pancakes stuffed with meat and salad, with a tasty topping?

2. What is a poussin?

3. The Austrian sachertorte took its name from the chef Franz Sacher. What is it?

4. Bhoona is the Hindi term for cooking spice in hot oil. What does the term bargar mean?

17. What would you expect to find in abundance in an Indian dish described as 'do-piaza'?

18. If an item of food is described as 'au naturel', how is it cooked?

19. The Indonesian dish gado-gado is a vegetable salad with dressing. What is the main ingredient of the dressing?

20. If you ordered pasta with 'supo di carne', what type of sauce would you expect?

21. Usually served in soup or as an entrée, what are quenelles?

22. What is abalone?

23. Lamingtons were named after a Governor of Queensland. What are they?

24. What name is given to herrings salted whole, then smoked?

25. Yams are used a good deal in West Indian cooking. What type of food are they?

1. In Germany, the Federal President is the head of state. What title is held by the head of government?

2. What do the letters ERM stand for?

3. Which party did George Bush belong to?

4. In which country were Five Year Plans the basis of economic planning after 1928?

5. Who founded the fascist party in Italy in 1919?

6. In which city is the headquarters of the European Commission of Human Rights?

7. What French term describes the forcible takeover of government by elements within the country?

8. In which year does China take control of Hong Kong?

9. To which party does Australian leader Bob Hawke, who first won power in 1983, belong?

10. In 1984, Indian troops were sent into which temple to dislodge a Sikh extremist leader?

11. What was the aim of the July Plot, hatched in 1944?

12. Milton Obote was president of which country?

13. Konrad Adenauer was Chancellor of West Germany from 1949 to 1963. Which party did he belong to?

14. The first-ever meeting between a reigning British monarch and a serving US President took place in 1918. Who was the President?

15. What name is given to the referral of proposed legislation to a direct vote by the electorate?

16. What was the subject of the Beveridge Report of 1942 in Britain?

17. Who launched the Cultural Revolution in China?

18. Which country had Jan Christian Smuts as premier between 1939 and 1948?

19. Where does the International Monetary Fund, an agency of the United Nations, have its headquarters?

20. What name is given to the military rulers of the country after an army takeover?

21. In the US, who was meant to benefit from 'affirmative action'?

22. Who suffered under the Cat and Mouse Act in England in the early part of this century?

23. Who was the prime minister of the Vichy government in France during World War II?

24. In which country is the financial clique called 'zaibatsu'?

25. Which British Prime Minister introduced the 'social contract' with the trade unions?

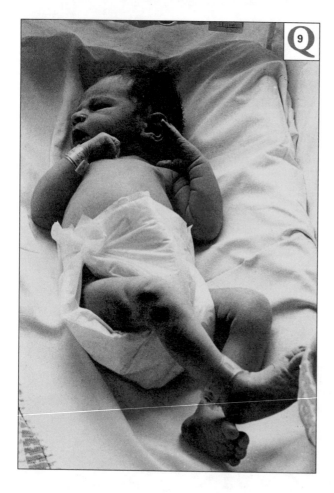

Q 9

4. Sometimes a baby is born with one or two of its first teeth already present. True or false?

5. What name is given to the jealousy sometimes shown towards a new baby by an older brother or sister?

6. At what stage in pregnancy does a mother begin to feel the baby's movements?

7. What attaches the baby to the placenta?

8. There are two types of sex chromosome, X and Y. Males have one X and one Y chromosome. What do females have?

9. Roughly how many hours a day does a baby normally sleep during the first three months?

10. What name is given to the tiny telescope mounted on the end of a hollow needle which doctors can pass through the abdomen into the uterus to check on the health of an unborn baby?

11. Modern researchers advise that babies should be put to sleep in what position?

12. Some babies suck their thumbs before they are born. True or false?

13. Which does a baby learn to do first, roll from his front on to his back or from his back on to his stomach?

1. Which doctors specialize in the care of pregnant women?

2. What name is given to the fluid, rich in antibodies, that precedes breast milk?

3. In a developing foetus, which organ makes blood cells?

14. What is the soft spot on the top of a baby's head called?

15. As babies develop in the uterus, their bodies are covered by fine, downy hair, which usually disappears before they are born. What is this hair called?

16. During the first week of life, most babies lose weight. When will they have regained their birth weight?

17. Over the first few weeks, babies learn to focus their eyes. At first, they can only see things clearly about what distance from their faces?

18. What is 'intra-partum care'?

19. Identical twins are formed if a fertilized egg divides in two parts and each half grows into a baby. How are fraternal twins formed?

20. Why might a baby be fed on soya milk?

21. What painful condition sometimes occurs in children up to three months of age, usually late in the day and lasting for only a short time?

22. A triple immunization often given to babies at two to three months of age is known as DTP. What does that stand for?

23. For what condition might a baby might be given phototherapy, during which it lies naked under a fluorescent light?

24. What is the purpose of amniocentesis during pregancy?

25. Some babies, especially those with low birth weight, stop breathing for very brief periods during sleep. What is this called?

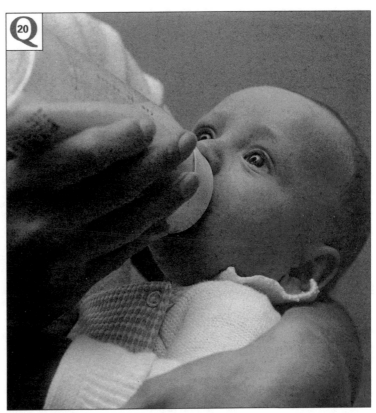

1. In 1988, who was the first woman since Margaret Court to win the tennis Grand Slam?

2. Who won two Olympic marathon titles – one barefoot, the other in shoes?

3. Which Nobel Prize winner wrote *For Whom the Bell Tolls* and *In Our Time*?

4. In which film did Bogart win his only Oscar?

5. Who was the only British Prime Minister this century to win three consecutive general elections?

6. Poet and essayist Octavio Paz won the Nobel Prize for literature in 1990. What nationality is he?

7. Which baseball team has won most World Series?

8. Who was the only world heavyweight boxing champion to remain undefeated throughout his entire professional career?

9. For which film did Dustin Hoffman win an Oscar, *The Graduate* or *Kramer v. Kramer*?

10. Linus Pauling was the only man to win two individual Nobel Prizes. What were they for?

11. Jodie Foster won an Oscar for *Silence of the Lambs* in 1992. For which film did she win it in 1989?

12. Which Belgian cyclist, nicknamed 'the Cannibal', won the Tour de France five times between 1969 and 1974?

Q11

13. Who won five Olympic golds in athletics in 1924?

14. Apart from the USA, only two countries have ever won the Olympic basketball championship. Which countries were they?

15. To whom is the Lawrence Trophy awarded annually?

16. Which grand-slam winning tennis player was nicknamed 'the Rocket'?

17. For which two films did Glenda Jackson win the Oscar for best actress?

18. Which author of *Lord of the Flies* and *Rites of Passage* won a Nobel Prize for literature in 1983?

19. Koichi Nakono won a record number of titles in which sport?

20. The 1994 Nobel Prize for Peace was awarded to Shimon Peres, Yasser Arafat and which other recipient?

21. At the Barcelona Olympics in 1992, who was the first British woman to win an Olympic track event since 1964?

22. For which film did Clint Eastwood receive an Oscar for best director in 1993?

23. Which member of the British royal family was once elected Sports Personality of the Year?

24. Holly Hunter won an Oscar for her role in which 1994 film?

25. Which of the following won the Nobel Peace Prize: Mikhail Gorbachev, Mother Teresa, Henry Kissinger, Willy Brandt?

Q 6

5. If you were whipping a rope, what would you be doing?

6. Which small sailing dinghy would be ideal for young beginners?

7. Which is the largest boat in Olympic competition?

8. The first sailor to circumnavigate the world alone was Captain Joshua Slocum, who set off from Rhode Island in 1895. How long did it take him?

9. What are Bruce, Danforth and Meon?

10. In canoeing, speed racing takes place on still water. On what type of water does slalom racing take place?

11. The international phonic alphabet is used in radio signalling for clarity. A is Alpha, B is Bravo. What is Y?

12. In the phonic alphabet, what is O?

13. Under which two bridges does the Oxford and Cambridge University Boat race pass?

14. What are halyards used for?

15. How long has yachting been an official Olympic sport?

16. Which boat skippered jointly by Robin Knox-Johnstone and Peter Blake broke the non-stop round the world record by five days in 1994?

1. What name is given to a light three-cornered headsail used to improve downwind performance?

2. How often does the Whitbread Round the World race take place?

3. What are the fastest sailing boats?

4. Who was the first woman to cross the Atlantic alone, in 1903?

17. The hull of the boat above the waterline is called what?

18. The tall sailing ship built in Germany as the *Horst Wessel* and confiscated after the war became the flagship of the US Coast Guard. What was it named?

19. What, in the world of sailing, is the IYRU?

20. Which British politican captained the winning team in the yacht *Morning Cloud* in the 1969 Sydney to Hobart Race?

21. In the international code of flag signals, what does a yellow flag with a black spot in the centre mean?

22. In 1905 the schooner *Atlantic* set a transatlantic racing record of 12 days 4 hours which was unbroken for 75 years. Who was the skipper?

23. Who was the Australian skipper who wrested the America's Cup from the US, after what seemed like an interminable run of wins, in 1983?

24. In a dinghy or small boat, what would you do with a thwart?

25. On which day of the year does the Sydney to Hobart Race begin?

1. What name is given to the study of the history of words?

2. In Italian cooking, what name is given to small dumplings made of mashed potato?

3. On which Hebridean island is Fingal's Cave?

4. Who dueted with Barbra Streisand in 'You Don't Bring Me Flowers'?

5. In the rhyme, how was Jack's head dressed after he fell down the hill?

6. What would you find in an arboretum?

7. Which country is often called 'the Emerald Isle'?

8. The songs 'My Funny Valentine' and 'The Lady is a Tramp' come from which musical?

9. Name the smallest planet in the solar system.

10. What name is given to a group of elk?

11. The bright spots of sunlight seen around the edge of the moon for a few seconds before and after an eclipse of the sun are called what?

12. What is agronomy?

13. What nationality was the painter El Greco?

Q4

14. If you made a tactless remark or a social error it might be described by which French expression?

15. Which state of Australia has the largest population?

16. What is called the 'fourth estate'?

17. In which country was the film *A Bridge Too Far* set?

18. Who said 'Russia is a riddle wrapped in a mystery inside an enigma'?

19. 'Decimate' is a word often used in an exaggerated sense. What does it actually mean?

20. Methuselah was a character in the Bible but in modern times methuselahs are containers for what?

21. Who painted *The Laughing Cavalier*?

22. The cocktail called Rusty Nail contains whisky and which liqueur?

23. What is a glockenspiel?

24. Who played the cabaret entertainer in *The Blue Angel*?

25. Which singer was nicknamed 'the last of the red-hot mamas'?

Geography and Travel • Holiday Spots

1. Golden coast
2. False
3. Palm Springs
4. Crete
5. Algarve, Portugal
6. Cornwall
7. Hawaii
8. Blessed or Fortunate Isles
9. Milford Sound
10. Marilyn Monroe
11. The south
12. The fortnight before Lent
13. May to November
14. Aswan
15. Balearics
16. Normandy
17. Sri Lanka
18. Rio de Janeiro
19. Great Barrier Reef
20. Capri
21. Indian
22. Fantasyland
23. Kenya
24. Utah
25. The Alps

Popular Culture • Detectives

1. Theo
2. Jessica Fletcher
3. Georges Simenon
4. Harriet Vane
5. Peugeot 403 Cabriolet
6. Violin
7. Derek Jacobi
8. In a cookie jar
9. Loretta Swit
10. Sam Spade
11. P. D. James's
12. Nancy Drew
13. John Forsythe
14. New Zealander
15. Tinker
16. Jane
17. St Mary Mead
18. Raymond Chandler
19. Humphrey Bogart
20. Hercule Poirot
21. Inspector Clouseau
22. Cannon
23. Father Brown
24. Amsterdam
25. Warren Beatty

Indoors and Out • Menumaster

1. Tacos
2. Baby chicken
3. Rich chocolate cake
4. Frying whole spices
5. Snacks served with a drink
6. A whole egg and toast covered with cheese and grilled
7. Chick-pea paste
8. Bean curd
9. Rolled and stuffed
10. A type of seaweed
11. Mince
12. Oeufs Bénédictine
13. Squid
14. Dolmades
15. Turkish delight
16. Fried eggs
17. Onion
18. It is uncooked
19. Peanuts
20. Meat sauce
21. A very light dumpling
22. A kind of shellfish
23. Chocolate cakes
24. Bloaters
25. Root vegetables

Past and Present • Political Affairs

1. Federal Chancellor
2. Exchange Rate Mechanism
3. Republican
4. USSR
5. Mussolini
6. Strasbourg
7. Coup d'état
8. 1997
9. Labour
10. Golden Temple at Amritsar
11. Assassination of Hitler
12. Uganda
13. Christian Democrat
14. Woodrow Wilson
15. Referendum
16. Social Security
17. Mao Ze Dong
18. South Africa
19. Washington DC, USA
20. Junta
21. Members of minority ethnic groups
22. Suffragettes
23. Henri Pétain
24. Japan
25. Harold Wilson

Youth World • Babycare

1. Obstetricians
2. Colostrum
3. Liver
4. True
5. Sibling rivalry
6. 18 to 22 weeks
7. Umbilical cord
8. Two X chromosomes
9. 14 to 18 hours
10. Fetoscope
11. On their backs
12. True
13. From front to back
14. Fontanelle
15. Lanugo
16. At about 10 days old
17. 20cm (8in)
18. Care given during labour and delivery
19. Two eggs are shed from the ovary and fertilized simultaneously
20. If he is allergic to cows' milk
21. Colic
22. Diphtheria, tetanus and pertussis
23. Jaundice
24. To check for genetic and developmental disorders
25. Apnoea

Famous Folk • Winners

1. Steffi Graf
2. Abebe Bikila
3. Ernest Hemingway
4. *The African Queen*
5. Margaret Thatcher
6. Mexican
7. New York Yankees
8. Rocky Marciano
9. *Kramer v. Kramer*
10. Chemistry and Peace
11. *The Accused*
12. Eddie Merckx
13. Paavo Nurmi
14. USSR and Yugoslavia
15. Scorer of the fastest first class cricket century
16. Rod Laver
17. *Women in Love* and *A Touch of Class*
18. William Golding
19. Cycling
20. Yitzak Rabin
21. Sally Gunnell
22. *Unforgiven*
23. The Princess Royal
24. *The Piano*
25. All of them

Sport and Leisure • Boats and Sailing

1. Spinnaker
2. Every four years
3. Catamarans
4. Gladys Gradeley
5. Binding the end to stop fraying
6. A pram dinghy
7. Soling
8. Three years
9. Anchors
10. Wild water
11. Yankee
12. Oscar
13. Hammersmith and Barnes
14. Hoisting sails
15. Since 1908
16. *ENZA New Zealand*
17. Topsides
18. *Eagle*
19. International Yacht Racing Union
20. Edward Heath
21. Altering course to port
22. Charlie Barr
23. John Bertrand
24. Sit on it
25. Boxing Day

Pot Luck

1. Etymology
2. Gnocchi
3. Staffa
4. Neil Diamond
5. With vinegar and brown paper
6. Trees
7. Ireland
8. *Pal Joey*
9. Pluto
10. Gang
11. Baily's beads
12. The study of crops and soils
13. Greek
14. Faux pas
15. New South Wales
16. The Press
17. Holland
18. Winston Churchill
19. To reduce by one-tenth
20. Champagne
21. Frans Hals
22. Drambuie
23. A musical instrument
24. Marlene Dietrich
25. Sophie Tucker

Q 5

1. Which French river is famed for the châteaux in its valley?

2. In which river are the 'thousand islands'?

3. What is the longest river in Australia?

4. The source of the Nile was a mystery for centuries. Now it is known to be two rivers, which unite at Khartoum. What are they called?

5. On which river does the city of Vienna stand?

6. What name is given to a flat stretch of land within a river valley, which is the remnant of an earlier flood plain, when the river was at a higher level?

7. The Rio Grande river forms part of the international boundary between the US and which country?

8. In which river was Jesus baptized?

9. Name the river that rises on the Tibetan Plateau of western China and has flooded more often and killed more people than any other.

10. Which river has the largest delta?

11. What is a delta?

12. How many rivers are there in Saudi Arabia?

13. Tower Bridge, over the River Thames, was opened in 1894. What makes it unique among London's bridges?

14. Which gulf does the Mississippi flow into?

15. In which country does the Zambezi River reach the sea?

16. What, in a river, is a meander?

17. The River Zambezi flows across the savannah of Zambia before plunging down Africa's most spectacular falls. What are they called?

18. On which American river is the Hoover Dam?

19. The Pied Piper of Hamelin cured the town's plague of rats by leading them into which river?

20. In which country is the River Po?

21. Which sea does the Nile flow into?

22. Francisco de Orellana explored it from Quito in Ecuador to the Atlantic in 1542 and called it the Rio Mar. By what name is it known now?

23. The third longest river in the world, the Yangtze in China, is famous for what spectacular features?

24. Which Canadian river rises in the Rockies as the Athabaska, leaves the Athabaska Lake as the Slave River, then changes its name as it leaves the Great Slave Lake?

25. The Ponte Vecchio in Florence was the only bridge over which river until 1218?

1. Whose autobiography is *A Long Walk to Freedom*?

2. To which genre do the novels of Zane Grey belong?

3. Which Jacqueline Susann novel sold nearly seven million copies in the first six months after its publication in 1966?

4. In which John Le Carré novel does George Smiley appear for the first time?

5. What story is told in *Exodus* by Leon Uris?

6. Two of the books in the Dollanganger series, by Virginia Andrews, are *Petals in the Wind* and *If There Be Thorns*. What is the first book?

7. Which novel brought Salman Rushdie a death sentence from Islam?

8. Name the most famous book written by Grace Metalious.

9. Which popular US novelist, with a string of best-sellers to her credit, is a descendant of the Lowenbrau brewery family and ran a PR firm called 'Supergirls' before becoming a novelist?

10. Stephen King's book *Misery* is about a writer who falls into the hands of his crazy number one fan. Who stars in the film with James Caan?

11. Which novel by Frederick Forsyth tells of an assassination attempt on Charles de Gaulle?

12. Who wrote *Saturday Night and Sunday Morning* and *Loneliness of the Long Distance Runner*?

13. In *Lolita* by Vladimir Nabokov, middle-aged Humbert Humbert lusts after the nymphet Lolita. How old is she?

14. Louisa May Alcott's *Little Women* concerns which New England family?

15. Germaine Greer is the author of the classic feminist work *The Female Eunuch*. What is her native country?

16. Which novel by Jeffrey Archer follows the fortunes of four MPs over 30 years from the time they take their seats in the 1960s?

17. *How to Save Your Own Life* and *Parachutes and Kisses*, by Erica Jong, both feature the same New York heroine. In which novel does her story begin?

18. Name the novel by Harper Lee in which a lawyer in America's deep south defends a negro accused of rape, with the action seen through the eyes of the lawyer's young daughter.

19. Who is the heroine of Barbara Taylor Bradford's *A Woman of Substance*?

20. *Where Eagles Dare*, by Alistair Maclean, follows a group of commandos sent to rescue an American general held prisoner by the Nazis in a Bavarian castle. In the film, who plays the commando leader?

21. Who wrote about Adrian Mole and about the British royal family living on a council estate?

22. Which Joseph Heller novel, set on a Mediterranean island in World War II, gave a new expression to the language?

23. Which English crime writer created a mystery herself by disappearing for a fortnight in 1926, only to be discovered at a Harrogate hotel?

24. Who caused a furore with his book *Diana: Her True Story* about the Princess of Wales?

25. *The Stud* was a 1978 film based on a book by Jackie Collins and starring her sister Joan. What was the follow-up film in 1979, also based on a Jackie Collins novel?

Q 4

1. In which country would you see the flightless emu in its natural habitat?

2. Which birds are the best known 'nest parasites'?

3. What is the scientific name for butterflies and moths?

4. Robins are known as friendly garden birds in western Europe and the American robin was named by settlers because of its red breast. What type of bird is the American robin?

5. What plant is known as the 'butterfly bush'?

6. Which bird is known for its ability to mimic human speech?

7. What type of bird is a raptor?

8. By what name is the blue peafowl commonly known?

9. How do butterflies extract the flower nectar on which they feed?

10. Where does the wood stork nest?

11. The life-cycle of the butterfly consists of four stages. What are they?

12. Which nocturnal, flightless bird gives a nickname to New Zealanders?

13. Legend says that the British monarchy will fall if which birds leave the Tower of London?

14. The *Hesperiidae* family of butterflies are often called 'skippers'. Why?

15. If a bird was vinaceous, what colour would it be?

16. How many families of butterflies are there?

17. Rooks are gregarious birds and their large twig nests can be seen grouped in tall trees. They often feed in mixed flocks and share communal winter roosts with which birds?

18. In what part of the world would you find butterflies called heliconius mimic, blue-green reflector and Cramer's mesene?

19. What sort of nests do swallows build?

20. How did the mockingbird get its name?

21. On a butterfly, what are eye-spots?

22. What is a cursorial bird?

23. The *Nymphalidae* family of butterflies are often called 'brushfooted butterflies'. Why?

24. What is described as a bird's 'nuptial finery'?

25. Blue-tits and great-tits are favourite garden birds and both are acrobatic feeders. How are great-tits distinguished from blue-tits in appearance?

1. Where was the first permanent English settlement in 1607?

2. In 1773 colonists boarded ships in Boston harbour, throwing cargo overboard as a protest against British taxes in the Boston Tea Party. What were the colonists disguised as?

3. In the American War of Independence, the British were surrounded at Yorktown, Virginia in 1781. Who led the American troops?

4. Eleven southern states broke away from the north in 1861 and formed their own union. What was this called?

5. The turning point of the war was the battle of Gettysburg. In which state is Gettysburg?

6. What was Billy the Kid's real name?

7. Who made his 'last stand' against the Sioux Indians in 1876?

8. In the most infamous western gunfight, at the OK Corral, the Earp brothers and Doc Holliday faced and fought the McLowery brothers and members of which other family?

9. Etta Place was the girlfriend of the Sundance Kid. Which actress played Etta in the film *Butch Cassidy and the Sundance Kid*?

10. Which President promised to 'bind up the nation's wounds' after the Civil War?

11. As immigrants poured into America, they were taken to an island in New York harbour for medical checks. Name the island.

12. Who broadcast 'Fireside Chats' to the American people in the 1930s?

Q16

17. Where did Shi'ite Muslim fundamentalists hold US embassy staff hostage in 1980?

18. During the Ford administration, George Bush acted as special envoy to which country?

19. In which scandal was Colonel Oliver North involved in 1986?

20. President Clinton was committed to appointing a woman as Attorney General but his first two choices came to grief in what was known as Nannygate. What was the problem in both cases?

21. Why were the rebellious students of the 1960s called the Spock Generation?

22. Which Caribbean island was invaded in 1983?

13. During whose presidency did the Korean war take place?

14. Where was the Bay of Pigs?

15. In 1960 an American U-2 reconnaissance plane was shot down over the Soviet Union and the pilot was sentenced to ten years imprisonment. Who was he?

16. Which president did Jimmy Carter challenge in 1976?

23. Where was a bombing campaign known as 'Rolling Thunder' carried out in 1965?

24. Who told the Americans in 1961 that his goal was to land a man on the moon by the end of the decade?

25. Name the independent candidate in the 1992 Presidential election.

Q 25

8. Name the world's smallest breed of horse.

9. What is a family of kittens called?

10. Llamas have been domesticated in South America, both as pack animals and for meat, hide and wool. What family do they belong to?

11. Which dog's present name comes from a character in Sir Walter Scott's novel *Guy Mannering*?

12. Which animal is known as sand rat or desert kangaroo?

13. What special purpose was the Tennessee walking horse was bred for in the southern US?

14. What were husky dogs used for in Iceland and Lapland?

15. Name the animal resulting from the mating of a donkey and a pony, if the sire was the donkey.

16. Toggenburg, Saanan and Anglo-Nubian are types of which animal?

17. Two distinctive breeds of working dog have been developed in Australia. One is known as the Australian cattle dog or Queensland heeler. What is the other?

18. What is the alternative name for the breed of dog known as the Russian wolfhound?

19. What type of animal is a guinea pig?

1. What is a male guinea pig called?

2. Where does the ragdoll breed of cat originate?

3. Goats can be house-trained. True or false?

4. Which dog is often used as a symbol of Britain?

5. How is the height of a horse measured?

6. What breed of cat is probably directly descended from the cats of ancient Egypt?

7. Which animals might be blue imperial, New Zealand white or angora?

20. If feline applies to the cat and canine applies to the dog, what word would apply to the horse?

21. Turkish van cats have a natural liking for something most cats loathe. What is it?

22. From which country did the poodle originate?

23. What is a female mouse called?

24. What is unusual about the coat of the Cornish rex cat?

25. Golden hamsters are one of our newest pets. When were they first bred in captivity?

Q9

Q 1

4. St Peter was the leader of the Apostles. He was given the name Peter by Jesus. What did it mean?

5. Who is the patron saint of artists and painters?

6. Hitler became Chancellor of Germany in 1933. Where did he address a rally of 200,000 people in September?

7. The carol 'Good King Wenceslas' commemorates the martyr who is patron saint of which country?

8. Who was the Italian founder of the Franciscan order?

9. How long a sentence of imprisonment was passed on David Berkowitz, the notorious 'Son of Sam' who terrorized New York in 1977?

10. In 1858 Saint Bernadette saw visions of the Virgin Mary. How old was Bernadette at the time?

11. With what emblem is St Agnes portrayed?

12. What does the name 'Beelzebub' mean?

13. According to tradition, who wiped the face of Jesus on the way to Calvary?

14. Where was Thomas à Becket murdered?

15. Burke and Hare were 19th-century grave-robbers and murderers and 'to burke' has passed into the language. What does it mean?

1. St Swithin is honoured on 15 July. If it rains that day, what will happen afterwards?

2. To which order of monks did St Bernard of Clairvaux belong?

3. Name the leader of a murderous 'family' in California who was described by the prosecutor at his trial as 'one of the most evil, satanic men who ever walked the face of the earth'.

16. Who is the patron saint of hopeless causes?

17. St John of the Cross was a Carmelite friar. What was his native country?

18. Dr Marcel Petiot was found guilty of 25 murders and guillotined in France in 1946. What did he pretend to his victims that he was running during World War II?

19. With what emblem is St Peter usually portrayed?

20. The English murderer George Joseph Smith drowned several wives for their insurance money. What were these murders popularly called?

21. Joan of Arc was a peasant girl who led the French army to victory in the 15th century. Which country was France fighting?

22. St Agnes was martyred in Rome and St Agatha in Sicily. What were they both dedicated to defending?

23. Who is the patron saint of cooks?

24. How did St Stephen die?

25. Ronald de Feo slaughtered his family at a Long Island house which later became notorious for terrifying happenings and was the subject of a book and a film. Where was it?

Q 8

1. What are netsuke?

2. Where did the willow pattern on china originate?

3. What kind of porcelain is called 'biscuit'?

4. How many spoons are there in an original set of Apostle spoons?

5. In furniture, what is a davenport?

6. Fabergé was official jeweller to the Russian Imperial court. What did he make specially for the Empress each year from 1884?

7. What is the usual colour of lacquer furniture?

8. In which country were fans invented?

9. If you had a rummer from Germany, what would you do with it?

10. What is scrimshaw?

11. The British call a high chest with seven or nine drawers a tallboy. What is it called in the US?

12. Carriage clocks were first produced as cheap, portable desk clocks in which country?

13. Fairings are popular with collectors. Originally, what were they?

14. In which English county has Wedgwood been produced since 1759?

15. What is a whatnot?

16. Button collecting is a popular hobby, especially in the US. In which century were buttons first worn on clothes?

17. Where does Belleek porcelain come from?

18. What is the name given to a design built up of tiny pieces of veneer?

19. Dutch Delftware is usually what colour?

20. Which country does the long, broad bench called an ottoman come from?

21. Chippendale was a master-craftsman, producing high quality furniture. What was his first name?

22. What is a prie-dieu?

23. Louis Quatorze furniture, from the second half of the 18th century, is massive, with ornate decoration. What is this style of furniture usually called?

24. A stick-back is the simplest form of which type of chair?

25. In the US a dumb waiter is a service lift. If you bought an early 19th-century dumb waiter in a saleroom, what would it be?

4. What comedy film earned Oscars for Clark Gable and Claudette Colbert in 1935?

5. Which is the world's largest residential palace?

6. Which game begins with a bully?

7. In what field did Rachel Heyhoe, later Heyhoe-Flint, achieve fame?

8. What would a cook add to a Welsh rarebit to make a buck rarebit?

9. British policemen are sometimes called 'bobbies', after the founder of the Metropolitan Police. Who was he?

10. Where in the US would you find Johns Hopkins university?

11. How many symphonies did Beethoven compose?

12. Which Shakespearean character wore yellow stockings, as the result of a trick?

13. 'True Love' and 'Now You Has Jazz' are songs from which musical?

14. In Canada, what is the RCMP?

15. Marc Chagall painted in a variety of styles, including Cubism. Which was his native country?

16. What nickname was given to Swedish singer Jenny Lind?

1. What would you do with parkin?

2. Name the small independent state set in the High Pyrenees between Spain and France.

3. In *An Englishman Abroad*, which actress meets spy Guy Burgess in Russia?

17. In heraldry, what is the name for red?

18. The characters Petruchio, Bianca and Katharina appear in which Shakespearean comedy?

19. What is the Latin term for 'in the year of our Lord'?

20. Hudson, the butler in *Upstairs, Downstairs*, was rejected for military service. What was his war work?

21. In the US, why would you win an Edgar?

22. What is the French phrase for a pen-name?

23. In which sport is the Stanley Cup awarded?

24. A sackbut is an earlier version of which instrument?

25. What type of car does Edward Woodward drive in *The Equalizer*?

Answers to Quiz 8

Geography and Travel • Rivers

1. Loire
2. St Lawrence
3. Murray River
4. White Nile and Blue Nile
5. Danube
6. River terrace
7. Mexico
8. Jordan
9. Yellow River
10. Ganges
11. An area formed from the sediment deposited at the mouth of a river
12. None
13. It is the only bridge that opens
14. Gulf of Mexico
15. Mozambique
16. A bend or curve
17. Victoria Falls
18. Colorado
19. Weser
20. Italy
21. Mediterranean
22. Amazon
23. Gorges
24. Mackenzie River
25. River Arno

Popular Culture • Bestsellers

1. Nelson Mandela
2. Westerns
3. *Valley of the Dolls*
4. *The Spy Who Came in From the Cold*
5. The creation of Modern Israel
6. *Flowers in the Attic*
7. *The Satanic Verses*
8. *Peyton Place*
9. Danielle Steel
10. Kathy Bates
11. *The Day of the Jackal*
12. Alan Sillitoe
13. 12
14. The March family
15. Australia
16. *First Among Equals*
17. *Fear of Flying*
18. *To Kill a Mockingbird*
19. Emma Harte
20. Richard Burton
21. Sue Townshend
22. *Catch 22*
23. Agatha Christie
24. Andrew Morton
25. *The Bitch*

Indoors and Out • Birds and Butterflies

1. Australia
2. Cuckoos
3. *Lepidoptera*
4. Thrush
5. Buddleia
6. Hill Mynah
7. A bird of prey
8. Peacock
9. Through a long, hollow feeding tube
10. In a treetop
11. Egg, caterpillar, pupa and adult
12. Kiwi
13. Ravens
14. They dart from flower to flower
15. Wine-coloured
16. Five
17. Jackdaws
18. Central and South America
19. Mud bowls built on to a wall or roof
20. It mimics other birds
21. Circular markings found on the wings
22. A ground-dwelling species
23. The male's front legs are covered with tufts of scales
24. Breeding plumage
25. By their black and white head pattern and white outer tail feathers

Past and Present • American History

1. Jamestown, Virginia
2. Native Americans
3. George Washington
4. The Confederacy
5. Pennsylvania
6. William Bonney
7. General Custer
8. The Clantons
9. Katharine Ross
10. Abraham Lincoln
11. Ellis Island
12. Franklin D. Roosevelt
13. Harry S. Truman's
14. Cuba
15. Gary Powers
16. Gerald Ford
17. Tehran
18. China
19. Iran-Contra Affair
20. Each had employed an illegal alien as nanny
21. Their behaviour was blamed on the permissive child-raising ideas of Dr Benjamin Spock
22. Grenada
23. Vietnam
24. John F. Kennedy
25. Ross Perot

Youth World • Favourite Animals

1. Boar
2. USA
3. False
4. Bulldog
5. In hands
6. Egyptian mau
7. Rabbits
8. Falabella
9. Litter
10. Camel
11. Dandie Dinmont
12. Gerbil
13. To carry plantation owners round their vast estates
14. To pull sleds
15. Mule
16. Goat
17. Australian kelpie
18. Borzoi
19. Rodent
20. Equine
21. Water
22. France
23. A doe
24. It is curly or wavy
25. 1930s

Famous Folk • Saints and Sinners

1. It will rain for 40 days
2. Cistercians
3. Charles Manson
4. The rock
5. St Luke
6. Nuremberg
7. Bohemia
8. St Francis of Assissi
9. 365 years
10. 14
11. A lamb
12. Lord of the Flies
13. St Veronica
14. Canterbury Cathedral
15. To murder by suffocation
16. St Jude
17. Spain
18. An escape route for those in danger from the Nazis
19. Keys
20. Brides in the Bath murders
21. England
22. Their virginity
23. St Lawrence
24. He was stoned to death
25. Amityville

Sport and Leisure • Antiques and Collectables

1. Small Japanese carvings in wood or ivory
2. Britain
3. Unglazed porcelain
4. 13
5. A small writing desk with a sloping surface
6. A jewelled Easter egg
7. Black with gold designs
8. Japan
9. Drink from it
10. Decorated or carved
11. Highboy
12. France
13. Small china ornaments won at fairgrounds
14. Staffordshire
15. A tiered stand, used to display trinkets
16. 14th century
17. Northern Ireland
18. Marquetry
19. Blue design on a white background
20. Turkey
21. Thomas
22. A small praying desk with a shelf for the knees and a higher shelf for the prayer book
23. Baroque
24. Windsor
25. A revolving stand with several tiers

china ornaments won at fairgrounds / objects made by sailors

Pot Luck

1. Eat it
2. Andorra
3. Coral Browne
4. *It Happened One Night*
5. The Vatican
6. Hockey
7. Cricket
8. A poached egg
9. Sir Robert Peel
10. Baltimore, Maryland
11. Nine
12. Malvolio
13. *High Society*
14. Royal Canadian Mounted Police
15. Russia
16. The Swedish Nightingale
17. Gules
18. *The Taming of the Shrew*
19. *Anno Domini*
20. Special constable
21. For writing a mystery novel
22. *Nom de plume*
23. Ice hockey
24. Trombone
25. Jaguar

1. What gas is released when rainforests burn?

2. What is hydropower?

3. In which country did 'Operation Tiger' begin, with the object of creating nature reserves for tigers?

4. Where was the world's largest oil spill?

5. What provides the entire diet of the endangered giant panda?

6. In 1961 an international organization was established to raise funds for conservation. Its first name was the World Wildlife Fund. What is it called now?

7. Which synthetic chemical, damaging to the environment, is still used in aerosol cans and in refrigerators?

8. What name is given to the heating up of the earth's atmospheric temperature?

9. In 1986 an accident at a nuclear power station in the USSR caused widespread contamination. Where did it happen?

10. What type of wood are teak and mahogany?

11. The snow leopard has been hunted for its spectacular coat, which is frosty-grey with dark rosettes. It is seldom seen but where is its habitat?

12. The power from burning wood and plant material is called what?

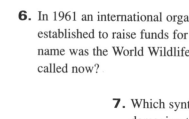

13. Which gas is produced from the rotting of household rubbish dumped on landfill sites?

14. The number of rhinos has been dramatically reduced because their horn is so highly prized in the Far East. What is it used for?

15. What name is given to the region in the stratosphere that absorbs the sun's ultra-violet rays and protects humans from its harmful effects?

16. Which substance produced in nuclear reactors can be used to make nuclear weapons?

17. Right whales were killed in such large numbers that they are now rare. How did they get their name?

18. What is the device for cutting the toxic fumes from car exhausts called?

19. Name the political party that grew up in Western Europe in the 1970s with conservation as its main aim.

20. Materials like glass, plastic and heavy metals are nonbiodegradable. What does this mean?

21. Which endangered animals inhabit the forests of the Virunga range of extinct volcanoes along the borders of Zaire, Rwanda and Uganda?

22. What metal is used to create nuclear power?

23. *Waldsterben* is the German name given to tree dieback due to air pollution, which was first noticed in the Black Forest in the late 1970s. What does the name mean?

24. The California condor is on the verge of extinction. What type of bird is it?

25. In 1979 a pressurized water reactor leaked radioactivity in the US. Where did this happen?

1. Who worked as a shop assistant, became an award-winning actress and then a British MP?

2. In which sport did Johnny Weissmuller win five Olympic gold medals before becoming Tarzan?

3. Which American astronaut became a US senator in 1974 but was unsuccessful in his bid to become a Democratic presidential candidate?

4. Before he studied medicine, what was Albert Schweitzer's occupation?

5. Which former *Neighbours* star had a 1992 hit with *Give Me Just a Little More Time*?

6. In which profession did Golda Meir, Israeli Prime Minister from 1969 to 1974, originally train?

7. Oliver Reed was once a bouncer for a strip club. True or false?

8. In which field did former actress Sheila Scott find fame in 1966?

9. Who played Walter Mitty and Hans Andersen, then went on to become Ambassador-at-Large for UNICEF?

10. What was Ernest Hemingway's job before he became a novelist?

11. Clint Eastwood became mayor of which American town?

12. Which member of the Monty Python comedy team wrote *Families and How To Survive Them* with Robin Skynner?

13. What was US President Hoover's original profession?

14. Which film actress became Minister of Culture in Greece?

15. What was Cleo Laine's job when she first met Johnny Dankworth?

16. Edward Woodward plays *The Equalizer*. What secret agent character did he play 18 years earlier, in another series?

17. Austrian motor-racing world champion Niki Lauda retired in 1985 to concentrate on his own business. What is it?

18. Ray Reardon and Christopher Dean both worked in the same job before they became snooker and ice dance stars respectively. What were they?

19. Who was a sports commentator, then a film actor, and later one of the leaders of the world?

20. Who began her film career playing Celie, a teenage bride in the deep south of America, and appeared as a singing 'nun' in two more recent films?

21. A US comedienne sometimes called 'the bitchiest woman in comedy', whose autobiography is entitled *Enter Talking*, won an Emmy for her talk show in 1990. Who is she?

22. What was Sir Walter Scott's original profession?

23. Neil Armstrong was the first man to walk on the moon. In 1971 he left NASA to do what?

24. Samuel Langhorne Clemens had several jobs before becoming famous as Mark Twain the novelist. Which job provided him with his pseudonym?

25. Who was Harry Palmer, and Alfie, and taught Rita a few things?

Q16

Q25

7. The part of a snail's body that remains inside the shell is protected by a thick skin. What is it called?

8. Aphids and leafhoppers are both a menace not only because they feed on plants but because they exude 'honey dew'. What does this encourage?

9. Are booklice really found in books?

10. Which is the most widely spread land bird in the world, found on every continent but Antarctica, and welcome because it preys on mice and voles?

11. Where does the scorpion carry its sting?

1. The 14th-century Black Death was brought to Europe by the fleas on which type of rat?

2. The boll weevil is the chief threat to which crop?

3. Why are earthworms the gardener's friends?

4. What is the only carnivore native to Australia?

5. In which country is the hedgehog considered sacred?

6. The house mouse is a prolific breeder. How many litters can it produce in a year?

12. Tigers will usually prey on animals like deer, antelope and monkey but they will sometimes raid villages in search of a a particularly tasty prey. What is it?

13. Mink are farmed for their fur but in the wild they often prey on poultry. What family do mink belong to?

14. Why is the vole a threat to trees and shrubs?

15. Which mosquitoes suck blood, the males or females?

16. Which creature is known for spoiling lawns with its burrowing habits?

17. The raccoon often steals fruit and vegetables from farmers. What name is given to the raccoon's home?

18. The caterpillar of which butterfly, common in Europe, the Mediterranean and North Africa, strips the leaves of the brassica family?

19. What are the two best-known types of blow-flies?

20. How do polecats mark their territory?

21. What do Americans call the poisonous spider known in Australia as the redback and in New Zealand as the katipo?

22. Which North American rodent, disliked by farmers, lives in large 'towns' with complicated patterns of interconnecting tunnels?

23. The wolverine, sometimes known as the skunk-bear or carijou, has another name that reflects its enormous appetite. What is it?

24. The mongoose can be a menace to birds and other wildlife in its natural habitat, but it is useful for what particular ability?

25. Where did the grey squirrel originally come from?

Q9

4. In which Dublin park were Lord Frederick Cavendish, chief secretary for Ireland, and his under-secretary T. H. Burke murdered in 1882?

5. Which organization was founded by Michael Collins in 1919?

6. In 1937 the Irish Free State changed its name to what?

7. What is the Republic of Ireland's lower chamber of parliament called?

8. Which organization has a name that means 'Ourselves Alone'?

1. Which British Prime Minister decided that the Union, the joining of English and Irish parliaments, was the answer to Ireland's problems?

2. What was the reason for the 1845 famine in Ireland?

3. What name was given to the rising of April 1916, when nationalists seized Dublin post office and proclaimed a republic?

9. Mairead Corrigan and Betty Williams founded which movement in 1976?

10. What are Fianna Fáil and Fine Gael?

11. How did Bobby Sands and Francis Hughes die in 1981?

12. Northern Ireland is divided into how many counties?

Q18

15. In the 1920s a special auxiliary force of the Royal Irish constabulary was employed by the British to combat Irish nationalists. Their popular name came from the colour of their uniforms. What was it?

16. The 'Guildford Four', who had been convicted of terrorist acts, were released when the Court of Appeal found their convictions unsound. How long had they served in prison?

17. Two years after the release of the 'Guildford Four', another group was released after a decision of the Court of Appeal. By what name were they popularly known?

18. Which war hero and member of the British royal family was killed by the IRA in 1979?

19. What do the initials INLA stand for?

20. Which US President visited Ireland in 1963?

21. Which famous London store was bombed in 1983?

22. The Anglo-Irish agreement of 1985 was much criticized. What did it promise Unionists about the status of Northern Ireland?

23. 1984 saw an attempt to kill members of the UK cabinet during the Conservative Party conference. In which town did this happen?

24. Who is the President of Sinn Fein?

25. What party does Ian Paisley lead?

13. In which year were British troops deployed in Northern Ireland to maintain law and order?

14. What name is given to the civil rights disorders in Northern Ireland?

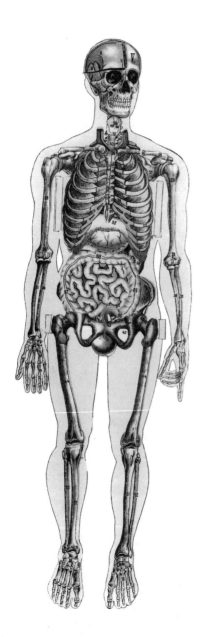

1. How many teeth are there in the first set, the 'milk' teeth?

2. The second set of teeth start coming through when a child is six or seven. How many teeth are there in this set?

3. A baby girl is born with thousands of egg cells in her ovaries. True or false?

4. What name is used for people who can use either hand equally well?

5. Where are the radius and the ulna?

6. What percentage of body weight do muscles account for?

7. Do arteries take blood away from the heart or to the heart?

8. What is produced by some white cells to kill disease organisms?

9. Which hormone controls a man's masculine appearance?

10. Is colour blindness more common in men or women?

11. How many bones make up the vertebral column?

12. The normal pulse rate for a baby is 120 beats per minute. How many beats is it in an adult?

13. If puberty occurs before the age of 10 in a boy, what is it called?

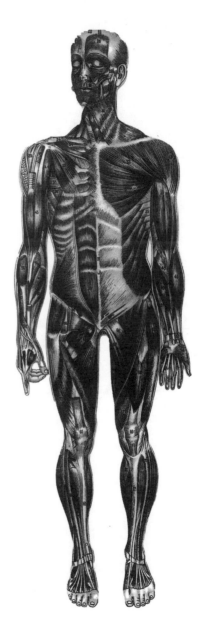

Q 6

14. What type of joint is the hip?

15. Girls usually stop growing by the age of 16 or 17. What age do boys normally stop growing?

16. What kind of acid, found in the stomach, dissolves food ready for digestion?

17. Where is the thyroid gland situated?

18. The rate at which the body uses up energy is called what?

19. Which part of the blood carries hormones around the body?

20. What is the first part of the small intestine called?

21. Are girls or boys more likely to be left-handed?

22. What is the smallest bone in the ear?

23. Give the common name for the clavicle.

24. A baby starts life with 300 bones. How many will it have as an adult?

25. What is the epidermis?

1. Name the young woman who loses her reason and drowns herself in *Hamlet*.

2. In *The Wizard of Oz*, who are the two wicked witches?

3. What is the first name of TV's Inspector Morse?

4. What is 'Crocodile' Dundee's first name?

5. When Clark Kent turns into his alter ego Superman, which reporter falls in love with him?

6. Who is the little boy who never grew up?

7. Arthur Daley's second minder is his nephew Ray. Who was the first minder?

8. Who saw Cock Robin die?

9. What is the problem with Cyrano de Bergerac's appearance?

10. Clara Peggotty is nurse to which young Dickens character?

11. In *Alice in Wonderland*, the Mad Hatter pours hot tea over which small companion?

12. Which couple war in the 1989 film directed by Danny De Vito and starring Michael Douglas and Kathleen Turner?

13. Who is the famous sidekick of Sherlock Holmes?

14. Who is Lady Chatterley's gamekeeper lover?

15. In *Citizen Kane*, what is Charles Foster Kane's newspaper?

16. What is the name of the nightclub singer in the play *I Am a Camera* and the film *Cabaret*?

17. In Beatrix Potter's books, what did Ginger and Pickles do until they were no longer able to pay the bills?

18. When Robin Hood becomes a titled gentleman, what is he called?

19. What is Just William's surname?

20. What is the profession of Indiana Jones?

21. Who is Phileas Fogg's servant who travels with him in *Round the World in Eighty Days*?

22. Holden Caulfield is a lonely, sensitive 16-year-old who leaves home in which novel by J. D. Salinger?

23. Joanna Lumley plays which part in *The New Avengers*?

24. In *Washington Behind Closed Doors*, what is the name of the President, played by Jason Robards?

25. Name the semi-autobiographical play by Eugene O'Neill which tells the story of a troubled family where the mother is a drug addict, her husband is an ageing former matinée idol, one of her sons is a drunk and the other is dying of consumption.

Q15

1. Who wrote the music for the Diaghilev ballets *The Firebird* and *Petrushka*?

2. Which opera was commissioned to celebrate the opening of the Suez Canal?

3. Singer Joan Sutherland is one of the best-known names in opera. Which country does she come from?

4. Which opera house is found in New York's Lincoln Center?

5. In which ballet does the leading ballerina dance the role of Odette-Odile?

6. What is the lowest female singing voice?

7. Name the Swiss hero featured in an opera by Rossini, first performed in 1829.

8. Benjamin Britten wrote the opera *Billy Budd*. Who starred as Billy in the film of the same name?

9. The fourth and last part of Wagner's Ring Cycle is called *Götterdämmerung*. What is its English name?

10. How many basic foot positions are there in ballet?

11. Who founded the Ballet Russe?

12. In *Amahl and the Night Visitors*, Amahl is a crippled shepherd boy. Who are the night visitors?

13. Which New Zealand soprano sang at the wedding of the Prince of Wales in 1981?

14. Who composed the music for *The Nutcracker*, *Sleeping Beauty* and *Serenade*?

15. The Royal Ballet, formerly known as the Sadler's Wells Ballet, was founded in 1931 by which dancer and choreographer?

16. The song 'Summertime' comes from which George Gershwin opera?

17. Which ballet tells the story of Franz, who falls in love with a mechanical doll, believing her to be a real woman?

18. Eight operas with the title *Turandot* have been written. Who wrote the most famous?

19. In 1987, what name did the Ballet Rambert take?

20. The opera *Rigoletto* is the story of the jester to the Duke of Mantua. What is Rigoletto's physical handicap?

21. Who is the choreographer of the ballets *Anastasia*, *Song of the Earth* and *Gloria*?

22. The author and broadcaster Ludovic Kennedy is married to which ballet dancer, star of the film *The Red Shoes*?

23. Three famous tenors sang in concert in 1990 and 1994. One tenor was Pavarotti. Who were the other two?

24. The 'Soldiers' Chorus' and 'Easter Fair Chorus' come from which Gounod opera?

25. Which Russian, born in 1890, became one of the world's most famous male dancers, but ended his carreer having succumbed to mental illness?

Q 11

1. Canada has two official languages. What are they?

2. Which boat is made from a wickerwork frame covered with a leather skin?

3. Who plays con-man Harold Hill in the 1962 musical film *The Music Man*?

4. If the British call him a tramp, what would Americans call him?

5. GATT is an abbreviation for which agreement?

6. In heraldry, what colour is vert?

7. Lewis Carroll was an Oxford professor as well as a writer. What was his subject?

8. US comedian Jimmy Durante was known by what nickname?

9. What kind of creature is a Jonathan Livingston?

10. Snooker was invented in which country?

11. Elton John's 'Candle in the Wind' is a tribute to which star?

12. In which decade were tea bags first launched?

13. What was the previous name of Taiwan?

14. Which animal would you find living in a citadel?

15. Who is the hero of *The Thirty-Nine Steps*?

16. British rule in India was known by the Hindi word for 'sovereignty'. What is it?

17. In the rhyme 'Hickory Dickory Dock', what time did the clock strike?

18. Which elderly actress won an Oscar for best actress in *Driving Miss Daisy*?

19. Where would you find a monument popularly known as 'the wedding cake'?

20. What nationality was the artist Whistler?

21. One of the two families in the TV programme *Soap* was called Tate. What was the other family called?

22. Every Muslim aims to make a pilgrimage to Mecca once in a lifetime. Where is Mecca?

23. Which Latin term warns the buyer to beware when buying goods?

24. Animals that can live either on land or in water are called what?

25. Who said: 'An appeaser is one who feeds a crocodile, hoping it will eat him last'?

Geography and Travel • Conservation

1. Carbon dioxide
2. Power from water
3. India
4. The Persian Gulf
5. The shoots and leaves of bamboo
6. World Wide Fund for Nature
7. Chlorofluorocarbons (CFCs)
8. Global warming
9. Chernobyl
10. Tropical hardwood
11. The mountain regions of central Asia
12. Biomass power
13. Methane
14. Medicine
15. Ozone layer
16. Plutonium
17. Hunters considered them the 'right' whales to kill
18. Catalytic convertor
19. Green Party
20. They cannot be broken down by living organisms
21. Mountain gorillas
22. Uranium
23. Forest death
24. New World vulture
25. Three Mile Island

Popular Culture • Career Moves

1. Glenda Jackson
2. Swimming
3. John Glenn
4. Professor of religious philosophy
5. Kylie Minogue
6. Teaching
7. True
8. Aviation: she flew solo round the world
9. Danny Kaye
10. Newspaper journalist
11. Carmel
12. John Cleese
13. Engineer
14. Melina Mercouri
15. Apprentice hairdresser
16. Callan
17. Lauda Air
18. Policemen
19. Ronald Reagan
20. Whoopi Goldberg
21. Joan Rivers
22. Law
23. Teach engineering at the University of Cincinatti
24. Pilot on the Mississippi; it was one of the river cries
25. Michael Caine

Indoors and Out • Friends and Foes

1. Black rat
2. Cotton
3. Burrowing improves aeration and drainage of the soil
4. Dingo
5. China
6. Five
7. A mantle
8. Black fungus, sooty mould
9. Yes
10. Barn owl
11. In the tail
12. Dog
13. Weasel
14. It gnaws at the base, causing the tree to die
15. Females
16. Mole
17. Den
18. Cabbage White
19. Bluebottles and greenbottles
20. With an unpleasant-smelling discharge
21. Black Widow
22. Prairie dog
23. Glutton
24. It kills snakes
25. North America

Past and Present • The Irish Question

1. William Pitt
2. A fungus attacked the potato crop
3. Easter Rising
4. Phoenix Park
5. Irish Republican Army
6. Eire
7. Dáil Eireann or the Dáil
8. Sinn Fein
9. Peace Movement
10. Political parties
11. As a result of hunger strikes
12. Six
13. 1969
14. The Troubles
15. Black and Tans
16. 14 years
17. 'Birmingham Six'
18. Earl Mountbatten
19. Irish National Liberation Army
20. Kennedy
21. Harrods
22. It would not be changed without the consent of the majority of the people
23. Brighton
24. Gerry Adams
25. Democratic Unionist Party

Youth World • Developing Body

1. 20
2. 32
3. True
4. Ambidextrous
5. In the arm
6. 40%
7. Away from the heart
8. Antibodies
9. Testosterone
10. Men
11. 24
12. 70
13. Precocious puberty
14. Ball and socket
15. 18
16. Hydrochloric acid
17. The base of the neck
18. Metabolic rate
19. Plasma
20. Duodenum
21. Boys
22. Stirrup bone
23. Collar bone
24. 206
25. The outer layer of skin

Famous Folk • Fictional Characters

1. Ophelia
2. The East and West Witches
3. It is never revealed
4. Michael
5. Lois Lane
6. Peter Pan
7. Terry McCann
8. The fly
9. He has an enormous nose
10. David Copperfield
11. The Dormouse
12. Barbara and Oliver Rose
13. Dr Watson
14. Oliver Mellors
15. *The Enquirer*
16. Sally Bowles
17. They kept a shop
18. Earl of Huntingdon
19. Brown
20. Archaeologist
21. Passepartout
22. *Catcher in the Rye*
23. Purdey
24. Monckton
25. *Long Day's Journey Into Night*

Sport and Leisure • Opera and Ballet

1. Stravinsky
2. *Aida*
3. Australia
4. Metropolitan Opera House
5. *Swan Lake*
6. Contralto
7. William Tell
8. Terence Stamp
9. *Twilight of the Gods*
10. Five
11. Diaghilev
12. The three kings
13. Kiri Te Kanawa
14. Tchaikovsky
15. Ninette de Valois
16. *Porgy and Bess*
17. *Coppelia*
18. Puccini
19. Rambert Dance Company
20. He is a hunchback
21. Kenneth MacMillan
22. Moira Shearer
23. Carreras and Domingo
24. *Faust*
25. Nijinsky

Pot Luck

1. French and English
2. Coracle
3. Robert Preston
4. A hobo
5. General Agreement on Tariffs and Trade
6. Green
7. Mathematics
8. Schnozzle
9. Seagull
10. India
11. Marilyn Monroe
12. 1920s
13. Formosa
14. Mole
15. Richard Hannay
16. Raj
17. One
18. Jessica Tandy
19. Rome: the monument to Victor Emmanuel II
20. American
21. Campbell
22. Saudi Arabia
23. Caveat emptor
24. Amphibians
25. Winston Churchill

PEOPLES

1. Which language is spoken by the descendants of Dutch and other immigrants who arrived in South Africa in the 17th century?

2. Name the race of hunter-gatherers of the African rainforests known for their small stature.

3. Where are the collective farms known as *kolkhoz*?

4. The Ainu are the aboriginal people of which country?

5. Approximately what percentage of the world's population is made up of Chinese?

6. Where does a Monegasque come from?

7. Name the nomadic people of northern Scandinavia.

8. The people of which country use zloty as currency?

9. Tok Pisin is now the official language of which country?

10. The Jains, who believe in complete non-violence, are a small religious community in which country?

11. Which people have often been called Eskimos, though they object to the name?

12. What are the indigenous Polynesian people of New Zealand called?

13. How did the Romany people get the name Gypsies?

14. What is the official language of Pakistan?

15. What is the official language of Iran?

16. In which part of South Africa would you be most likely to meet Zulus?

17. Where do women wear kimonos?

18. What is the language of the people of Haiti?

19. In which country are the Kikuyu the dominant ethnic group?

20. A murderous sect of Hindus that flourished in the 18th and 19th centuries specialized in violence against travellers. They have given their name to the language, describing a brutal and violent person. What is it?

21. What currency is used by people in Libya, Iraq and Jordan?

22. In which country would you meet Ibos?

23. Where do Walloons live?

24. What are the Paiute, Shoshone and Algonquin?

25. The Bedouin are desert nomads who scorn agricultural work. What is their occupation?

Q 14

1. In which continent did the poncho – a circular or rectangular piece of cloth with a hole for the head – originate?

2. What is a 'barbour', originally designed by John Barbour in 1890, but becoming popular for country wear this century?

3. Where would you wear gaiters?

4. Which hairdresser created the 'wash 'n' wear bob' in 1965?

5. In the 18th century, what was a banyan?

6. Which US designer created the influential 'prairie look', with denim skirts worn over layered white petticoats, in 1978?

7. What name is given to a divided skirt?

8. In which decade did the so-called 'peacock revolution' take place?

9. What were stays?

10. How did Americans come to use the name 'pants' to describe what the British call trousers?

11. Which designers were responsible for Lady Diana Spencer's wedding dress in 1981?

12. What were 'hot pants'?

13. What are espadrilles?

14. Which designer launched the 'New Look', with its small waist and full skirt, in the 1940s?

15. What was a fichu?

16. Which British designer closely associated with the punk movement launched the 'New Romantic' and the 'Pirate Look' in the late 1980s?

17. What shape was the mob cap of the 19th century?

18. The bustle, which made dresses stand out at the back, was eventually made from wire. What was it originally made from?

19. What is a dirndl skirt?

20. In which decade of the 19th century was the crinoline invented?

21. The 'A' line was created by Christian Dior in 1955. What shape was an 'A' line dress?

22. In the UK, 'Sloane Rangers' dress in timeless, classic clothes. What are their equivalent in the US called?

23. What was the chief feature of a poke hat?

24. What type of clothes are characteristic of the Gothic style, which became popular in the late 1980s?

25. The designer Giorgio Armani, who launched his own label in 1975, became famous for his suits and jackets. He is identified with which style for executive women?

1. Which plant takes its name from the Latin *lavare*, meaning to wash, because of its use in toilet preparations?

2. Which country do gladioli originally come from?

3. Which drug is derived from the poppy?

4. Which flower is sometimes called 'cut and come again' or 'youth and old age'?

5. Which flower is named after the Swiss botanist Charles Godet?

6. Give the collective name for the sepals of a flower.

7. Which perennial flowering herb with orange-yellow flowers is used in treatments for bruises and sprains?

8. What does 'dimorphoteca' mean in relation to a plant?

9. What colours will hydrangeas growing in acid soil normally be?

10. Which flowers can be floribunda or hybrid tea?

11. The flower called after the 16th-century German physician and herbalist Leonhart Fuchs is known as what?

12. How is the dahlia propagated?

13. What name is given to the male reproductive organ of a flower?

14. The flower sometimes known as bird of paradise was named after Queen Charlotte of Mecklenburg-Strelitz, wife of the English king George III. What is it?

15. Which flower has varieties including De Caen and St Brigid?

16. What is the popular name for *Impatiens*?

17. In which country is the growing and breeding of orchids centred?

18. The drug digitalis, a heart stimulant, comes from which flower?

19. Gaillard de Marentonneau, the French patron of botany, gave his name to which flower?

20. Which flowering tree has the botanical name *Prunus triloba*?

21. What name is given to the joint at which leaves are born on a stem?

22. What is the country of origin of lupins?

23. Which flower features in a song from *The Sound of Music*?

24. Give the popular name for antirrhinum.

25. Which type of begonia would be used as a show plant in containers, *Begonia semperflorens* or *Begonia tuberosa*?

1. Name the ex-prime minister of Italy who came under investigation after allegations of corruption.

2. Who was the American serial sex murderer killed by fellow inmates in prison in 1994?

3. Which boxer, sentenced to 10 years (four suspended) for rape in Indianapolis in 1992, was released in 1995?

4. George Michael lost his long-drawn-out battle with his recording company in 1994. Name the company.

5. In South Africa, much controversy has raged around Winnie Mandela. From which government post was she fired by her estranged husband?

6. How were businessmen Ernest Saunders, Gerald Ronson, Jack Lyons and Anthony Parnes linked in 1990?

7. Who married Michael Jackson soon after the scandal of alleged child abuse?

8. The film *Quiz Show*, directed by Robert Redford, concerns the scandal that rocked America in the 1950s. Name the quiz show involved.

9. Whose autobiography, entitled *My Lucky Stars: A Hollywood Memoir*, drew an unflattering portrait of Frank Sinatra and Dean Martin?

10. Qubilah Bahiyah Shabazz was charged with allegedly hiring a hitman to kill the leader of Nation of Islam. She is the daughter of which militant black leader?

11. Which British athlete, former Commonwealth 800 metres gold medalist, was banned for four years for alleged drug use?

12. When Spain celebrated its first royal wedding for 89 years, who was the bride?

13. Heart-throb tennis star Henri Leconte married Marie Sara. What is her claim to fame?

14. In a media context, what does 'outed' mean?

15. Camilla Parker-Bowles, friend of the Prince of Wales, announced her divorce in 1995. What is her husband's name?

16. What much-publicized confession did US talk show host Oprah Winfrey make on a programme about drugs?

17. Which top US comedy series star has accused her parents of abusing her as a child – accusations they strenuously deny?

18. John Wayne Bobbit hit the headlines when he was mutilated by his vengeful wife. What is her name?

19. A British advertising agency, known for publicizing the Conservative Party, was the scene of a boardroom battle, resulting in the resignation of the Chairman, though the firm bore his name. What was the firm?

20. Pamela Anderson of *Baywatch* is a favourite with the media. Name her pop-star husband.

21. Name the Hollywood 'madam' convicted of running a prostitution ring in a blaze of publicity.

22. French footballer Eric Cantona, playing for Manchester United, was disciplined after a violent episode at which ground?

23. In 1994 Andrew Lloyd Webber replaced the lead in his latest musical when it opened on Broadway because 'she couldn't sing well enough.' She then sued him. Name the actress and the musical.

24. Which British actress, star of *Eastenders*, was in the headlines twice within a short space of time over incidents in cars?

25. O. J. Simpson's trial for murder monopolized the American media. What was his wife's name?

1. *Gunfight at the OK Corral* (1957) stars Burt Lancaster as Wyatt Earp. Who stars as Doc Holliday?

2. Give the title of the 1989 TV mini-series based on Larry McMurtry's Pulitzer Prize-winning novel.

3. Who plays the man with no name in *High Plains Drifter*?

4. Which comedy duo went *Way Out West* in 1937?

5. In *High Noon*, marshal Will Kane faces a gunman seeking revenge, against the wishes of his new Quaker bride. What is the film's theme song?

6. Who directs and stars in *Dances with Wolves*?

7. In the TV series *Maverick*, which of the Mavericks is played by James Garner?

8. What was Clark Gable's (and also Marilyn Monroe's) last film?

9. Yul Brynner, Steve McQueen, Brad Dexter, James Coburn and Horst Buchholz are five of *The Magnificent Seven*. Who are the other two?

10. 'Oh, What a Beautiful Morning' is the opening number of which western musical?

11. In the TV series, what aliases do Hannibal Heyes and 'Kid' Curry use?

12. Richard Harris plays an English aristocrat captured by which Indian tribe in *A Man Called Horse*?

13. The classic western *Stagecoach* made John Wayne a star. In which US setting was it filmed?

14. Which family lived on the Ponderosa ranch in *Bonanza*?

15. In *Unforgiven*, Clint Eastwood plays a retired gunfighter. How is he trying to earn a living?

16. Who directed the movies *Major Dundee* and *Junior Bonner* and the TV series *Gunsmoke* and *Have Gun, Will Travel*?

17. Three friends going through a mid-life crisis take a cattle drive vacation in *City Slickers*. Which veteran actor plays their ageing trail boss?

18. 'There's No Business Like Show Business' and 'Doin' What Comes Naturally' come from which musical?

19. Bob Hope stars in the comedy western *The Paleface* with which 1940s sex symbol?

20. In the long-running TV series *Wagon Train*, who plays the wagon-master?

21. *They Died with their Boots On* is the story of which flamboyant figure of the Old West?

22. Who directed the spoof western *Blazing Saddles*?

23. In *Seven Brides for Seven Brothers*, Howard Keel plays the eldest brother. Who plays the baby of the family?

24. Barbara Stanwyck stars as a wealthy ranch-owner in which 1960s TV series?

25. In which film does Spencer Tracy play a one-armed stranger arriving in a hostile town?

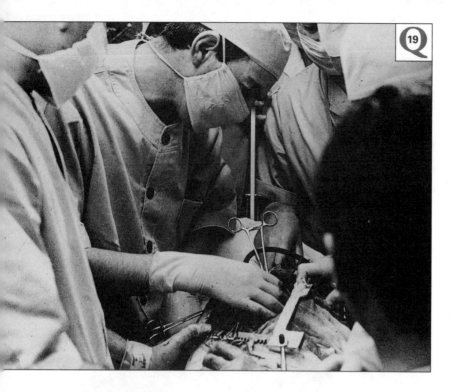

5. Where was the British army hospital where that most famous of nurses Florence Nightingale worked to lamplight?

6. The ideas of Karl Marx had a dramatic effect and lasting effect on the politics and political ideologies of the 20th century. What was his most famous work?

7. Which prolific American inventor counted among his patents the printing telegraph, the microphone and gramophone?

8. Name the French philosopher who put forward his ideas, which were influential in the French Revolution, in the *Social Contract*?

1. In 1969 Neil Armstrong and Buzz Aldrin walked on the moon. Who stayed behind in the command module?

2. Who introduced the science of psychoanalysis, the investigation of the unconscious mind?

3. Which British philosopher and noted campaigner against nuclear weapons wrote the *History of Western Philosophy* and *Principia Mathematica*?

4. Alexander Graham Bell, inventor of the telephone, made the first long-distance call in 1892 from New York to which city?

9. Which missionary found the Victoria Falls in 1855 and set out to trace the source of the Nile, only to be 'lost' for a time in Africa?

10. Who set out his revolutionary ideas on the evolution of man in *The Origin of Species*?

11. What was the achievement of Bruce McCandless in space in 1984?

12. Andrei Sakharov campaigned for human rights in the USSR and was sentenced to internal exile in 1980. When was he released?

13. Name the three Pankhursts, mother and two daughters, who campaigned for votes for women in Britain in the 1880s.

14. What startling theory did Polish astronomer Copernicus put forward?

15. The first message sent in his special code in 1844 was 'What hath God wrought'. Who was he?

16. Frank Whittle was a pioneer in what field?

17. Name the Scot who invented a rainproof fabric, still used for raincoats.

18. Buffalo Bill's favourite weapon was the 'six-shooter'. Who had patented the revolver?

19. In which decade did Christiaan Barnard perform the first heart transplant?

20. The American Frederick Douglass was advisor to President Lincoln during the Civil War. Why was this remarkable?

21. What did Elisha Otis instal for the first time ever in a New York store in 1857?

22. Who invented a system to reduce background noise on audio equipment in 1967?

23. In what field did Friedrich Froebel pioneer?

24. Which new form of medicine did Samuel Hahnemann pioneer in the 19th century?

25. Mother Teresa is famous for her work among the poor in which city?

1. Which West Indian captain led his team in the most Test matches?

2. Who captained the first 'rebel' tour of South Africa?

3. How many players are there in an ice hockey team?

4. Who was the first man to win the Grand Slam in tennis?

5. In 1975 an Australia versus England cricket match had to be abandoned because of vandalism. Where was this?

6. How many innings would each side normally have during a game of baseball?

7. What are sandlotters?

8. In a game of fives, what do players use to hit the ball?

9. Which is the only tennis championship where women play the best of five sets?

10. Which batsman made the greatest number of centuries in his cricket career?

11. The first metal tennis racquets appeared in the 1920s. What were the strings made of?

12. At the beginning of an ice hockey match, the referee drops the puck on the ice between the sticks of opposing players. What is this procedure called?

13. Which Australian Test cricket player was nicknamed 'the unbowlable'?

14. In tennis, what score is called 'deuce'?

15. Who did Pete Sampras beat in the singles finals at Wimbledon in 1994?

16. In softball, how is the ball pitched?

17. The distances between bases are longer in softball than baseball. True or false?

18. If a cricket umpire raises both arms above his head, what is he signalling?

19. Which game was originally called 'sticky' by its detractors?

20. Who is the only West Indian cricketer to make a hundred hundreds?

21. What are the following: yorker, googly and chinaman?

22. In baseball, the fielding side is divided into three sections. What are they?

23. Rounders is usually played by women or children. How many innings does each team have?

24. If the server in tennis throws up a ball, attempts to hit it and misses, does it count as a fault?

25. Which baseball legend does Tommy Lee Jones play in a 1994 film?

Q 24

1. Which Victorian novelist created the fictional county of Barsetshire?

2. What do the French call the English channel?

3. 6 June 1944 is known as D-Day. What does the D stand for?

4. Name the largest island in the Caribbean.

5. Which composer did Dirk Bogarde play in *Song Without End*?

6. What would you be doing in a sulky?

7. In which TV series would you have heard about an organization called THRUSH?

8. Who painted a pile of Campbell's soup cans?

9. The film *Amadeus* was the story of which composer?

10. The following are models of which car: Riviera, Skylark and Skyhawk?

11. What is the currency of Iceland?

12. The Westchester Cup is awarded in which sport?

13. What modern convenience did Sir John Harrington design and instal for Queen Elizabeth I in her palace in Richmond, Surrey?

14. The works of which Italian painter include *St George and the Dragon*, now found in the Louvre, and *Coronation of the Virgin*, in the Vatican gallery?

15. In 1973 Cape Kennedy reverted to its former name. What is it?

16. Which gangster was nicknamed 'Baby Face'?

17. What type of animal is a cavicorn?

18. In medieval times, what would you be doing if you threw down the gauntlet?

19. Which country in Central America is known by the Spanish words for 'rich coast'?

20. In air travel, what does ETA stand for?

21. A famous novel is based on the real-life adventures of Alexander Selkirk. What is it called?

22. In which film did Bill Murray play a TV weatherman?

23. Gracie Fields sang about the 'cast-iron plant' by its other name. What is it?

24. What is boxer Barry McGuigan's nickname?

25. Which pop singer had hits with 'Delilah' and 'Green, Green Grass of Home'?

Q22

Answers to Quiz 10

Geography and Travel • Peoples

1. Afrikaans
2. Pygmies
3. Russia
4. Japan
5. Over 25%
6. Monaco
7. Lapps
8. Poland
9. Papua New Guinea
10. India
11. Inuit
12. Maoris
13. They were wrongly thought to come from Egypt
14. Urdu
15. Farsi
16. Natal
17. Japan
18. French
19. Kenya
20. Thug
21. Dinar
22. Nigeria
23. Belgium
24. They are all tribes of Native Americans
25. Herding animals

Popular Culture • Fashion

1. South America
2. A waxed cotton jacket
3. Below the knee
4. Vidal Sassoon
5. A dressing gown
6. Ralph Lauren
7. Culottes
8. 1960s
9. Corsets stiffened with whalebone
10. Early trousers were similar to the leggings known as pantaloons
11. David and Elizabeth Emanuel
12. Very short shorts
13. Canvas shoes with braided cord soles
14. Christian Dior
15. A triangular shawl
16. Vivienne Westwood
17. A puffed crown with a deep frill
18. Horsehair
19. A full skirt gathered at the waist
20. 1850s
21. Narrow shoulders and wide hips
22. Preppies
23. A large brim
24. Black clothes, often with fringes and tears
25. The wide-shouldered look

Indoors and Out • Flowering Plants

1. Lavender
2. South Africa
3. Opium
4. Zinnia
5. Godetia
6. Calyx
7. Arnica
8. It produces two different kinds of seed
9. Blue and mauve
10. Roses
11. Fuchsia
12. By division of tubers
13. Stamen
14. Strelitzia
15. Anemone
16. Busy Lizzie
17. USA
18. Foxglove
19. Gaillardia
20. Flowering almond
21. Node
22. North America
23. Edelweiss
24. Snapdragon
25. *Begonia tuberosa*

Past and Present • Gossip, Gossip

1. Silvio Berlusconi
2. Jeffrey Dahmer
3. Mike Tyson
4. Sony
5. Deputy Minister of Arts, Culture, Science and Technology
6. They were the Guinness Four
7. Lisa Marie Presley
8. *Twenty-One*
9. Shirley MacLaine
10. Malcolm X
11. Diane Modahl
12. The Infanta Elena
13. She is the world's only female bullfighter
14. Homosexuals named without their consent
15. Andrew
16. She had used cocaine
17. Roseanne
18. Lorene
19. Saatchi and Saatchi
20. Tommy Lee
21. Heidi Fleiss
22. Crystal Palace
23. Faye Dunaway in *Sunset Boulevard*
24. Gillian Taylforth
25. Nicole

Youth World • Westerns

1. Kirk Douglas
2. *Lonesome Dove*
3. Clint Eastwood
4. Stan Laurel and Oliver Hardy
5. 'Do Not Forsake Me, Oh My Darlin''
6. Kevin Costner
7. Bret
8. *The Misfits*
9. Charles Bronson and Robert Vaughn
10. *Oklahoma*
11. Smith and Jones
12. Sioux
13. Monument Valley
14. The Cartwright family
15. Pig farming
16. Sam Peckinpah
17. Jack Palance
18. *Annie Get Your Gun*
19. Jane Russell
20. Ward Bond
21. George Armstrong Custer
22. Mel Brooks
23. Russ Tamblyn
24. *The Big Valley*
25. *Bad Day at Black Rock*

Famous Folk • Pioneers

1. Michael Collins
2. Sigmund Freud
3. Bertrand Russell
4. Chicago
5. The Crimea
6. *Das Kapital*
7. Thomas Edison
8. Jean-Jacques Rousseau
9. David Livingstone
10. Charles Darwin
11. The first untethered space walk
12. 1986
13. Emmeline, Sylvia and Christabel
14. That the earth moved round the sun
15. Samuel Morse
16. Jet propulsion
17. Charles Macintosh
18. Samuel Colt
19. 1960s
20. He was born a slave
21. A passenger elevator
22. Dolby
23. Kindergarten education
24. Homeopathy
25. Calcutta

Sport and Leisure • Bat and Ball

1. Clive Lloyd
2. Graham Gooch
3. Six
4. Fred Perry
5. Headingley
6. Nine
7. Amateur baseball players
8. The hand
9. Virginia Slims
10. Jack Hobbs
11. Piano wire
12. Face off
13. Bill Woodfull
14. Forty-all
15. Goran Ivanisevic
16. Underarm
17. False
18. A boundary six
19. Lawn tennis
20. Viv Richards
21. Styles of bowling
22. Battery, infield and outfield
23. Two
24. Yes
25. Ty Cobb

Pot Luck

1. Anthony Trollope
2. La Manche
3. Day
4. Cuba
5. Franz Liszt
6. Harness racing
7. *The Man from Uncle*
8. Andy Warhol
9. Mozart
10. Buick
11. Krona
12. Polo
13. A flush lavatory
14. Raphael
15. Cape Canaveral
16. George Nelson
17. One with hollow horns
18. Issuing a challenge to a duel
19. Costa Rica
20. Estimated time of arrival
21. *Robinson Crusoe*
22. *Groundhog Day*
23. Aspidistra
24. Clones Cyclone
25. Tom Jones

Q 4

1. In which Austrian town would you be able to visit Mozart's birthplace?

2. A bronze statue of Captain Bligh, of the *Bounty* mutiny fame, stands in Sydney, New South Wales. Why?

3. On which Christian site in Jerusalem does the Church of the Holy Sepulchre stand?

4. Name George Washington's home in Virginia, USA.

5. The Casa Guidi, where Elizabeth Barrett and Robert Browning lived after their elopement and marriage, now belongs to the Browning Institute. Which Italian city is it in?

6. Lizzie Borden's name became notorious when she was tried for the murder of her father and stepmother. The house in which the murders took place still stands in which Massachusetts town?

7. Which famous literary figure lived in the English town of Stratford-upon-Avon?

8. Name the novel that Victor Hugo wrote about the bellringer of a Paris cathedral.

9. Who attained enlightenment under a tree at Bodhgaya, in Bihar, India?

10. The Little Bighorn Battlefield National Monument, marking the scene of Custer's momentous defeat, is in which American state?

11. The writer often called 'Denmark's most famous son' was born in Odense, where his birthplace is now a museum. Who was he?

12. Which palace, now a top tourist attraction, was home to Henry VIII and is supposedly haunted by two of his wives?

13. Jesus gave a famous sermon on what is now known as the Mount of Beatitudes in the Jordan valley. The mount stands above which stretch of water?

14. Which New York square, at the heart of Greenwich Village, gave its name to the title of a novel by Henry James?

15. Name the Scottish poet who is remembered in museums at his birthplace in Alloway, Strathclyde and at the Tam O'Shanter Inn in Ayr.

16. Oscar Wilde's grave is in the Père Lachaise cemetery in Paris, where it was moved nine years after his death. Which famous sculptor produced the headstone?

17. Which Ernest Hemingway novel, set in the Spanish Civil War, was made into a film starring Ingrid Bergman?

18. In which German city can you visit Beethoven's birthplace and attend a concert in the Beethovenhalle?

19. The Captain Cook Memorial Museum is on New Zealand's Bay of Islands. In which ship did he sail round the country in 1769?

20. Laura Ingalls Wilder set the *Little House on the Prairie* books in Missouri but the original 'little house' and the farmhouse Charles Ingalls built in 1887 can be seen in which state?

21. Chartwell was Winston Churchill's home for 40 years. In which English county is Chartwell?

22. Which American state, where the restored home and law offices of Abraham Lincoln are situated, as well as the great man's tomb, is often called 'Land of Lincoln'?

23. The Napoleon museum is found in the Louis XV wing of the French palace in which he lived. Which palace is it?

24. Wild Bill Hickok and Calamity Jane are both buried above the town in South Dakota where Wild Bill was murdered. Name the town.

25. Which Jerusalem street, following the path taken by Jesus on his way to Golgotha, is now marked with the 'Stations of the Cross'?

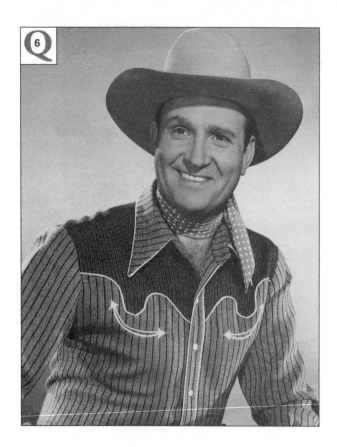

6. Gene Autry was the most successful of all singing cowboys to break into films. Name his horse.

7. Which country singer appeared in a US television series in the 1980s with her sisters Irlene and Louise?

8. Whose 1992 hit 'Achy Breaky Heart' led to a country music dance with the same name?

9. Which country star took her name from a hamburger stand?

10. The first female solo singer elected to the Country Music Hall of Fame in 1973 died in a plane crash in 1963. Who was she?

11. What is Stonewall Jackson's real name?

12. Name the vocalist who was born in England, grew up in Australia and was a country singer in the 1970s before going on to a more lucrative career in films like *Grease*.

13. Who is the 'Coalminer's Daughter'?

14. Which star, known for his country music, wrote the all-time favourite 'Country Roads'?

15. Who made the award-winning double platinum album *Trio* with Linda Ronstadt and Dolly Parton?

16. Which country music legend was nicknamed the 'Drifting Cowboy'?

1. Who recorded an album live in Folsom prison?

2. What are the first names of the Everly Brothers?

3. Which singer starred with John Wayne in *True Grit*?

4. Name Dolly Parton's Smoky Mountain theme park.

5. Who was known as the 'Singing Brakeman' and was later called the 'Father of Country Music'?

17. By what name is Virginia Wynette Pugh better known?

18. Which star, who began as Randy Traywick, then became Randy Ray before changing his name a second time, is said to be the 'first of the new traditionalists'?

19. Who wrote and performed 'Big Bad John' in the 1960s and later had hits with 'Stand Beside Me' and 'IOU'?

20. The 'International Ambassador of Country and Western Music' was the first American Western singer to perform in Russia and Czechoslavia. Who is he?

21. Which singer married Kris Kristofferson in 1973?

22. One of the richest men in country music, owner of a huge farm in Georgia, had one of his biggest hits with 'Islands in the Stream', a duet with Dolly Parton. Name him.

23. Which singer wrote 'Honeysuckle Rose' for the film of the same name and played Robert Redford's manager in *The Electric Horseman*?

24. In which town is the Grand Ole Opry?

25. Name the singer who starred with Jane Fonda and Lily Tomlin in the film *9 to 5*.

1. Which type of beans are used in Boston baked beans and in the French dish cassoulet?

2. The European types of sweet pepper are called paprikas. What do the Spanish call them?

3. Carrots are rich in which vitamin?

4. What vegetable is traditionally used in moussaka?

5. Tomatoes are now grown widely throughout the world, but where do they come from originally?

6. To which family does the globe artichoke belong?

7. What is Indian dhal made from?

8. By what name is the Lima or Madagascar bean often known?

9. Which type of garden peas are most used for canning and freezing?

10. In which country did the turnip originate?

11. Which name is given to the sun-dried peppers used to spice up Tabasco sauce and cayenne pepper?

12. Cabbage, kale and brussel sprouts are all members of which family?

13. Which vegetable is hollowed out and used as a lantern at Hallowe'en?

14. The chief pulse crop of India is called Bengal gram. By what name is it more commonly known?

15. There are two types of celery. One is the trenching variety. What is the other?

16. Potatoes are a crop of world-wide importance. Who were the first people in Europe to make great use of the potato in the early 17th century?

17. Chicory (endive) leaves are used in salads. Chicory is also dried, roasted and ground and mixed into which beverage?

18. Which vegetable would you find in Dubarry soup?

19. Beetroot is the main ingredient of which Russian soup?

20. What is the only cereal crop with American origins?

21. Which small type of cucumber is grown for pickling, where the immature fruits are soaked in brine and treated with boiling vinegar?

22. Kohlrabi is a cross between which vegetables?

23. Asparagus contains which vitamins?

24. What can be cherry, pear or potato-leaved?

25. Which vegetables are used in the famous New Orleans Creole dish gumbo?

5. Lenin was the leading light of which revolutionary party in Russia?

6. Where were the Russian royal family shot in 1918?

7. The gladiator Spartacus led a slave revolt in Rome in 71BC. Who played Spartacus in the 1960 film of the same name?

8. A notorious massacre of 2000 Huguenots who had gathered in Paris in August, 1857, took place on which saint's day?

9. Which leader of the Cuban revolution took power in 1959?

10. In which year did the massacre of pro-democracy students in Tiananmen Square, Beijing, take place?

11. Which Italian ship was hijacked in the Mediterranean in October 1985?

12. What was the nationality of the gunman who shot Pope John Paul II in Rome in 1981?

13. Who led the liberal movement which was put down by the Russians in Czechoslovakia in 1968?

14. Riots in Los Angeles followed the acquittal of four white police officers on charges of beating up a black man in 1991. Who was he?

15. What revolution took place in Iran in 1979?

1. Which political group imposed dictatorship in France after the Revolution?

2. Who took over the reins of power in France after the Revolution?

3. In 1857, in the Indian Mutiny, sepoys serving under British officers refused to handle cartridges. Why?

4. In China, a young nationalist movement known as the 'Society of Harmonious Fists' rose against foreign influences in 1900. The rebellion was known by the society's nickname. What was it?

16. The Belgian Congo became independent in 1960 after nationalist riots. In 1971 it changed its name to what?

17. Pam Am Flight 103 was blown up over Lockerbie in 1988. In what had the bomb been planted?

18. Who was forced into exile from the Philippines in 1986?

19. Two million Armenians were massacred as a result of religious intolerance between 1895 and 1922. Which government was attempting to eliminate Armenia as a nation?

20. Which country revolted against the rule of the USSR in 1956?

21. In what year did General Franco become head of state in Spain after the Civil War?

22. In February 1993 a car bomb planted by Islamic Fundamentalists went off in the underground parking garage of which New York building?

23. In which capital city was there a suicide bomb attack on the US Embassy in 1976?

24. An airliner belonging to which country was hijacked and taken to Entebbe airport in 1976?

25. In which Jordan field were three airliners blown up by Arab guerillas in 1970?

Q⑤

MYTH AND FAIRYTALE

Q 8

1. What was special about the relationship between Castor and Pollux?

2. Which epic poet wrote the *Iliad* and the *Odyssey*?

3. In Aborigine legend, the world was formed in Dreamtime. In these stories, who provides the first light of dawn by lighting a fire to prepare a torch to carry through the day?

4. In the Grimm brothers' fairytale, why did the Sleeping Beauty fall asleep for 100 years?

5. What was the name of King Arthur's magic sword?

6. Who wrote an opera about Hansel and Gretel?

7. According to Irish mythology, what natural wonder was the beginning of a pathway built by the great warrior Finn McCool to link the coasts of Ireland and Scotland?

8. Pan was a mischievous, pipe-playing Greek god who was only half man. What was the other half?

9. In which mythology would you find Balder, Freyja and Loki?

10. How many labours did Hercules have to perform to atone for his crimes?

11. What did Cinderella leave behind when she fled from the ball?

12. The Greeks called him Eros. What did the Romans call him?

13. In ancient Canadian legend, what was the oldest and wisest creature on earth before man came to the Americas?

14. What did the Delphic oracle prophesy that Oedipus would do to his parents?

15. Thumbelina, a tiny girl not half as big as a thumb, was grown from a beggar's gift to a peasant woman who befriended her. What was it?

16. Which planet was named after the goddess of love?

17. Who was condemned to carry the world on his shoulders for making war on the gods?

18. Maui is the great hero of Maori legend. Which New Zealand island do the Maoris call Te Ika a Maui, meaning 'Maui's fishhook'?

19. What was the occupation of Snow White's seven dwarfs?

20. Medusa was one of the Gorgons. What did she have for hair?

21. Which Greek dramatist wrote *Oedipus Rex*, *Antigone* and *Electra*?

22. What high office did Dick Whittington eventually fill?

23. In Greek mythology, which river did souls have to cross to get to Hades?

24. Whose wife was the Egyptian goddess Isis?

25. Who played Hans Christian Andersen in the 1952 film?

Q 4

5. How many children did John and Jackie Kennedy have?

6. Which brother did Ethel Skakel marry?

7. Which brother died when his plane exploded while on a World War II mission?

8. What political party did J. F. K. represent?

9. Which state did J. F. K. represent as senator?

10. What new feature appeared in the presidential campaign of 1960 when John F. Kennedy and Richard Nixon debated issues?

11. How old was J. F. K. when he was elected President?

12. What was the name of the young woman who died in 1969 when the car that Edward Kennedy was driving plunged off a bridge?

13. How did J. F. K.'s sister Kathleen die?

14. What was the international crisis during Kennedy's presidency that took the world close to nuclear war?

15. Which Kennedy sister was divorced from actor Peter Lawford?

16. In which year was J. F. K. assassinated?

17. Who shot Lee Harvey Oswald?

1. How many brothers and sisters did John F. Kennedy have?

2. Rose Kennedy, matriach of the family, died in January 1995. How old was she?

3. What was the first name of Rose's husband?

4. What was Jacqueline Kennedy's maiden name?

18. Who was sworn in as President immediately after the assassination?

19. Where is J. F. K. buried?

20. Which commission investigated the circumstances of the assassination?

21. Which brother married Joan Bennett?

23. John F. Kennedy was the first Catholic President of the US. True or false?

23. Who shot Robert Kennedy?

24. Where was Robert Kennedy assassinated?

25. John F. Kennedy Jnr has spent a year working on a new political publication called *George*, after George Washington. What was his previous job in Manhattan?

Q21

6. Which team has won eight team gold medals in Olympic Games dressage?

7. What age horses run in Triple Crown races in the US?

8. Name the jockey who overcame cancer to win the 1981 Grand National.

9. Ireland has produced some of the world's finest thoroughbred stock. Which racecourse is the home of all the Irish Classics?

10. The three-day event is still referred to as the *militaire* on the Continent because of its origins. Why?

11. Pierre Durand, France's Olympic gold medal winner in 1988, was still a part-time showjumper at the time, becoming full-time only in 1989. What was his previous profession?

1. What nationality is showjumping star Frankie Sloothaak?

2. In horse-jumping, what is the penalty for three refusals?

3. Where were the first World Equestrian Games held?

4. Name the horse that won the Derby by the greatest margin ever in 1981 and later disappeared.

5. How many players are there in a polo team?

12. In show-jumping, how many faults are incurred if horse and rider fall?

13. What relation are the showjumping riders Liz Edgar and David Broome?

14. How many fences in the Grand National are jumped twice?

15. What is the major race in Australia?

16. Which best-selling novelist wrote *Riders* and *Polo*?

17. Who was the first woman to win an individual gold medal in the Olympic Games in an equestrian event?

18. In horse-racing, what is a stayer?

19. The US race Arlington Million was first run in 1981 at Arlington Park, in which city?

20. Caroline Bradley, who died in 1983, was one of the world's best woman riders. She had a famous partnership with which horse?

21. Which showjumping rider holds most individual Olympic medals as individual rider and most titles as individual winner in World Championships?

22. In the film *National Velvet*, on which horse did Velvet Brown win the Grand National?

23. Where would riders encounter the Derby Bank?

24. The richest day's sport in the world is a US race meeting, held in October or November. What is it?

25. Puissance is a test of jumping ability. Where does the name come from?

Q3

1. Who painted *The Night Watch*?

2. What would you make in a samovar?

3. Patrice Lumumba was the premier of which African country?

4. In which year was synchronized swimming first included in the Olympic Games?

5. Who said that a cauliflower is nothing but a 'cabbage with a college education'?

6. In the St Valentine's Day Massacre, members of Bugs Moran's gang were gunned down by members of which other gang?

7. Which character did Felicity Kendall play in TV's *The Good Life*?

8. Andrew Bonar Law was British Prime Minister from 1922 to 1923. In which country was he born?

9. Who was assassinated by Nathuran Godse in 1948?

10. What is an animal's pug?

11. Which country is divided into 23 cantons?

12. In what type of painting did the artist Giovanni Bellini specialize?

13. Who would eat Halal meat?

14. In many countries, some insects are regarded as delicacies. Which insects are the most popular snacks?

15. What is unusual about the Chinese Crested dog?

16. Which father and daughter topped the charts with 'Something Stupid' in 1967?

17. Name Shirley MacLaine's actor brother.

18. In which country was Laurens van der Post born?

19. King George V changed the name of the British royal family to Windsor. What had it been previously?

20. The Parthenon in Athens belongs to which order of architecture?

21. Who was Liza Minelli's famous mother?

22. What animal married the Owl and Pussycat after they had gone to sea together?

23. *Sophie's Choice*, a novel by William Styron, was filmed in 1982. Who played Sophie?

24. Amy is a girl's name that comes from Old French. What does it mean?

25. The 'Star-Spangled Banner' became the US national anthem by Act of Congress in 1931. Who wrote the words?

Geography and Travel • In the Footsteps

1. Salzburg
2. He was governor of New South Wales
3. The site of the crucifixion
4. Mount Vernon
5. Florence
6. Fall River
7. Shakespeare
8. *The Hunchback of Notre Dame*
9. Buddha
10. Montana
11. Hans Christian Andersen
12. Hampton Court
13. Sea of Galilee
14. Washington Square
15. Robert Burns
16. Jacob Epstein
17. *For Whom the Bell Tolls*
18. Bonn
19. *Endeavour*
20. South Dakota
21. Kent
22. Illinois
23. Fontainebleau
24. Deadwood
25. Via Dolorosa

Popular Culture • Country and Western

1. Johnny Cash
2. Don and Phil
3. Glen Campbell
4. Dollywood
5. Jimmy Rodgers
6. Champion
7. Barbara Mandrell
8. Billy Ray Cyrus
9. Crystal Gayle
10. Patsy Cline
11. Stonewall Jackson
12. Olivia Newton-John
13. Loretta Lynn
14. John Denver
15. Emmylou Harris
16. Hank Williams
17. Tammy Wynette
18. Randy Travis
19. Jimmy Dean
20. George Hamilton IV
21. Rita Coolidge
22. Kennie Rogers
23. Willie Nelson
24. Nashville, Tennessee
25. Dolly Parton

Indoors and Out • Vegetable Crop

1. Haricot beans
2. Pimiento
3. Vitamin A
4. Aubergine (eggplant)
5. South America
6. The daisy family
7. Lentils
8. Butter bean
9. Marrowfat
10. Greece
11. Chillies
12. Brassica
13. Pumpkin
14. Chickpea
15. Self-blanching
16. The Irish
17. Coffee
18. Cauliflower
19. Bortsch
20. Corn
21. Gherkins
22. Cabbage and turnip
23. B and C
24. Tomato
25. Okra, green peppers, celery and onions

Past and Present • Revolution and Riots

1. Jacobins
2. Maximilian Robespierre
3. They believed they were coated with cow and pig grease
4. Boxer Rebellion
5. Bolsheviks
6. Ekaterinburg
7. Kirk Douglas
8. St Bartholomew's Day
9. Castro
10. 1989
11. *Achille Lauro*
12. Turkish
13. Alexander Dubcek
14. Rodney King
15. Islamic revolution
16. Zaire
17. In a radio/tape recorder
18. Ferdinand and Imelda Marcos
19. Turkish government
20. Hungary
21. 1939
22. World Trade Center
23. Beirut
24. France
25. Dawson's Field

Youth world • Myth and Fairytale

1. They were identical twin brothers
2. Homer
3. The Sun Woman
4. She pricked her finger on a spindle
5. Excalibur
6. Humperdinck
7. The Giant's Causeway
8. Goat
9. Norse
10. 12
11. A glass slipper
12. Cupid
13. The turtle
14. Kill his father and marry his mother
15. A barleycorn
16. Venus
17. Atlas
18. North Island
19. Diamond miners
20. Serpents
21. Sophocles
22. Lord Mayor of London
23. Styx
24. The wife of Osiris
25. Danny Kaye

Famous folk • The Kennedys

1. Eight
2. 104
3. Joseph
4. Bouvier
5. Three; one died in infancy
6. Robert
7. Joseph
8. Democrat
9. Massachusetts
10. The first-ever live TV presidential debate
11. 43
12. Mary Jo Kopechne
13. In a plane crash
14. Cuban missile crisis
15. Patricia
16. 1963
17. Jack Ruby
18. Lyndon B. Johnson
19. Arlington National Cemetery
20. Warren Commission
21. Edward
22. True
23. Sirhan B. Sirhan
24. Ambassador Hotel, Los Angeles
25. Assistant district attorney

Sport and Leisure • Horsy Sports

1. Dutch
2. Elimination
3. Stockholm
4. Shergar
5. Four
6. Germany
7. Three-year-olds
8. Bob Champion
9. The Curragh
10. It originated as a test for officers' chargers
11. Lawyer
12. Eight
13. Brother and sister
14. 14
15. Melbourne Cup
16. Jilly Cooper
17. Marian Mould
18. A horse that can gallop at racing pace over 2.4 km (1½ miles) or further
19. Chicago
20. Milton
21. Hans Günter Winkler
22. The Pie
23. Hickstead, Sussex
24. Breeders' Cup Day
25. It is French for 'power'

Pot Luck

1. Rembrandt
2. Tea
3. The Congo
4. 1984
5. Mark Twain
6. Al Capone's
7. Barbara Good
8. Canada
9. Gandhi
10. Footprint
11. Switzerland
12. Devotional pictures of the Madonna
13. Muslims
14. Grasshoppers
15. It is hairless
16. Nancy and Frank Sinatra
17. Warren Beatty
18. South Africa
19. Saxe-Coburg-Gotha
20. Doric
21. Judy Garland
22. Turkey
23. Meryl Streep
24. Loved
25. Francis Scott Key

12

1. What is the longest river in India?

2. China was the birthplace of two religions. One is Taoism, what is the other?

3. The tsetse fly, found in Africa, spreads what disease?

4. Which country, the most populated in Africa, is often called 'the Giant of Africa'?

5. What is a calabash?

6. Which country is the largest producer of tungsten?

7. The world's highest active volcano is in Ecuador. What is it called?

8. In which country is the ancient town of Timbuktu?

9. What is the largest and most sparsely populated state in Central America?

10. Rwanda obtained its independence from which country in 1962?

11. Why are the Blue Mountains of Jamaica so called?

12. When does the wet season begin in India?

13. What is puja?

14. The OAU was set up in 1963 at the conference of Addis Ababa, its aim to promote unity among African states. What do the initials stand for?

15. Varanasi is one of the most sacred of Hindu cities. Pilgrims bathe from the 'ghats', or stairs, in which river?

16. What is Columbia's largest export?

17. Name the capital and chief port of Nigeria.

18. The Ruwenzori mountains are found on the border between which countries?

19. The highest mountain in the world is found in the Himalayas. What does 'Himalayas' mean?

20. The most devastating floods in Bangladesh were in 1970, before the country gained independence. What was it called at that time?

21. The Live Aid concert was organized to raise money for the famine victims of which country?

22. Which fertile state in India is often called the 'granary of India'?

23. What name is given to the ruler of a Muslim state?

24. The Masai Mara game park in Kenya is on the Serengeti Plain. What is the dramatic setting of the second most popular Kenyan game park, Amboseli?

25. Which mountain range is known as the 'roof of the world'?

Q 22

5. Which poet invited Maud to come into the garden?

6. Barbara Cartland, one of the world's most prolific novelists, extols the virtue of vitamin supplements and what natural food?

7. In *Gone with the Wind*, Rhett Butler loves Scarlett O'Hara. Who does Scarlett love?

8. Clark Gable and Carole Lombard were both movie idols when they met, eloped and married in secret. How did she die in 1942?

9. Which character sings 'If Ever I Would Leave You' in *Camelot*?

10. In Shakespeare's *Romeo and Juliet*, Romeo belongs to the Montagu family. Which family does Juliet belong to?

11. Why does Miss Havisham, in *Great Expectations*, live as a recluse in a white dress and veil?

12. Which couple married in Canada in 1964 and again in 1975 in Botswana?

13. 'Stranger in Paradise' and 'This is my Beloved' are songs from which musical?

14. Which classic screen love story begins with Alec removing a cinder from Laura's eye on a railway station and progresses to a score by Rachmaninov?

15. Who is Hiawatha's beloved in the poem of that name by Longfellow?

1. The love story of which writer is portrayed in *Shadowlands*?

2. The songs 'If I Loved You' and 'You'll Never Walk Alone' come from which musical?

3. In which country did the Duke of Windsor and his wife take up residence after his abdication?

4. Who married his *Days of Thunder* co-star?

16. During the making of which film did Humphrey Bogart and Lauren Bacall meet and fall in love?

17. Who plays the insomniac widower in *Sleepless in Seattle*?

18. Which poet's love is like 'a red, red rose that's newly sprung in June'?

19. In *Dr Zhivago*, who has a passionate affair with the hero?

20. Which character washes a man right out of her hair in *South Pacific*?

21. Who plays the two characters who plan a sexy vacation in Spain and then fall in love by mistake in *A Touch of Class*?

22. In which novel by Charlotte Brontë does a governess marry the master of Thornfield Hall?

23. Where do two ex-lovers meet under dramatic circumstances in *Casablanca*?

24. In which Jane Austen novel does Elizabeth Bennet fall in love with Mr Darcy?

25. When is St Valentine's Day?

1. What name is given to the dragonfly larva that hatches from the egg?

2. Where does the mandarin duck nest?

3. How would you distinguish an alligator from a crocodile, at a glance?

4. The papyrus plant, once plentiful in the Nile Delta, is now an endangered plant in Egypt. What was papyrus used for in ancient Egypt?

5. Daphnia and cyclops are types of which creature?

6. What are the smallest type of plants found in a pond called?

7. The pondskater uses its hind legs as rudders and its middle legs as oars. What are the front legs for?

8. What do the plants Canadian pondweed, bladderworts, milfoil and hornwort have in common?

9. Dippers are found in Europe, the Americas, West Africa and Asia, feeding on snails, tadpoles and larvae. How do they find their food?

10. How does the male stickleback fish attract a mate?

11. What is the largest and heaviest water-bird of freshwater lakes and rivers?

12. The Australian platypus is a monotreme. What is a monotreme?

13. When do some drakes go into 'eclipse' plumage?

14. Which flowers had the reputation as a symbol of immortality in ancient times?

15. What is the otter's home called?

16. The plants with poker-shaped heads that usually feature in pictures of Moses in the bulrushes, are not true bulrushes. What are they?

17. What name is given to young fish, especially salmon and trout?

18. Female frogs lay their eggs in water. What do they hatch into?

19. The water spider spends its whole life under water. How does it create a place to mate and lay its eggs?

20. What is a beaver's home called?

21. The medicinal leech produces a chemical which can have a use in medical practice. What does it do?

22. For its first three years in the river, a salmon is known as a 'parr'. When it migrates to the sea it is known as what?

23. The heaviest snake is the water boa of northern South America. What is it usually called?

24. Water lettuce is a floating plant with rosette leaves which is often used to coat the surface of tropical ponds and fish tanks as it keeps the water cool and fresh. What is its disadvantage?

25. The Jaçana bird has long, widespread toes that enable it to walk across leaves in its search for insects and seeds. What is its nickname?

Q 12

1. In which decade of the 19th century was the Ku Klux Klan originally founded?

2. What do the initials WASP stand for?

3. What was the meaning of 'apartheid'?

4. What was the Holocaust?

5. In 1937 Hitler told a sitting of the Reichstag that Germans needed *Lebensraum*. What did this mean?

6. Which Jews were first boycotted under Hitler's anti-Semitic decrees?

7. Who took control of the ruthless SS from 1929?

8. Chelmno was the first example of an important instrument of Hitler's plans. What was it?

9. Josef Goebbels was Hitler's right-hand man. How did he die?

10. Adolf Eichmann, who was personally responsible for the operation of extermination centres, escaped after the war. Where was he eventually kidnapped by Israeli agents?

11. Where was the largest Jewish ghetto, the scene of an uprising in 1943?

12. The battle of Wounded Knee in 1890 involved which minority ethnic group?

13. In America, what do the initials CORE stand for?

14. What did the 'Jim Crow' laws, enacted in various American states, seek to do?

15. 'The Little Rock Nine' were black students who took their places in a previously segregated High School against strenuous local opposition. In which American state is Little Rock?

16. In 1955 Rosa Parks refused to give up her seat to a white man in a bus in Alabama and was imprisoned as an agitator. What incident followed?

17. In the early 1960s, South African police enforced security laws run by BOSS. What do the initials stand for?

18. What are the 'Bantustans'?

19. Which South African 'black consciousness' leader died from severe brain damage while in police custody in 1977?

20. What is Soweto short for?

21. Which notorious massacre took place at a South African township in 1960, when police opened fire on a crowd demonstrating against the pass laws?

22. In which year was Nelson Mandela sentenced to life imprisonment?

23. Who took over from Mandela as ANC leader?

24. What church did civil rights leader Martin Luther King belong to?

25. In the 1970s the Rhodesian government found itself fighting with ZAPU and ZANU. ZAPU was the Zimbabwe Africa People's Union. What was ZANU?

Q5

4. Scott Baio plays the title character in *Bugsy Malone*. Who plays Tallulah?

5. How old was Judy Garland when she appeared in *The Wizard of Oz*?

6. In which film do three children, played by Hayley Mills, Alan Barnes and Diane Holgate, find a killer they believe to be Jesus Christ?

7. Which teenage singer-actor of the 1930s went on to star with Gene Kelly in *Singin' in the Rain*?

8. Eight-year-old Margaret O'Brien stars in *Our Vines Have Tender Grapes*. Who plays her Wisconsin farmer father?

9. Ricky Schroder made his debut at age nine in a film about prize-fighting, with Jon Voigt and Faye Dunaway as his parents. Name the film.

10. How old was Tatum O'Neal when she won the Best Supporting Actress award for *Paper Moon*?

11. In which film do youngsters Jon Whiteley and Vincent Winter find a baby on a Scottish hillside and decide to keep it as a pet?

12. *Home Alone* made Macaulay Culkin a star. Name the 1995 film in which he plays a youngster who becomes a millionaire after his parents are killed in a plane crash.

13. Bette Davis plays a former child star grown old and embittered in which film?

1. Who starred as Helen Keller at the age of 16 and as Helen's teacher in a TV version of the same work 17 years later?

2. Which father and daughter star in *Tiger Bay*?

3. In which film does Lukas Hass play a young Amish boy who sees a murder ?

14. Deanna Durbin was a teenage singer-actress who launched her film career along with Judy Garland in a short film called *Every Sunday* in 1936. What is her nationality ?

15. What role does young Henry Thomas play in *ET*?

16. Which member of a well-known acting family plays one of the Banks family in *Mary Poppins*?

17. The 1947 version of *Miracle on 34th Street* stars a child actress who later went on to star as Gypsy Rose Lee. Who is she?

18. In a classic western Brandon de Wilde plays Joey, idolizing a former gunfighter who comes to the rescue of homesteaders menaced by an all-powerful cattle baron. Name the film.

19. Which child star of the 1970s made her debut as a director with *Little Man Tate*, about the problems of a child genius?

20. Which child actress is the eldest of *The Railway Children*?

21. Tatum O'Neal appeared in *Bad News Bears* which revolved around which sport?

22. Which former child actress became US ambassador to Czechoslovakia in the late 1980s?

23. Linda Blair gives an electrifying performance as the girl possessed by demons in *The Exorcist*. Who wrote the book on which the film is based?

24. Mark Lester plays the title role in *Oliver!* Who plays the Artful Dodger?

25. As a child, Roddy McDowall tugged at the heartstrings in *How Green Was My Valley*. In the 1960s he appeared in a science fiction film which was to inspire several sequels as well as animated cartoons and a TV series. Name it.

Q21

1. Who was the first king of Israel?

2. In which country has Queen Margrethe II reigned since 1972?

3. Which German ruler did Queen Victoria's eldest daughter marry in 1858?

4. Who is the only son of Prince Rainier of Monaco?

5. Which royal house ruled Austria from the 15th century to 1918?

6. For how long did Lady Jane Grey reign in England in 1553?

7. Juan Carlos was restored to the Spanish throne after Franco's death. He married a princess from which country?

8. Who plays King Faisal in the 1962 film *Lawrence of Arabia*?

9. Which Roman general became Cleopatra's lover and ruled Egypt with her?

10. Brian Boru became king of which country in 1001?

11. Who was the legendary first king of Rome, ruling for 40 years?

12. Madame du Barry was the influential mistress of which French king?

13. The rulers of the Netherlands, currently represented by Queen Beatrix, belong to which royal house?

14. Where was Princess Elizabeth when she heard that her father had died and she was Queen of Britain?

15. Which Babylonian king conquered the kingdom of Judah and sacked Jerusalem, sending the Hebrews into captivity in Babylon?

16. Which king of Prussia was chosen as the first emperor of Germany in 1871?

17. What Australian city was named after the wife of William IV of Britain?

18. In which kingdom did the house of Wittelsbach reign?

19. Which French king re-established the Bourbon dynasty after the downfall of Napoleon, reigning from 1815 to 1824?

20. At what age did Queen Victoria come to the throne?

21. Peter II was the last king of Yugoslavia. After his exile in 1945, who came to power in the country?

22. In which country were Simeon, Boris, Ferdinand and Ivan Shishman kings?

23. Who was technically the last Tsar of Russia, becoming Emperor in 1721?

24. In the film *The Madness of King George*, who plays Queen Charlotte?

25. Which of Henry VIII's wives outlived him?

1. After how many penalty points is a contestant in a wrestling bout eliminated?

2. What used to be called a battledore?

3. When did Torvill and Dean first win the World Ice Dancing Championship?

4. Which immigrants introduced nine-pin bowling to the US?

5. On how many pieces of apparatus do men compete in international gymnastic competition?

6. On how many pieces of apparatus do women gymnasts compete?

7. At the beginning of a basketball game, the referee throws up the ball in the centre circle. What is this called?

8. A table tennis game is won by the first player to reach how many points?

9. Ice hockey has its historical roots in which country?

10. A game of pool is made up of an agreed number of 'sections', each played to an agreed point requirement. What are these sections called?

11. What is special about a three cushion billiard table?

12. Which is the most successful country in Olympic boxing?

13. Whose set of rules was adopted in boxing in 1865?

14. What is the nickname of basketball player Irvine Johnson?

15. In November 1994 who regained the world heavyweight boxing title he lost 20 years earlier to Muhammad Ali ?

16. In which sport is the Uber Cup awarded?

17. What is the lowest possible score to conclude a game of darts?

18. In which sport might you see an Endocircle, Elgrip swing or Voronin hop?

19. When is a spare scored in ten-pin bowling?

20. In 1985 Steve Davis came close to winning his third successive world title with a lead of 8–0 but his opponent came from behind to beat him. Who was he?

21. Basketball has five players a side. How many does netball have?

22. In an American game of squash, both server and receiver can score. True or false?

23. How many balls are used in a game of pool?

24. Badminton became an Olympic sport quite recently. Give the year.

25. Which British boxer had a left hook, with which he once floored Muhammad Ali, known as 'Enery's 'ammer'?

1. In dice, what are 'snake eyes'?

2. Who caught the German war-criminal Adolf Eichmann after World War II?

3. Which famous group was led by Guy Gibson in World War II?

4. In heraldry, what is a creature in a lying position called?

5. Which actress stars in *Anatomy of a Murder* and *Days of Wine and Roses*?

6. Halley's Comet, named after Edmond Halley who calculated its orbit, will next reappear in which year?

7. Name the singer who had hits with 'Pretty Woman' and 'Only the Lonely'.

8. Which school of architecture was associated with Walter Gropius?

9. What is the middle name of the Princess of Wales?

10. Name the sauce made from mayonnaise, chopped capers and onions and served with fish?

11. What was the first Rolls Royce model called?

12. Which is the largest of the Canadian provinces?

13. In which sea are the group of islands called Tristan da Cunha?

14. In 1991 *Dances with Wolves* won an Oscar for best picture. Who won the best director award for the same film?

15. What name is given to a male swan?

16. What is the unit of weight used to measure gemstones?

17. In which musical does a Scottish village become visible for only one day in every hundred years?

18. What is a group of porpoises called?

19. Who wrote *The Birthday Party* and *The Caretaker*?

20. Which film star said: 'You are not drunk if you can lie on the floor without holding on'?

21. On which part of the body would you wear puttees?

22. Which city was often painted by Canaletto?

23. What is the capital of Burma?

24. Rachel, a name that appears in the Old Testament, comes from the Hebrew. What does it mean?

25. What do the novelist J. R. R. Tolkien's initials stand for?

Geography and Travel • Third World

1. Brahmaputra
2. Confucianism
3. Sleeping sickness
4. Nigeria
5. A gourd, hollowed out to hold liquids
6. China
7. Cotopaxi
8. Mali
9. Nicaragua
10. Belgium
11. There is a bluish haze over them
12. June
13. A form of religious worship for Hindus
14. Organization of African Unity
15. Ganges
16. Cocaine
17. Lagos
18. Uganda and Zaire
19. Abode of snow
20. East Pakistan
21. Ethiopia
22. Punjab
23. Emir
24. Below Mount Kilimanjaro
25. Karakoram

Popular Culture • Romance

1. C.S. Lewis
2. *Carousel*
3. France
4. Tom Cruise
5. Tennyson
6. Honey
7. Ashley Wilkes
8. In a plane crash
9. King Arthur
10. Capulet
11. She was jilted on her wedding day
12. Elizabeth Taylor and Richard Burton
13. *Kismet*
14. *Brief Encounter*
15. Minnehaha
16. *To Have and Have Not*
17. Tom Hanks
18. Robert Burns
19. Lara
20. Nellie Forbush
21. Glenda Jackson and George Segal
22. *Jane Eyre*
23. Rick's bar
24. *Pride and Prejudice*
25. 14 February

Indoors and Out • Pond and River Life

1. Nymph
2. In a hole in a tree
3. The alligator's teeth do not project when the jaw is closed
4. Paper and sails
5. Water-fleas
6. Algae
7. Grabbing insects for food
8. They all float on the water surface
9. They dive into the water and walk along the bottom
10. He dances for her
11. Mute swan
12. An egg-laying mammal
13. Outside the breeding season
14. Waterlilies
15. Holt
16. Reed mace
17. Alevin
18. Tadpoles
19. It spins a web between plants that acts as a diving bell
20. Lodge
21. It prevents blood clotting
22. Smolt
23. Anaconda
24. It spreads quickly
25. Lily-trotter

Past and Present • Race Relations

1. 1860s
2. White Anglo-Saxon Protestant
3. Separate development
4. Persecution and destruction of Jews by the Nazis
5. Living space
6. Shopkeepers, doctors and lawyers
7. Heinrich Himmler
8. Extermination camp
9. He shot himself
10. Argentina
11. Warsaw
12. Native Americans
13. Congress of Racial Equality
14. Limit the rights of blacks
15. Arkansas
16. A boycott of buses by the blacks
17. Bureau of Social Security
18. South African homelands
19. Steve Biko
20. South-West Township
21. Sharpeville massacre
22. 1964
23. Oliver Tambo
24. Baptist
25. Zimbabwe African National Union

Youth World • Young Stars

1. Patty Duke
2. John and Hayley Mills
3. *Witness*
4. Jodie Foster
5. Seventeen
6. *Whistle Down the Wind*
7. Donald O'Connor
8. Edward G. Robinson
9. *The Champ*
10. 10
11. *The Kidnappers*
12. *Richie Rich*
13. *Whatever Happened to Baby Jane?*
14. Canadian
15. Elliott
16. Karen Dotrice
17. Natalie Wood
18. *Shane*
19. Jodie Foster
20. Jenny Agutter
21. Little League baseball
22. Shirley Temple Black
23. Peter Blatty
24. Jack Wild
25. *Planet of the Apes*

Famous Folk • International Royalty

1. Saul
2. Denmark
3. Frederick III
4. Prince Albert
5. Hapsburg
6. Nine days
7. Greece
8. Alec Guinness
9. Mark Antony
10. Ireland
11. Romulus
12. Louis XV
13. Orange
14. Kenya
15. Nebuchadnezzar
16. William I
17. Adelaide
18. Bavaria
19. Louis XVIII
20. 18
21. Tito
22. Bulgaria
23. Peter the Great
24. Helen Mirren
25. Catherine Parr

Sport and Leisure • Indoor Sports

1. Six
2. Badminton racquet
3. 1981
4. Dutch and German
5. Five
6. Three
7. Jump ball
8. 21
9. Canada
10. Blocks
11. It has no pockets
12. USA
13. Marquess of Queensberry
14. Magic
15. George Forman
16. Badminton
17. Two
18. Men's gymnastics
19. When a player knocks down all 10 pins with both balls in a frame
20. Dennis Taylor
21. Seven a side
22. True
23. One white ball and 15 numbered object balls
24. 1992
25. Henry Cooper

Pot Luck

1. Two
2. Dr. Simon Wiesenthal
3. The Dambusters
4. Couchant
5. Lee Remick
6. 2061
7. Roy Orbison
8. Bauhaus
9. Frances
10. Tartare sauce
11. Silver Ghost
12. Quebec
13. Atlantic
14. Kevin Costner
15. Cob
16. Carat
17. *Brigadoon*
18. A school
19. Harold Pinter
20. Dean Martin
21. On the legs
22. Venice
23. Rangoon
24. Ewe
25. John Ronald Reuel

QUIZ

13

Q 23

1. Which town gives its name to the French national anthem because so many of its revolutionaries marched on Paris in 1792?

2. Where is the oldest oracle in Greece, dedicated to Zeus?

3. What would you find in the Prado, Madrid?

4. Name the Scottish royal residence bought by Queen Victoria and Prince Albert as a summer home in 1848.

5. What does the Bayeux tapestry record?

6. Where is the headquarters of the World Health Organization?

7. What is the smallest state in the world?

8. Which European city consists of 118 islands linked by 400 bridges?

9. In which German town is a passion play performed every 10 years?

10. The leaning Tower of Pisa is a popular tourist attraction. What is it?

11. In which part of Paris is the Cathedral of Notre Dame?

12. Monte Marmolada is the highest peak in which mountain range?

13. In which country would you find the ports of Cartagena, Santander and Bilbao?

14. In the old song, which Irish mountains 'sweep down to the sea'?

15. Which country is sometimes called the 'Hexagon' because it is roughly six-sided?

16. In which mountain range would you find the ski resort of St Moritz?

17. What do the frescoes on the ceiling of the Sistine Chapel in Rome, painted by Michelangelo, depict?

18. In which Italian town is a horse race called the Palio run around the main piazza?

19. What is the oldest part of the Tower of London, built for William the Conqueror?

20. Name the flat, marshy area of south-east France, famous as a breeding ground for bulls and horses.

21. On which French bridge, according to the song, did everyone dance in a ring?

22. In which city would you find the statue of the Little Mermaid?

23. In which country would you find flamenco dancers?

24. What is the highest peak in the Alps?

25. Which wall was built across the north of England to defend the northern frontier of the Roman empire?

1. Which British actress played Sable Colby in *Dynasty*?

2. Name the former star of *Neighbours* who had a 1990 hit with 'Another Night'.

3. Both *Brookside* and *Emmerdale Farm* have introduced lesbian characters. Who are they?

4. In *Eastenders*, who was sent to prison after a drink-drive accident?

5. *Home and Away* takes place in which seaside resort?

6. Name the three founder members of Ewing Oil in *Dallas*.

7. In *Falcon Crest*, what was Angela Channing's maiden name?

8. Which brewery owns the Rover's Return in *Coronation Street*?

9. The Colbys was a short-lived spin-off of *Dynasty*. Who appeared in the series as the glamorous Maya Kumara?

10. In *Neighbours*, who ran over Cheryl Stark after an argument?

11. What is the name of the restaurant set up by Barry and Max in *Brookside*?

12. In *Knots Landing*, who is Gary and Val's eldest daughter, a central character in early episodes of Dallas?

13. In *Dynasty*, Pamela Sue Martin first played Fallon. Who took over from her?

14. Which three women monopolized the Snug of the Rover's Return in the early days of *Coronation Street*?

15. In *Home and Away*, how did Bobby receive her fatal injury?

16. *Falcon Crest* is set in which valley?

17. Who set fire to Frank's car lot in *Eastenders*?

18. Which member of the Ewing clan had heart surgery in *Dallas*?

19. In what street do the characters from *Neighbours* live?

20. Who shot Blake Carrington in the last episode of *Dynasty*?

21. In *Coronation Street*, which two friends run the cafe?

22. Who plays Greg Sumner in *Knots Landing*?

23. Who temporarily replaced Barbara Bel Geddes as Miss Ellie?

24. How did 'Dirty Den' die in *Eastenders*?

25. The spoof series *Soap* featured a butler who had his own spin-off series. What was his name?

Q 8

4. If a plant is described as 'suspensa', what does it mean?

5. What useful piece of gardening equipment did Edwin Beard Budding invent in 1830?

6. Fertilizers contain N P & K in various proportions. What do the initials stand for?

7. Which type of vegetable crop is most susceptible to damage from pests?

8. At what time of year would you divide chrysanthemums and michaelmas daisies?

9. Which of the following are grown from corms: hyacinth, gladiolus, daffodil, tulip, crocus?

10. In what part of the world have most successful seaside shrubs evolved?

11. What would you use secateurs for?

12. When a mulch is applied to the surface of the soil, what does it do?

13. What does it mean when a plant is named *exotica*?

14. What can be tent, barn or T-shaped?

15. Who sailed with Captain Cook to Australia and was responsible for bringing thousands of plants back to England, where he founded Kew Gardens?

16. Calcareous soils are rich in what?

1. What does the pH scale measure?

2. When growing seedlings, what is a cold frame used for?

3. What name is given to an insecticide which is absorbed into the plant sap stream from an application to the soil?

17. Which crops can be sown earlier in open ground: onions or cauliflowers?

18. What name is given to a cross between botanically distinct species?

19. Blackberry bushes need lime-free soil. True or false?

20. When mowing a lawn, you might use a cylinder or a rotary mower. Which would you use if you wanted a striped effect?

21. Layering is a way of propagating plants. What does it mean?

22. What name is given to the type of weedkiller that does not kill established weeds but helps to prevent germination for up to three months?

23. Spinach will deteriorate if it is allowed to grow long enough to 'bolt'. What does that mean?

24. What does it mean if a plant is described as *prostratus*?

25. Among the most serious diseases that attack roses are black spot and rust. What type of diseases are these?

4. In which country is the Zapatista guerilla movement active?

5. Who is Jean Luc Dehaene?

6. How did Dehaene hit the headlines in mid-1994?

7. Tony Blair is Leader of the Labour Party in Britain. What is his wife's name?

8. Who was returned to power in Haiti with American help?

9. Who became the Speaker of the House in America in 1995?

10. In 1997 the countries of the world begin work on a major space project to be completed in 2002. What is it?

11. Alija Izetbegovic is President of which country?

12. Eurotunnel has suffered a number of teething troubles, including too few passengers on the high-speed London-Paris and London-Brussels train service. What is this service called?

13. When did the IRA announce a complete cessation of military operations?

14. Which British bank crashed as a result of unwise derivatives trading?

1. Name the company headed by Richard Branson.

2. In which country is the town of Grozny, besieged by the Russians in 1994?

3. Who resigned as director of the CIA at the end of 1994?

15. Name the Formula One driver who agreed terms with McLaren and signed to partner Mika Hakkinen at the age of 42.

16. In Australia the OSW, created by the Whitlam government in 1974, was recently in the news. What do the initials stand for?

17. 2500 UN peacekeeping troops pulled out of which country in February 1995?

18. How many members did the European Union have in December 1994?

19. Which countries joined the European Union in January 1995?

20. Who was the first woman to head MI5?

21. Algeria has endured several years of conflict between the government and which extremist group?

22. Bill Gates has been called the richest man in America. How does he make his money?

23. Which country suffered a devastating earthquake in 1995?

24. In Britain, the ordination of women priests was adamantly opposed until recently. In which decade were women priests first allowed in New Zealand?

25. What is Bill Clinton's 'three strikes' policy?

Q 14

1. In windsurfing, what is the uphaul?

2. How do wetsuits keep the wearer warm in water?

3. How many pieces are used in backgammon?

4. What name is given to computer games in which characters move from one level to another collecting objects to score points?

5. In what game do players 'peg out'?

6. How many dragon colours are there in mah jong?

7. When playing darts, the darts are thrown from behind a line. What is the line called?

8. What name is given to a kind of underwater hockey played between teams?

9. How many players take part in a game of Solo?

10. What are the crouch roll, pike fall and springheader?

11. What name is given to the horizontal lines of squares on a chessboard?

12. If you were rolling dice chanting 'baby needs new shoes' what would you be playing?

13. What does 'judo' mean?

14. What name is given to the flat surface of a skateboard?

15. How many skittles are used in table skittles?

16. 'Dungeons and Dragons' is one of the best known of the original computer games. What type of game is it?

17. In stud poker, how many cards are dealt before the betting starts?

18. How many pieces are there in a Rubik's cube?

19. What is BMX short for?

20. What is buddy diving?

21. In Scrabble, what bonus is gained if a player puts down all seven tiles in one turn?

22. What are PBM games?

23. In wild card poker, what is a wild card?

24. In the original Space Invaders, which is worth more points, a flying saucer or a column of space invaders?

25. What name is given to the gear system of racing and mountain bikes, whereby the chain is thrown from one sprocket onto the next?

Q16

1. What is Linford Christie's native country?

2. By what name is Edson Aro Arantes do Nascimento better known?

3. Racing driver Jochen Rindt suffered a fatal crash in practice for which event in 1970?

4. Who is regarded as the first boxing champion?

5. Why was Muhammad Ali stripped of his heavyweight title in 1967?

6. What ended the playing career of tennis star Arthur Ashe in 1979?

7. Who was the first man to sail non-stop round the world?

8. In which sport is Adrian Moorhouse well known?

9. Which US baseball player was once married to Marilyn Monroe?

10. Name the Canadian hockey player, probably the best in the history of the National Hockey League, who plays with the Edmonton Oilers and the Los Angeles Kings.

11. Josiah Shackford made the earliest known single-handed Atlantic crossing in 1786. Which country did he start from?

12. In which year did Daley Thompson first win the Olympic Decathlon?

13. In 1985, which 17-year-old was the youngest winner of the Wimbledon men's singles title?

14. Who has acted as captain most often in Test Matches?

15. Which British footballer was transferred to the Italian club Lazio in 1992 for £5.5 million?

16. The South African runner Zola Budd was given British citizenship to enable her to compete in the Olympic Games in which year?

17. Why is the New York Yankee stadium called 'the house that Ruth built'?

18. Who was the first French World Drivers Champion?

19. In which sport is Peter Oosterhuis well known?

20. Which heavyweight boxer was nicknamed the 'Manassa Mauler'?

21. Canadian sprinter Ben Johnson was disqualified from his winning event in 1983 for his use of steroids. In which event had he previously set a record?

22. Who was known as 'the Kaiser'?

23. Name the yachtsman who circumnavigated the world solo in 1970–71 and had previously rowed across the North Atlantic with a companion.

24. Graham Hick was his country's youngest professional cricketer at the age of 17. Which country was it?

25. Which woman was the outstanding athlete of the 1988 Olympics, winning three golds and a silver in sprints and relays?

Q 5

1. Which country pioneered orienteering ?

2. What would you do with a cagoule?

3. Who led the team of mountaineers who first succeeded in climbing Everest?

4. What is a terminal moraine?

5. How long is a marathon?

6. When did the 'Golden Age of Mountaineering' – the 11 years in which 180 great peaks were climbed for the first time – begin?

7. In rock climbing, what does rappel mean?

8. What is the science of map-making called?

9. Which is the world's oldest annual race, which first took place in 1897?

10. Name the Alaskan mountain climbed for the first time in 1913.

11. Which athlete set a 100 metres record in Japan in 1991?

12. Which American broke that 1991 record in 1994?

13. In mountaineering, what is a cornice?

14. What would you do with dubbin?

15. On a snowy mountain, what is glissading?

16. Magnetic north is the north to which the compass needle always points. What is grid north?

17. When climbing, what would you be doing if you were traversing?

18. What name is given to metal spikes hammered into rock as anchors?

19. What is a couloir?

20. The first ascent of K2 was in 1954. What nationality was the team?

21. The Boston Marathon, run on or around April 19 every year, commemorates what event?

22. In mountaineering, what are the 'voies normales'?

23. Which is older, the London or the New York marathon?

24. In which year was the London Marathon first held?

25. In 1985 an American millionaire became, at 55, the oldest man to scale Everest and the first to climb to the highest points of all the continents. Name him.

Q18

1. Which group's first album is *Piper at the Gate of Dawn*?

2. In which sport did Richard Meade become famous?

3. Who was the husband of Messalina?

4. Americans call it a bill. What is it called in Britain?

5. George IV tried to have his marriage to Caroline of Brunswick dissolved in 1820. On what grounds?

6. Which film featured the song 'Bright Eyes'?

7. Who painted the *Blue Boy*?

8. What is the name given to an area of low atmospheric pressure along the equator, and sometimes used for a person who is feeling depressed?

9. In which film did Marilyn Monroe sing 'That Old Black Magic'?

10. Mel Brooks is married to which actress?

11. What type of acid is normally used in car batteries?

12. What year links an overture by Tchaikovsky and Napoleon's retreat from Moscow?

13. What are the major suits in bridge?

14. Trevor Huddleston, a priest who later became an archbishop, wrote a book called *Naught for your Comfort*. What was it about?

15. What do superstitious actors call Shakespeare's *Macbeth*?

16. Who wrote about a traffic warden called Rita?

17. What, according to the saying, can you never make out of a sow's ear?

18. The Pole Star, the brightest star in the constellation of Ursa Minor, is known by what other name?

19. Who had a hit with 'The Ballad of Bonnie and Clyde'?

20. Cocker, clumber and springer are types of which breed of dog?

21. Bruce Willis, Sylvester Stallone and Arnold Schwarzenegger are the owners of which London restaurant?

22. What animal is a mandrill?

23. Name the Russian born novelist, a naturalized American, who wrote *The Fountainhead* and *Atlas Shrugged*.

24. In which sport might the participants have to battle through a tie-break?

25. What drink was often called 'old Tom'?

Answers to Quiz 13

Geography and Travel • European Tour

1. Marseilles
2. Dodona
3. Works of art collected mainly by Spanish royalty
4. Balmoral
5. Scenes from the 1066 Norman invasion of England
6. Geneva
7. The Vatican
8. Venice
9. Oberammergau
10. The free-standing campanile (bell-tower) of the cathedral
11. Ile de la Cité
12. Dolomites
13. Spain
14. Mountains of Mourne
15. France
16. The Alps
17. The Creation
18. Siena
19. The White Tower
20. The Camargue
21. Avignon
22. Copenhagen
23. Spain
24. Mont Blanc
25. Hadrian's Wall

Youth World • Fun and Games

1. The rope used to pull the sail out of the water
2. By trapping water between the body and the suit
3. 30
4. Platform
5. Cribbage
6. Three
7. The hockey
8. Octopush
9. Four
10. Dives
11. Ranks
12. Craps
13. The gentle way
14. Deck
15. Nine
16. A role-playing fantasy game
17. Two: one face up, one face down
18. 26
19. Bicycle Motocross
20. Diving with companions
21. 50 points
22. Play by mail games
23. It represents any card the player decides on
24. Flying saucer
25. Derailleur gear system

Popular Culture • Soaps: Then and Now

1. Stephanie Beacham
2. Jason Donovan
3. Zoe Tate and Beth Jordache
4. Pat Butcher
5. Summer Bay
6. Jock and Jason Ewing and Digger Barnes
7. Gioberti
8. Newton and Ridley
9. Bianca Jagger
10. Julie Martin
11. Grants
12. Lucy Ewing
13. Emma Samms
14. Ena Sharples, Martha Longhurst and Minnie Caldwell
15. In a speedboat incident
16. Tuscany valley
17. Phil Mitchell
18. Jock
19. Ramsay Street
20. Captain Handler
21. Gail Tilsley and Alma Barlow
22. William Devane
23. Donna Reed
24. He was shot
25. Benson

Famous Folk • Sporting Personalities

1. Jamaica
2. Pélé
3. Italian Grand Prix
4. James Figg
5. He refused to be drafted into the army
6. Heart trouble
7. Robin Knox-Johnston
8. Swimming
9. Joe Di Maggio
10. Wayne Gretzky
11. France
12. 1980
13. Boris Becker
14. Clive Lloyd
15. Paul Gascoigne
16. 1984
17. Baseball player Babe Ruth brought so much money to the club
18. Alain Prost
19. Golf
20. Jack Dempsey
21. 100 metres
22. Franz Beckenbauer
23. Chay Blyth
24. Zimbabwe
25. Florence Griffith-Joyner

Indoors and Out • Gardening Know-how

1. Acidity and alkalinity of the soil
2. Hardening off the seedlings, so that they get used to outdoor conditions
3. Systemic
4. Hanging down or weeping
5. Lawnmower
6. Nitrogen, phosphorus, potassium
7. Members of the cabbage family
8. Spring
9. Gladiolus and crocus
10. Australia and New Zealand
11. Pruning
12. It prevents the growth of weeds and helps retain moisture
13. It is of foreign origin
14. Cloches
15. Joseph Banks
16. Chalk
17. Onions
18. Hybrid
19. True
20. Cylinder
21. Inducing a stem or shoot to grow roots while still attached to the parent plant
22. Residual weedkiller
23. Develop flowering shoots
24. It is ground-hugging
25. Fungal

Sport and Leisure • Walking, Running, Climbing

1. Sweden
2. Wear it
3. John Hunt
4. An accumulation of stones and debris left across a valley by a glacier which has since retreated
5. 42.195 km (26 miles 385 yards)
6. 1854
7. Descending by rope by means of mechanical brake devices
8. Cartography
9. Boston Marathon
10. Mount McKinley
11. Carl Lewis
12. Leroy Burrell
13. An overhanging mass of snow formed by the wind along the edge of a ridge
14. Put it on boots to keep them supple
15. A way of descending a snow slope by sliding
16. The north indicated by the grid on maps
17. Moving sideways without gaining altitude
18. Pitons (pins and pegs)
19. A gully or small open valley
20. Italian
21. Paul Revere's ride through Boston
22. The most regularly climbed routes
23. New York
24. 1981
25. Dick Bass

Past and Present • In the News

1. Virgin
2. Chechnya
3. James Woolsey
4. Mexico
5. Prime Minister of Belgium
6. John Major vetoed him as European Union successor to Jacques Delors
7. Cherie
8. Jean-Bertrand Aristide
9. Newt Gingrich
10. The construction of Space Station Alpha
11. Bosnia
12. Eurostar
13. August 1994
14. Barings
15. Nigel Mansell
16. Office of Status of Women
17. Somalia
18. 12
19. Austria, Finland and Sweden
20. Stella Rimington
21. Islamic Salvation Front
22. In computer software
23. Japan
24. 1960s
25. The life sentence given to criminals found guilty three times of certain federal offences

Pot Luck

1. Pink Floyd
2. Three-day eventing
3. Emperor Claudius
4. A banknote
5. Caroline's adultery
6. *Watership Down*
7. Thomas Gainsborough
8. Doldrums
9. *Bus Stop*
10. Anne Bancroft
11. Sulphuric acid
12. 1812
13. Spades and hearts
14. His experiences in South Africa
15. 'The Scottish Play'
16. Lennon and McCartney
17. A silk purse
18. North Star
19. Georgie Fame
20. Spaniel
21. Planet Hollywood
22. Baboon
23. Ayn Rand
24. Tennis
25. Gin

1. In which capital city would you travel on klongs and visit wats?

2. Which country produces most of the world's dates?

3. In which European mountain range is Andorra?

4. What country was once called Bechuanaland?

5. Where was Graham Greene's novel *The Comedians* set?

6. On which Hawaiian island is Waikiki beach?

7. In which country would you be if you lived in a houseboat on Dal Lake?

8. In which country does the heroine of *Shirley Valentine* take her life-changing holiday?

9. Which country has the oldest flag in the world?

10. In which city would you find the Spanish riding school with its famous Lippizaner horses?

11. 600 statues stand on Easter Island. In which ocean does this island lie?

12. Name the country once known as Hibernia.

13. In which Australian territory is Ayers Rock?

14. Which countries are linked by the Khyber Pass?

15. Where would you find the ports of Limassol, Larnaca and Kyrenia?

16. Which is the only walled city in North America to be declared a World Heritage Treasure by UNESCO?

17. In which country would you find Cossack dancing?

18. Where would you travel on vaporetti instead of buses?

19. Which country has most borders with other countries?

20. Where would you find the geysers and hot springs of the Rotorua district?

21. If you were travelling through the Cascade Mountains, where would you be?

22. Which country has the red maple leaf on its flag?

23. Unique animal and bird species including platypus, wombat and kookaburra are found in which country?

24. Name the most prolific film-producing country in the world.

25. Which island situated off the tip of the Sorrento peninsula in Italy has the Grotta Azura as one of its main tourist attractions?

HORROR MOVIES

Q

6

1. *The Fly*, a 1986 remake of the 1958 film, tells the story of a scientist who makes a mistake in an experiment and metamorphoses into a human fly. Who plays the scientist in the more recent film?

2. *The Innocents*, starring Deborah Kerr, was based on the novel *The Turn of the Screw*. Who wrote the novel?

3. Which film concerns a man-eating shark lurking off the beaches of a fictional resort called Amity?

4. Who directed *The Birds*?

5. Which story was filmed in 1925, 1943 and 1962 and was made into a musical by Andrew Lloyd Webber?

6. What power does the title character in *Carrie* possess?

7. Who is the father of *Rosemary's Baby*?

8. Which motel does Anthony Perkins run in *Psycho*?

9. Which actor became the archetypal monster with his starring role in Frankenstein in 1931?

10. Which character appears most often in horror films?

11. What is the name of the ghostly, scarred killer of *Nightmare on Elm Street* and several sequels?

12. Heather Langenkamp, who starred in *Nightmare on Elm Street*, played herself a decade later in another 'Nightmare' film. What was its title?

13. What is the name of the psychopathic killer played by Anthony Hopkins in *The Silence of the Lambs*?

14. In which film does Vincent's Chucky doll come to life as a demonic killer?

15. Who plays the devil incarnate to three sex-starved witches in *The Witches of Eastwick*?

16. How old is the vampire telling his story to a journalist in *Interview with the Vampire*?

17. Which 13-year-old actress is *The Little Girl Who Lives Down the Lane* in the 1977 Canadian film?

18. In *Cape Fear* Robert de Niro plays ex-convict Max Cady, who terrorizes a lawyer's family. Who plays the role in the previous version in 1962?

19. What is the link between Harvey Stephens, Jonathan Scott-Taylor and Sam Neill, stars of a trio of horror films?

20. In the 1958 Hammer film *Dracula* (in the US *The Horror of Dracula*) Peter Cushing plays Van Helsing. Who plays Dracula?

21. Which spoof horror film, which has become a cult movie, includes the songs 'Dammit Janet', 'The Time Warp' and 'Touch Me'?

22. Who directed the 1994 film *Mary Shelley's Frankenstein*?

23. In *The Shining*, based on Stephen King's novel, what is 'shining'?

24. Some critics compare *Halloween* to *Psycho*, which stars Janet Leigh. Name her daughter, who stars in *Halloween*.

25. Heather O'Rouke plays a child stalked by evil spirits in *Poltergeist* and its two sequels. What is the child's name?

1. What are sometimes known as cake urchins or sea biscuits?

2. How does a cuttlefish catch its prey?

3. What type of creature is a mudskipper?

4. Which group of creatures includes slugs, snails, octopuses and chitons?

5. What are the two basic types of barnacle?

6. How did the lantern fish get its name?

7. What can be cut-throat, moray or culper?

8. What is the study of shells called?

9. Why is a pilot fish so called?

10. How does a mussel feed?

11. Horns made from shells have been used by many civilizations. Which shells are usually used?

12. Lobsters are red when cooked. What colour are they when alive?

13. Dolphins live together in groups. What are these groups called?

14. How can dolphins be distinguished from porpoises?

15. What is a young pilchard called?

16. Why is the basking shark harmless?

17. How do hermit crabs differ from other crabs?

18. Lampreys are jawless fish. How do they feed?

19. What are oarweed, furbelows and dabberlocks?

20. Why do divers often fear barracudas more than sharks?

21. Abalones are sea snails. What is the abalone or ear shell best known for?

22. How does the scorpion fish get its name?

23. Helmet shells take their name from their resemblance to the helmets of Roman gladiators. What item of jewellery is traditionally carved from bullmouth helmet shells?

24. Which fish uses a 'rod and line' to catch other fish, using a long fin growing from its forehead, with a lure-like a bait on the end of it?

25. Which are the largest whales?

1. The world's most powerful warship to date was launched in 1907. What was it called?

2. The final section of the longest continuous stretch of railway in the world was completed in 1917. Name the railway.

3. Emily Davison threw herself in front of the King's horse at the Derby in 1913. What cause was she trying to promote?

4. Who were the original allies of the British Empire in World War I?

5. One of the factors that brought the United States into the First World War was the sinking of a British liner which was carrying Americans. Name the liner.

6. Britain's War Minister appeared on the famous World War I recruiting poster. Who was he?

7. The League of Nations was formed in 1919. What did it become in 1945?

8. Where was Hitler when he wrote *Mein Kampf*?

9. Which English-speaking country gave women the vote in 1901?

10. Which country built the series of fortifications called the Siegfried Line?

11. Which British prime minister announced in 1937 that the result of a European conference would guarantee 'peace in our time'?

12. In 1940 a fleet of small ships evacuated British and French troops from which port?

13. About what battle did Churchill say 'Never in the field of human conflict was so much owed by so many to so few'?

14. Which Russian city was cut off by the Germans for nearly 18 months in the early 1940s?

15. What name was given to the atomic bomb that devastated Nagasaki in 1945?

16. Which European city was blockaded by the Russians after World War II and was saved by a massive airlift of supplies?

17. What popular name was given to the European Recovery Programme which provided aid for rebuilding after World War II?

18. What was tested on Bikini Atoll in the Pacific in 1954?

19. Name the first space traveller in Sputnik II.

20. Which President brought American troops out of Vietnam?

21. When the Viet Cong took over Saigon, what did they name it?

22. The eastern region of Nigeria declared independence in 1968, but the country was united again in 1970. What was the independent republic called?

23. Ian Smith was premier of which country?

24. Under what name do we know Vladimir Ilyich Ulyanov?

25. The Berlin Wall was breached in 1989. For how long had the border been closed?

1. Who plays the robot gunfighter in *Westworld*?

2. Name the director of *Close Encounters of the Third Kind*.

3. What is a cyborg?

4. Ian Holm plays Ash in *Alien*. What is odd about Ash?

5. Who wrote the first major novel about a war with alien invaders?

6. In the *Six Million Dollar Man* who was the actress who played the Bionic Man's wife?

7. Who was the actress who played the female equivalent of the Bionic Man?

8. In the classic film *The Invasion of the Body Snatchers*, where do the duplicate bodies grow, in preparation for their takeover?

9. Who plays *The Prisoner*?

10. *Cocoon* tells the story of the members of a retirement community who are rejuvenated when a group of aliens take up residence nearby. Where is the action set?

11. What is cryogenics?

12. In what car does Michael J. Fox go to the future?

13. William Shatner as James Kirk is the first captain of the starship Enterprise. Who is the second?

14. In which *Star Trek* film does the crew go back to 20th-century Earth to collect whales?

Q13

17. Which pop star plays an alien in *The Man Who Fell to Earth*?

18. In which TV series is Dr David Banner strangely transformed when he becomes angry?

19. *Star Wars* is the first film of a trilogy. Name the other two films.

20. In which novel and film do mobile giant plants attack humans?

21. Which character makes a series of quantum leaps?

22. In *Planet of the Apes*, what proves to the hero that the world he knows has been blown up?

23. Who stars in the title role of *The New Adventures of Superman*?

24. In *Total Recall* Schwarzenegger stars as a construction worker who comes to believe that he is a secret agent. Which planet does he travel to in order to discover the truth?

15. In what year is the TV series *Babylon 5* set?

16. The TV series *Battlestar Galactica* was the subject of lawsuits from 20th-Century Fox because they alleged it was a 'steal' from which film?

25. Which author wrote the famous *Foundation* saga that won the Hugo Award for Best All-Time Novel Series?

Q 19

1. What was distinctive about the appearance of Israeli commander General Moshe Dayan?

2. General Eisenhower commanded US forces in Europe in World War ll and later became the US President. Which party did he represent?

3. Which Carthaginian general took elephants and troops over the Alps?

4. What date was predicted as the date of Julius Caesar's death?

5. Which American general led the Confederate armies in their only run of successes in the Civil War?

6. What relation was Earl Mountbatten of Burma to Queen Victoria?

7. Which Chinese general set up the right-wing government in Taiwan in 1949 when he was expelled from the mainland by Communist forces?

8. Which German field marshall was played by James Mason in the 1951 film?

9. Who led the Boer army against the British and became Prime Minister of South Africa in 1910?

10. Which English soldier and statesman created the New Model Army?

11. Under what name do we know Francisco Paulino Hermengildo Teodulo Franco y Bahamonde?

12. In 1429 Joan of Arc led the French army to victory over the English. Which city were they besieging?

13. General de Gaulle was a gallant soldier and President of France from 1956 to 1969. What is the appropriate meaning of the name 'de Gaulle'?

14. Which 19th-century South American leader was known as the Liberator?

15. Where was Napoleon exiled in 1813?

16. After his final defeat at Waterloo in 1815, where was Napoleon exiled?

17. Name the general who commanded the US forces in the Far East in World War II and in the Korean War.

18. Which Roman statesman and general married Caesar's only daughter Julia, though he later led forces against Caesar in the civil war?

19. Give the first names of Viscount Montgomery of Alamein.

20. Which British general was besieged at Khartoum in 1885?

21. Who played the title role in the 1970 film *Patton: Lust for Glory*?

22. Which Marshal of France was appointed Commander-in-Chief of the Allied armies in 1918?

23. Claus von Stauffenberg, the World War II German general, is best remembered for what?

24. For what brutal action of the American Civil War is General Sherman best remembered?

25. Which revolutionary leader, whose first name was Ernesto, adopted the name Che?

Q 25

4. Which team won a record fifth Super Bowl title in American football in January 1995?

5. How many forwards are there on each side in hockey?

6. How does the size of teams differ in Rugby League and Rugby Union?

7. A record transfer fee was paid by Juventus to Bari for which Association Football player?

8. The first women's soccer World Cup was held in China in 1991. Who won?

9. In Rugby, where does the ball go when it goes into touch?

10. Australian Rules Football is unique to Australia. How many team-members are playing at any one time?

11. What, in American football, is spearing?

12. American footballer George Blanda holds the record for the number of games played in the NFL. How many seasons did he play?

13. Which country won the World Cup for the fourth time in 1994?

14. Women's lacrosse has 12 team-members playing at any one time. How many does men's lacrosse have?

1. Which Brazilian World Cup star was known as 'the little bird'?

2. In the World Cup, which was the first country to win the Jules Rimet trophy twice?

3. In American football, how many points are awarded for a field goal?

15. American football is a fast-growing sport in Europe. When was the European Football League formed?

16. In American football, what is a pass that travels either behind or along the line of the scrimmage called?

17. Name the nations that take part in the Five Nations Rugby Championships.

18. How many times has Switzerland, home of FIFA, staged the World Cup?

19. Where was the rugby World Cup played in May and June 1995?

20. The first Olympic hockey game was played in 1908. Who won?

21. In which country was the hockey World Cup first played on an artificial surface?

22. The Big Four Bowl games in American football include the Rose Bowl and Cotton Bowl. Name the other two.

23. Which English footballer was known as 'the wizard of the dribble'?

24. In soccer, what is an indirect free kick?

25. Which French Rugby Union player gained his hundredth cap in 1994?

Q

Q 9

1. Where would you visit the Great Slave Lake?

2. In Cecil B. De Mille's name, what does the initial B stand for?

3. Which East German ice skater was 1984 Olympic champion and by 1990 had won four world titles?

4. The TV series *Inspector Morse* is set in which English town?

5. In the Bible, who wore a coat of many colours?

6. Sodium hydroxide is commonly known by what name?

7. What is the general term used to describe the islands of the central and south Pacific, including Australia and New Zealand?

8. At which festival is the Golden Rose award given?

9. In the 1958 film *Summer Holiday*, where was Cliff Richard's double-decker bus heading?

10. What branch of science deals with heat and energy?

11. In Roman times, by what name was Istanbul known?

12. Where would you find a crevasse?

13. What is the popular name for timpani?

14. In which country would you find the Sutherland Waterfall?

15. Who, in the nursery rhyme, had 10,000 men?

16. In the Bible, which is the shortest of the four Gospels?

17. Which film did the Beatles make for television?

18. What colour sari would a Hindu bride wear?

19. In the TV series *Happy Days*, what was Fonz's first name?

20. How many parts of speech are there?

21. What type of food is Dunlop?

22. The Nazis invaded which part of Britain in 1940?

23. Complete this quotation from Shaw's *Man and Superman*: 'It is a woman's business to get married as soon as possible and a man's . . .'

24. In computer language, what name is given to the part of the memory which holds data while it is waiting to be used?

25. What do D. H. Lawrence's initials stand for?

Geography and Travel • Where in the World?

1. Bangkok
2. Iraq
3. Pyrenees
4. Botswana
5. Haiti
6. Oahu
7. Kashmir
8. Greece
9. Denmark
10. Vienna
11. Pacific
12. Ireland
13. Northern Territory
14. Pakistan and
   Afghanistan
15. Cyprus
16. Quebec
17. Russia
18. Venice
19. China
20. North Island of New
   Zealand
21. Washington State, USA
22. Canada
23. Australia
24. India
25. Capri

Youth World • Science Fiction

1. Yul Brynner
2. Steven Spielberg
3. Part man, part machine
4. He is a malfunctioning
   android
5. H.G. Wells
6. Farrah Fawcett-Major
7. Lindsay Wagner
8. In pods
9. Patrick McGoohan
10. Florida
11. The science of freezing
   living creatures and
   bringing them back to
   life again
12. DeLorean
13. Captain Picard, played
   by Patrick Stewart
14. *Star Trek IV. The
   Voyage Home*
15. 2259
16. *Star Wars*
17. David Bowie
18. *The Incredible Hulk*
19. *The Empire Strikes
   Back* and *Return of the
   Jedi*
20. *The Day of the Triffids*
21. Dr Sam Beckett
22. The remains of the
   Statue of Liberty
23. Dean Cain
24. Mars
25. Isaac Asimov

Popular Culture • Horror Movies

1. Jeff Goldblum
2. Henry James
3. *Jaws*
4. Alfred Hitchcock
5. *Phantom of the Opera*
6. Telekinesis
7. Satan
8. Bates Motel
9. Boris Karloff
10. Dracula
11. Freddy Krueger
12. *Wes Craven's New
   Nightmare*
13. Hannibal Lector
14. *Child's Play*
15. Jack Nicholson
16. 200 years
17. Jodie Foster
18. Robert Mitchum
19. They all play Damien,
   the anti-Christ, in *The
   Omen* and its sequels
20. Christopher Lee
21. *The Rocky Horror
   Picture Show*
22. Kenneth Branagh
23. Psychic ability
24. Jamie Lee Curtis
25. Carol Anne

Famous Folk • Military Leaders

1. He wore a black eye-
   patch
2. Republican
3. Hannibal
4. The Ides of March (15
   March)
5. Stonewall Jackson
6. Great-grandson
7. Chiang Kai-Shek
8. Rommel
9. Louis Botha
10. Oliver Cromwell
11. General Franco
12. Orléans
13. 'Of France'
14. Simón Bolívar
15. Elba
16. St Helena
17. General Douglas
   MacArthur
18. Pompey
19. Bernard Law
20. General Gordon
21. George C. Scott
22. Foch
23. The conspiracy to
   assassinate Hitler
24. The destructive march
   through Georgia and
   burning of Atlanta
25. Che Guevara

Indoors and Out • Sea and Shore

1. Sand dollars
2. It shoots out long
   tentacles at speed
3. Fish
4. Molluscs
5. Acorn and goose
6. It has a row of light-
   producing organs down
   each side of its body
7. Eels
8. Conchology
9. It swims close to larger
   fishes as though
   guiding them
10. By filtering small
   particles from water
11. Conch and triton
12. Blue
13. Schools
14. By their beaked snouts
15. Sardine
16. It feeds on plankton
   only
17. Their rear part is not
   covered by shell
18. They are parasites,
   preying on other fish by
   sucking their blood
19. Seaweeds
20. They hunt by sight and
   will attack any flashing
   metal object
21. The rainbow mother-of-
   pearl sheen on the
   inside of the shell
22. From its many sharp
   spines, which can be
   poisonous
23. Cameo brooches
24. Angler fish
25. Blue whales

Sport and Leisure • On the Field

1. Garrincha
2. Italy
3. Three
4. San Francisco 49ers
5. Five
6. Rugby League has 13
   players a side, Rugby
   Union has 15
7. David Platt
8. USA
9. Out of play over the
   sidelines
10. 18
11. Diving head-first at an
   opposing player
12. 26
13. Brazil
14. 10 in each team
15. 1985
16. A lateral
17. England, Ireland,
   Scotland, Wales and
   France
18. Once
19. South Africa
20. Scotland
21. Canada
22. Super Bowl and Orange
   Bowl
23. Stanley Matthews
24. A kick from which a
   goal cannot be scored
   until the ball has been
   touched by another
   player
25. Philippe Sella

Past and Present • Making of the Modern World

1. *HMS Dreadnought*
2. Trans-Siberian Railway
3. Women's suffrage
4. France and Russia
5. *Lusitania*
6. Lord Kitchener
7. United Nations
8. In jail
9. Australia
10. Germany
11. Neville Chamberlain
12. Dunkirk
13. Battle of Britain
14. Leningrad
15. Fat boy
16. Berlin
17. The Marshall Plan
18. The hydrogen bomb
19. Laika, a dog
20. Nixon
21. Ho Chi Minh City
22. Biafra
23. Rhodesia
24. Lenin
25. 28 years

Pot Luck

1. Canada
2. Blount
3. Katarina Witt
4. Oxford
5. Joseph
6. Caustic soda
7. Oceania
8. Montreux
9. Athens
10. Thermodynamics
11. Byzantium
12. In a glacier
13. Kettledrums
14. New Zealand
15. The grand old Duke of
   York
16. Mark
17. *Magical Mystery Tour*
18. Red
19. Arthur
20. Eight
21. Cheese
22. Channel Islands
23. 'To keep unmarried for
   as long as he can'
24. Buffer
25. David Herbert

INDEX

Picture Acknowledgements:

(Abbreviations Key: T = Top, B = Below)

Barnaby's Picture Library: 10, 15, 16, 23, 24 (Gerald Cubitt), 28 T, 36, 37, 39, 43 (B. Gibbs), 46 (David W. Corson), 50, 51, 54 T, 58, 59, 69, 72, 73, 74, 79, 82, 87, 90, 95, 101, 104, 105, 107 (Lesley Howling), 121, 123, 124 (G. Clyde), 126, 127, 128, 132, 137 T, 141, 145, 154 (H. Kanus), 158, 159, 162, 163, 169, 172, 176, 177, 195, 203 (© Richard Gardner), 212, 216, 220 T, 222 (Andrew Besley), 244. **Popperfoto**: 11, 12, 13, 18, 21, 22, 28 B, 29, 34, 42, 48, 49, 53, 55, 56, 57, 64, 68, 71, 75, 77, 78, 83, 84 (Both), 85, 86, 88, 93, 100, 106, 108 TL, 110, 111, 112, 113, 118, 119 (© David Brown), 125, 129, 131, 136, 137 B, 139, 140, 142 (Greg Newton), 144, 154, 156, 157, 160, 161, 166, 167, 173, 178, 179, 182, 183, 185, 187 (Bob Thomas), 190, 191, 193, 196, 204, 208, 209, 214, 220 B, 221, 223, 229, 230, 232, 233 (© Hector Mata), 234, 235 (Bob Thomas), 238, 239, 240, 248, 251, 252, 253, 256, 257, 258 (Bob Thomas). **Hulton Deutsch Collection**: 14, 17, 20 (Both), 35, 38 (Both), 47, 52, 54 B, 60 B, 65, 70, 76, 89, 92, 94, 96, 97, 102, 108 B, 109, 130, 143, 146, 147, 150, 168 (Mckenzie), 174, 175, 184, 196, 198, 200, 201, 202, 205, 210, 215, 218, 219, 226, 227, 236, 237, 250, 254, 255, 259. **Kobal Collection**: 19, 25, 30, 31, 60 T, 91, 103, 114, 115, 120, 138, 151, 164, 165, 180, 181, 186, 192, 211, 217, 228, 241, 245, 246, 247. **Robert Harding Picture Library**: 40, 41, 231, 248. **Syndication International**: 61, 66, 67 (Both), 194 (Bernard Alfieri). **Bridgeman Art Library** 133, 148 (all), 149, 199. **Haldane Mason**: 32, 33, 122. **Frank Lane Photo Agency**: 213 (© Mark Newman)

Every effort has been made to trace the copyright holders and we apologise in advance for any unintentional omissions. We would be pleased to insert the appropriate acknowledgement in any subsequent edition of this publication.